LITTLE GODS

TIM PRATT

PRIME BOOKS
Canton, Ohio

LITTLE GODS

Published in the United States by **Prime Books, Inc.**
P.O. Box 36503, Canton, OH 44735
www.primebooks.net

ISBN: 1-894815-82-3 (hardcover)
ISBN: 1-894815-83-1 (paperback)

CONTENTS

"This is for Heather, my own little goddess of joy."

INTRODUCTION TO LITTLE GODS

by Michaela Roessner

Tim Pratt was pretty much raised by wolves. Three fierce, intelligent, independent she-wolves.

There. Now I've got your attention.

The fact that they were, respectively, his mother, great-aunt, and great grandmother is almost beside the point—he was the only cub in their pack. In this day and age, it's a tenuous existence for such creatures. Living on the fringes of society, trying to suss out interactions with the predominant free-standing, uppity, techno-primate culture. It takes a lot of savvy, a willingness to warily study in depth those who surround you. Those who represent at one moment potential prey, and the next potential predator.

Is it any wonder that these she-wolves immersed themselves in the contemplation of all that is bizarre, wondrous, and inexplicable in human society? They transferred the voraciousness of the hunt for prey to a voraciousness for reading, for knowledge. Is it any wonder that Tim was raised in dens lined with books? Or that the first novel he read, at the tender age of eight, was that great testament to humanity's cruelty, intolerance, and strangeness, Stephen King's *Carrie*?

It was only a matter of time before Tim waded his way through dens'-worth of King, Asimov, Heinlein, Herbert, Card, to finally alight upon the first volume of *The Year's Best Fantasy*. There, lying in wait for him, were Charles de Lint's "Uncle Dobbin's Parrot Fair" and Jonathon Carroll's "Friend's Best Man." They pounced. He read them. Since then he has been theirs: a writer of the vast panoply of mythos that, though often unseen, permeates contemporary life.

Being raised by wolves might explain why Tim first wrote about other animals as much if not more than about people. His earliest published work was "A Day in the Life of a Spider," written in third grade. A fourth grade piece featured an alternate dimension full of talking alligators.

He requested and received an electric typewriter from his mother and stepfather. By his mid-teens he was following the journeyman writer's time-honored and hide-toughening apprenticeship of submitting to and getting rejected by genre magazines. Further conditioning exercises were administered by high school teachers who insured Tim that the odds of his succeeding as a writer were about as good as the odds of his someday walking on the moon. One assumes that these former teachers are currently pooling together funds to buy him a nice NASA moonwalk suit.

He attended college at Appalachian State University in Boone, North Carolina. There he at last began to enjoy his natural inheritance of "The Luck of the Wolves." (I know, you thought the phrase was "The Luck of the Irish," but the original traditional good fortune was bestowed upon things lupine.) A special residential program for freshmen and sophomores called Watauga College recruited him. Watauga offered an interdisciplinary curriculum, drawing in faculty from all over the University's different departments and letting them teach their passions. It gathered together as students artists, writers, actors, dancers, musicians and foreigners. And who could be more foreign than a raised-by-wolves fable writer?

At Watauga he encountered a poetry professor who helped transform his writing. Even more importantly, every few years Orson Scott Card taught a "writers' book camp" for Watauga during spring break. Tim applied, and was accepted for one of the half-a-dozen slots. During this ten-day intensive he wrote under pressure, was critiqued by peers in the program and by Card, and received enough encouragement to keep going. By his last year in college he'd begun to make sales to some small presses.

In the summer of 1999 he attended the Clarion writing workshop at Michig n State University, which is where I first encountered him. At Clarion a different professional speculative fiction author presides each week over the six-week length of the workshop. The atmosphere is intense. Rather than a traditional teacher/student learning relationship, the focus is more that of established professionals working with potential eventual peers in the field to broaden their horizons and hone their skills. The impression I had of Tim was that he was a naturally gifted storyteller. I had no idea at the time that he'd already paid considerable dues in the form of the gruntwork necessary to become a writer, logging in hundreds of thousands of words as he developed his craft. At Clarion he sharpened his technical proficiency, but more importantly learned about "artistic stuff." He especially listened when Tim Powers took him to task for writing "silly, gimmicky" stories—that he should be writing stories that mattered to him. After Clarion Tim eventually moved to California, to Santa Cruz. There he lived for a year while working as an office manager for an archetypally California-style business: a wheelchair design/disabled advocacy firm. It was during this time that he met, in Oakland, Pre-Raphaelite beauty and fellow writer, Heather Shaw, to whom he is now engaged. So of course Tim then moved to Oakland, where he currently works as assistant editor for *Locus Magazine*.

So . . . what can you expect from this wolfkin?

Like Orpheus, Tim plumbs the dark depths, seeking to retrieve the beloved, transformed. But in Tim's case the beloved isn't a wife, an individual, a single thing. The beloved are those old, old templates of our souls, the archetypes that guide us: the god of choice at the crossroads; the witch; the stolen magical child; the ideal of the superhero; neglected and abandoned deities; the too-clever thief, and, of course, Orpheus himself. Archetypes too often ignored and then lost. Tim's gift is to climb with them out of the abyss of the forgotten, bringing them back into the light and back to life. Who else but a child raised himself in mythos could spin for you these tales of evil bicycles, the sacrifices of broken-hearted monsters, owl dinners, metamorphing secret agents, and a little goddess of cinnamon and brown sugar?

— **Michaela Roessner**

LITTLE GODS

"I wish I could be a little goddess of cinnamon," my wife Emily says, closing her eyes and leaning in close to the spices. I'm used to Emily saying things like that, so I don't take any notice, just nod and pick up a bottle of peach nectar off the shelf, slosh it around, wrinkle my nose. I know all the gunk in there is supposed to be fresh natural goodness, but to me it just looks like gunk. Emily says that I deny the truth of natural origins. Emily likes peach nectar, so I put the bottle in the basket.

"A little goddess of cinnamon," Emily repeats. "Or brown sugar." She crosses her arms, her silver-and-brass bracelets tinkling together.

"As opposed to a big goddess of cinnamon?" I move on down the aisle with my basket over my arm.

"Little things get little gods," Emily says. "It's only natural." She trails after me, running her finger along the shelves, pausing to sniff at the black teas, to open the lid on a jar of sugar-free gumdrops. Emily is always prodding, smelling, caressing—she says that she is experiencing the world.

"So big gods are for big things, then? Like, say, whales?"

Emily sighs behind me. "Big things like . . . I don't know . . . love."

"How about hate? Jealousy?"

"Sure. But I wouldn't want to be one of those, nothing so big." She squeals in delight. "Ooh! Chocolate-covered espresso beans!"

"I didn't realize those were in season," I say dryly, but she isn't paying attention to me, has darted off to get a plastic bag to fill with candied caffeine. She'll be up all night, and she'll keep me up with her. That might be nice. Sometimes she likes to make love all night when she's had a lot of caffeine; other times she gets jittery and talks wistfully of the days when she smoked cigarettes.

Emily dances down the aisle, long skirt swaying, silver bells around the hem jingling. She shakes her bag of espresso beans like a maraca.

"Goddess of chocolate?" I say. "Would you go for that?"

"Sure. But I'd be even more particular. Goddess of dark chocolate. Goddess of Mexican hot chocolate. Goddess of hot fudge on a wooden spoon."

"Those are awfully small gods. It'd take a lot of them to keep the world running."

"Well, sure." She looks around the otherwise uninhabited aisle in an amusingly furtive way, then opens the plastic bag, removes a bean, and pops it into her mouth. "The big gods—the gods of abstractions and ideals—they're like CEOs, figureheads, upper management. I mean, the goddess of joy may get paid well, but where would her operation be without the god of hot showers, the goddess of hot sex, the avatar of angel food cake? I'd be just as happy to have one of those lower-level positions, one with nice, clearly defined responsibilities, a comprehensible mission."

"I love you," I say, feeling warm toward her all of a sudden, my Emily with her corkscrew black hair, her squinched-in-thought features, her clothes she's made mostly with her own hands, sewn all over with suns and moons. My flaky angel who reads the stars and knows how to make bread rise, bring flowers to life, tune a mandolin, make my heart beat beautifully along with her own. My Emily, who believes in little gods of tuna casserole and stained glass.

She takes my hand and squeezes it. We go toward the checkout. There is some commotion up front, I can't see what—a crowd milling around, someone talking hurriedly and sharply. I don't pay attention, just push through toward the front, Emily's hand in mine, tugging her along—she can be distracted ten times in ten seconds, and I want very much to get her home, to get into the hot tub with her, to talk about the little gods of kissing-her-belly, rinsing-her-hair, touching-her-face.

When I get to the checkout I see him, just a boy really, not even seventeen. He wears a mask like the Lone Ranger's, but his is just cheap black plastic with a rubber band to hold it on, something picked up from the 99-cent bin at an after-Halloween sale. He has a gun, though, and it jerks all over as he aims it here and there, warning people away from the exits, threatening the cashier, who just stands perfectly still, as if her brains have been scooped out or drained off. Emily doesn't see the boy, the robber-boy; she is looking off to the side at a display of kiwi and passion fruit, oblivious, she can sometimes be so oblivious. "Ooh," she says, and pulls her hand away from me and starts toward the fruit, moving on a course tangential to the boy-thief, the gun-boy.

"Emily, no," I say, and she turns toward me with her eyebrows raised, and in turning she bumps into a dump-bin full of suckers and packs of gum, her hip thumping the display hard and making a little candy avalanche. The boy with the gun jerks his arm up, startled by my voice or the movement or the sound of falling candy or perhaps just strung too tightly with the frustration of the motionless cashier who won't goddammit put the money in the bag like he told her. I don't know if the boy means to do it or if it happens by accident but the gun goes off with a crack and a stink (small god of lead, small god of expanding gases) and Emily goes down, goes over, tumbles into the candy display and it falls down with her. She hits the ground in a rain of neatly-wrapped sugar, the little bag of espresso beans falling from her hand, and she doesn't move, and the front of her is all red.

The boy-thief, killer-boy, runs away. Someone screams. Someone says something very calmly about calling an ambulance.

I drop my basket. The bottle of peach nectar tumbles out. It hits near my feet and explodes. Small god of the sound of breaking glass. Small god of small wet fragments.

Two days after Emily's funeral, with her parents finally gone and everything settled except for the pain in my head, I put a chair out on the back deck and sit looking at the birdhouse Emily made last year. A family of jays lived there for a while, but they're gone now, nothing left inside but bits of straw and sticks and string. My chest seems sometimes as empty as that birdhouse, and other times I think I've been filled with something hot and foul and gooey, cough syrup heated on the stove, thickened with molasses or blood.

I have trouble with time and living. Clocks don't make sense. I cry. I'm too hot, or too cold. The covers stultify me, and I can't sleep on my bed (our bed), so I stay in the living room on the couch, with my eyes closed so that I can't see anything, not the watercolors Emily hung on the redwood walls, not the flowers she cut the morning we went to the grocery store, now dying in the vase. Nothing but the inside of my eyes.

It's better outside, with just the natural world pressing around me, rather than the substance of the life Emily and I made together. Emily used to call this house our haven, our safe place, and I thought it would be so always. I never expected it to become a bleak museum of grief.

I watch the sky for a while, the sun moving, and gradually realize that my throat is dry; I haven't had anything to eat or drink since Emily's parents left. I get up and go to the door, part of my mind wondering why I bother, why I waste time keeping body together when soul is sundered. But it's easier just to go along, to move without thinking. I go into the house, into the kitchen, and the first thing I notice is the smell of divinity fudge cooking, that sweetness that is almost too cloying, a sweetness that Emily loved far more than I did. Then I see the woman standing at the stove and think for a bright leaping moment that it is my wife, my Emily, somehow returned to me—but this woman is too tall, and her dress is too black—raven's-wing black, slice-of-night black—with no designs or silver threads. Emily would never wear anything so dark, and anyway, she is dead.

I move closer, wondering who this black-dressed, black-haired woman is, why she is in my kitchen, but I don't really care—I am not ultimately very interested. Perhaps she is a friend of Emily's. Perhaps she is a thief.

She turns toward me, and her face is pale, white as sugar. She holds a wooden spoon. A large pot stands on the stove, empty and gleaming, and yet she moves the spoon inside as if stirring something, and the smell of divinity fudge rises up. I am suddenly furious (and even that feels strange, because I have felt nothing at all for days now, except sometimes a dull ache with sharp edges). Who is this woman, to come into my home, to touch Emily's things?

I snarl at her and she drops the spoon with a clatter, her mouth opening in surprise as if *I'm* the one who should not be here. I step forward, not knowing what will happen, whether I'll grab her or hit her or just firmly take her arm. Before I can touch her I am blasted in the face with a wave of hot air, and that air carries smells—divinity fudge, vanilla cookies, incense, rainwater, cinnamon, Emily's skin. Emily's skin. A hundred other smells, too, all of them keying instantly to memories of my wife, all of them bringing up fragments of images and moments. Memories that a week ago would have been sweet now twist like corkscrews, jabbing like knives, reminding me of all I've lost. I go down on my knees, my eyes closed against that scented wind, my chest twisting and contracting as if there's some horrible crab behind my ribcage, writhing. I put my forehead on the cold linoleum and sob.

The smell, the storm of smells, fades. I lift my head, blinking, looking for the pale woman in black.

She is gone. There is no pot on the stove, no spoon. The kitchen smells like dust and nothing else at all.

I check the doors and windows, somewhat surprised to find that they are locked. I don't remember locking them, but perhaps Emily's father did so before he left. He is a large and capable man, slow-moving and sad, like a great and ponderous planet in erratic orbit. He would have locked the doors and windows for me. But that means no woman could have gotten in, and that means my mind is coming loose, not just hiding under a stone but actually coming loose, imagining things, imagining even the scents of grief.

I sit on the couch again and lean my head back, my eyes closed. I feel smothered, as if a wet curtain has been draped over me, stifling my breath. It's not enough that my wife dies in a grocery store on a springtime afternoon; I have to lose my mind, too. But why do I need my mind, with my mind's closest best companion gone?

I hear something like the movement of a bird and open my eyes. There is something on my ceiling, above the rafters, something like a black cloth pinned up at the corners and center—a drape, a canopy. I look at it blankly, trying to understand it with my eyes. After a moment I realize it is not just cloth but a woman in a long black dress. The woman is suspended somehow in the center of the ceiling, looking down, and her impossibly long skirts are spread out all around her, covering the ceiling. I did not see the woman at first because her skin is nearly as black as her dress, and her eyes are dark too, and she is not smiling, so I cannot even see her teeth. This is of course not the same woman I saw in the kitchen, but for some reason my first thought is: *They're sisters.* Which makes no sense, as the other was white, and this one is black.

The woman's skirts begin to sag, billowing, falling down toward me, and I feel my sense of suffocation double, now it is like lying facedown in the mud while wet, mildewed mattresses are piled on top of me. I gasp and struggle to my feet, staring up at the woman on my ceiling. I grope blindly and my hand finds a paperweight on the end table, a lump of volcanic glass that Emily picked up on our honeymoon in Hawaii. It seems terribly heavy, but I am angry now, angry beneath the wet burlap suffocation, and I manage to lift the weight.

I hurl the chunk of rock at the woman on the ceiling. It hits her in the stomach and bounces off, landing on the coffee table with a *crack.* She squawks like a blackbird. Her skirts draw in quickly like windowshades snapping shut, and then she's gone, nothing on my ceiling but abandoned spiderwebs.

I sit back down, the oppressive weight suddenly gone, making me feel impossibly light by comparison—as if I could float away, as if no one I loved had ever died, as if the sun were filling my veins. But that thrill leaches slowly away, returning to me to the grayness, the neutrality, that I've felt since Emily died.

I fall asleep, which is really only another flavor of oblivion.

I wake to find a man dressed in a threadbare black suit sitting on the edge of the hearth, cleaning his fingernails with a folding pocketknife. I immediately think of him as a preacher, as he resembles somewhat the country preacher of the small church my family attended when I was young, though he is clearly not the same man. He has black hair, a bit mussed, and a single heavy eyebrow that looks almost too hairy to be real. His face is middle-aged, hale and hearty, and when he looks up at me his eyes are blue and twinkling.

"Boo," he says, softly.

"Who are you?" I demand, irritable from being just-awake, irritable at all these incomprehensible intrusions, all these distractions from the grayness of my first week without Emily, the first of who knows how many weeks I'll be able to bear.

"I'm here to help," he says, sounding sure and self-satisfied. "A couple of the girls told me there was something funny about you, that you could see them, so I came to investigate things personally. And here I am, and here you are, seeing me." He stands up, folds his knife, taps it against his palm. He makes a peculiarly medieval sort of bow. "I'm the King of Grief, Gatekeeper of the Dead Places, and a Gambler of Bad Fortunes."

I don't know what to make of him. "Those women . . . ," I say.

He waves his hand dismissively. "Just little goddesses, handmaids, field workers, don't mind them. The one in the kitchen was the goddess of scents with sad associations, the one with the big black skirt was the goddess of heavy hearts. You don't need to think about them. I've taken a personal interest in you, because of your . . . peculiar vision. You can see us, and that means you're a special man, a man who deserves more than bad luck."

I look at him blankly; it is as if I am observing all this through a pane of dirty glass, as if it is taking place inside an aquarium. Little gods of grief? Like Emily's little gods of joy, of love? Is this the route my madness has taken, to make me inhabit a darker version of the world my wife imagined? How can this man be the King of Grief, with his threadbare suit, his greasy hair? Just looking at him, I know he has bad breath, and his teeth are crooked when he smiles. His eyes shine, but it seems to me that the shine is like that of oil on a rain puddle—full of rainbows, but ultimately foul. Still, who am I to question my own delusions, to question the face of a god?

He sits back down on the hearth and leans forward, elbows on knees, rubbing his hands together briskly. "Now then. What will you give me to get Emily back?"

I sit up straighter, as if I've been given an electric shock, and the grayness recedes, replaced by a furtive and desperate kind of hope. "What?" I say. "What do you mean?"

He looks annoyed, his single eyebrow bristling and drawing down. "A *bargain*," he says, enunciating plainly. "You've heard the stories, haven't you? A man goes into the underworld to fetch out his dead wife, a woman gathers the dismembered pieces of her lover and begs the gods to put him back together, it's a classic tale, and here you are, in the middle of it. But it's a *bargain*, and I need something in return, if you want Emily back."

"Anything," I say, not caring if this is a delusion, not caring if I've gone insane—better an insane world with Emily alive than a sane world without her. But of course that's a contradiction in terms; no world in which my beautiful wife is dead can be called sane.

"Your left eye?" he asks, flicking open his pocketknife, showing me the shiny blade. He grins, and there are bits of gristle and meat stuck in his teeth. "That's more or less what Odin gave up for wisdom—is your dead wife worth as much to you?"

I think of the knife, the blade, the pain that would come, my vision forever dimmed—but I'd have Emily. Would I give up an eye to look upon her again?

I don't even question. If I'm insane, insane enough to see and hear this, then my mind is lost beyond redemption. But if it's real, if this offer is real, how can I refuse it, how can I even risk a hesitation?

"Give me the knife," I say, holding out my hand. "I'll do it."

He laughs heartily. "Good man! But you're too eager, that's no way to bargain. Your left eye is hardly anything, after all. Perhaps if you also sacrificed an ear. Van Gogh cut off his ear for a whore—is your wife worth as much flesh as a whore, hmm?"

I clench my fists, furious, and say, "Don't toy with me. I'll give anything for my wife. If you are who you say, you know that."

"Oh, yes," he says, voice suddenly like velvet, but even that image is rotten, and I imagine tattered red velvet eaten by moths. "I know. But would you give your life? Would you plunge this blade"—and suddenly the blade is longer, ten inches long, a foot, length sliding from the hilt like a cat's claw from a paw—"into your eye, into your brain, knowing your death would bring your wife back to life?"

I hesitate. Death? By my own hand?

"I see," he says, sounding satisfied, flipping the knife closed. "I thought you wouldn't. I mean, just because you caused her death, that's no reason for you to give up your own life."

I tremble, but not from anger, from something different, more brittle, more sharp. "I didn't," I whisper. "The boy, the boy with the gun—"

"He just wanted money," the man said. "But you had to shout at Emily, call the boy's attention to her, startle her, startle him. If you'd just kept your mouth shut, she wouldn't be dead. And yet you"—his contempt is total, I am as useless as the gristle caught in his teeth—"you won't give up your life for hers."

He is right. He is absolutely right. "Give me the knife," I say. "And give Emily back to the world."

"That's my boy," he says, and flips the knife over, and holds it out to me—

The sound of wings, battering at glass. Both of us look at the windows, and there are butterflies there. No, not butterflies, white moths. The man, the King of Grief, whimpers. "Shit," he says.

I smell dust.

A woman glides into the room from the kitchen. She has olive skin and otherworldly, golden eyes. Her long dark hair is pulled back in a simple ponytail, and she wears white pants and a white shirt; they could be silk pajamas. Her feet are bare. She looks at the man on the hearth. "You," she says, and the disappointment in her voice is heavy and inescapable. The man cringes. "Get out of here," she says.

"I was only doing my job," he mutters, folding his knife.

"Away," she says, and the command in her voice is the command of the mind moving a muscle—it cannot possibly be disobeyed.

The man looks at me, scowls, and then climbs headfirst up the chimney. A moment later his feet disappear from view.

I wonder who this woman can be, to reprimand the King of Grief, and I hate her for driving him away on the cusp of my absolution, my sacrifice for Emily's salvation.

"He is no King," she says, looking at me, and in her eyes I see long years of looking at gray slabs of stone, of peering through air thick with dust. "He is a petty thing with pretensions, and I regret to admit that he is one of mine." She sits down beside me on the couch, and it is this unassuming, perfectly normal gesture as much as anything that makes me believe her. "I am the goddess of grief," she says matter-of-factly, and I don't hear the grandiosity, the capitalization-of-words, that I heard when the man said something similar. "He is the little god of guilt and bargains. A natural part of grief, for many, and therefore necessary to my employment . . . but his spirit is meaner than those of most of my helpers. When he realized you could see us, that he could interact with you directly . . ." She shrugs. "He chose to violate all protocols and do so. I apologize for his behavior."

I nod. Tentative, hopeful, I say, "What he said, about bringing Emily back, about bargains, can you . . . " But I trail off, because her eyes are sad now, full of twilight. I slump. I put my face in my hands but don't cry.

"I'm sorry," she says, and I believe her, but it doesn't help.

"If there are gods, then is there something more, a place we go when we die, will I ever see her again?"

"I am concerned with the living," she says simply. "Grief is my work, from beginning to end. The causes of grief, the resolutions . . . I cannot speak to those things."

I am not angry, only empty. I wonder if I am not angry because she does not wish me to be angry, if she controls me that much.

"It is . . . unusual, your situation," she says. "Not unheard-of, but rare. A loss such as yours can sometimes trigger deeper understanding, deeper vision. Needless to say, this changes everything. The process is made more complicated. By seeing us, knowing we're here, you interfere with our work."

"I think I can be devastated without your help," I say, but without as much bite as I would wish.

"Oh, yes." She nods, her hands folded neatly in her white lap. "Without a doubt. You can be destroyed by your loss, emptied out and drained. But without our help . . . it is unlikely that you will come out whole on the other side."

"It's supposed to get easier with time," I say.

She smiles, perhaps, but the light touches her slantwise, so I can't be sure. "Yes. I make it so."

"I don't care. Without Emily, nothing matters." And then, bitterly: "And it *is* my fault that she died."

"I can help," she says, and I hear the pattering of moths again, white moths against the windows. "The process is broken, but . . . I can make you forget. Carry away your memories, carry away your pain. This house and everything in it"—she makes a sweeping gesture—"is an engine of grief. But that engine cannot run smoothly, now; your perception ruins that. Let me soothe you. Let me make it easy. Let me take it all away."

The moths are inside now, flying around her head, and I remember reading once about a sort of moth that drinks tears to survive, clustering around weeping eyes to drink. I wonder if these are that sort of moth, and think: of course they are. They can drink my pain away, and leave cool white flutterings where the hurt used to be. That's her offer, her gift.

Anger penetrates my grayness. "No," I say. "No, no, no. No forgetfulness. I loved her. I won't give that up."

She brings her hands together, as if in prayer, and kisses her fingertips. The moths swarm together for a moment, then disappear like candle flames going out. "Then another way," she says, and puts her gentle hand on my knee. "We'll find another way."

I do cry, then.

She stays with me. She holds me while I shiver on my too-empty bed. She makes me drink water, but she won't let me take pills; instead, she sings to me when sleep won't come, and though I suspect the songs are funeral dirges from some lost civilization, they serve as lullabies. She says that everything will be all right, and from her, how can I doubt it? And yet, of course, I do. I doubt it.

She washes my sheets, clearing away the dust, taking away the scent of Emily that clings to the fabric. She opens the drapes to let light in. I talk about loss, my loss, and she listens somberly. She watches while I rage, when I punch my fist against the wall until my knuckles are bloody, and in the presence of her patient eyes I calm down, I sit. I am not angry at the house. She says little, but somehow her presence helps me. The grayness of the days just after Emily's death is gone; I am plunged headlong into the furnace, into the boiling pool, into the whirlwind of my life without her.

After the first two weeks, the goddess doesn't stay every day. She leaves me to sort through pictures, clothes, musical instruments, books—these are Emily's earthly remains, as much as the body I saw buried, and I divide them, some to go to her family, some to be given away, some to be kept deep in a closet. I feel as if I'm burying her all over again.

The goddess comes every few days, and though I tell her that I feel so broken and torn-apart at times that I fear I'll never be whole, she never offers me the solace of her tear-drinking moths again. I hate her for that, but I am also grateful. She is the queen of grief, and she wants me to pass through the dark and the tunnels and the shadows of her kingdom, and emerge into the light on the other side.

I ask her if she was ever human, if her helpmeets ever were, if Emily might, perhaps, have her wish fulfilled—become a goddess of ice water on hot days, goddess of warm oil on sore muscles, goddess of breath in a sad lover's lungs. The queen wraps her arms around me, and the smell of dust that surrounds her is almost sweet. "What I am, I have always been," the queen says. "And as for others, who knows? If it pleases you to imagine your wife in such a way, do."

Like all her comfort, it is somewhat cold and all too truthful, but I accept her words as best I can.

She leaves that night, after brewing me a cup of black tea and kissing my forehead. My grieving is not done, she says, but the time for her direct intervention is past. From now on, the process will proceed on its own. From now on, it's up to me.

My first moment of happiness comes three months after Emily's death. I sit on a bench in a little park near the sea cliffs, watching the sailboats in the bay. Sailboats have no particular association for me—I never went sailing with Emily, she never particularly exclaimed over the grace of wind-driven boats. Watching the colorful sails in the water, I find myself smiling, a true smile that won't turn to poison in a moment, that isn't a smile over something Emily said or did. This is a smile of the rest of my life.

I see a woman on the sea cliffs, and at first I think it is the queen of grief because she has the same sort of presence, the same sort of *bigness,* but this woman is dressed in yellow, not white. Her dress seems to be composed entirely of gauzy scarves. She dances lightly along the precipice, and when her face turns toward me for an instant it is a morning star, a sunrise after a long night, a sudden downpour of water in the desert. I recognize her in the deepest chambers of my heart—this is the goddess of joy. And behind her come other women and men, dancing in colorful costumes, feathers and shawls and hats and capes—the retinue of joy, her small gods. The goddess of joy leaps into the air over the water and shatters into light, becomes motes of brightness drifting, becomes the reflection of sunlight on the waves. The small gods follow, jumping after her, whooping and singing and laughing, and I find myself still smiling as they, too, turn to light.

The last of the small gods hesitates on the cliff. She wears a purple dress sewn all over with stars and moons. She turns her head toward me, her hair a cloud of soft black corkscrews, hiding her face. My breath stops. I look at her, wondering—do I know that shape, that hair, that stance?

I smell, faintly, a trace of cinnamon on the wind, and nothing has ever been sweeter.

The small goddess (of cinnamon, of one man's love) leaps from the cliff, and turns to light.

I sit, watching, until her brightness merges with the sparkles on the surface of the water, and then I walk away, mouthing a prayer of thanks to the small gods of waking up in the morning, the small gods of drawing breath, the small gods of holding on.

THE FALLEN AND THE
MUSE OF THE STREET

"Pretty wild place," Madisen said, stepping aside to avoid a drunk retching his way out of a strip club. Madisen splashed through a puddle of rainwater and beer, breaking up the reflection of neon signs and streetlights. The air smelled of liquor, smoke, and sweating bodies.

Samaelle snorted. "Gomorrah was a wild place. This is a playground. Why couldn't we go to Bangkok?"

Madisen took her arm. At six-foot-two, Samaelle topped him by four or five inches. They strode down the middle of the street, and the crowd of drunken pedestrians parted before them, unaware of the angels in their midst. "Eight-year-old prostitutes make me uncomfortable, and Beelzebub is there, testing plagues. You know how he feels about me. I like New Orleans."

"Bangkok's better," she said stubbornly. Samaelle had relinquished her armor and black wings in favor of a tank top and ragged denim shorts. She kept her sword, strapped firmly to her back, but no mortal would see it. They never did, until the last moment.

A red-bearded man with a dozen strands of beads hanging around his neck lurched toward them. "Aren't you hot in that?" he asked, pointing at Madisen's red velvet tuxedo.

"I've been hotter," Madisen said, stepping past him.

They passed under a wrought-iron balcony packed with leering, shouting people. Dance music thundered out of the bar below. "Hey!" someone called. "Hey, Red! Show me your tits!"

Samaelle looked up and pointed to herself. The man on the balcony nodded and held out a handful of beads. Samaelle smiled.

The man squawked and tumbled headfirst over the railing. The small portion of the crowd that noticed gasped. A moment later the man stood, unharmed by his fall to the street, and let out a whoop of triumph. He high-fived random members of the crowd. People applauded.

Madisen tugged her arm. "Samaelle, we've talked about the value of subtlety."

"You didn't have to cushion him," she said, irritated. "It was only a one-story drop. You're no fun any more."

"I don't want a repeat of our last vacation."

Samaelle rolled her eyes. "It was only a small village."

They shouldered their way through the crowd, passing drunk college girls lifting their shirts for beads, hard-bitten middle-aged women drinking daiquiris, and serious bald men with video cameras. "We could have at least come during Mardi Gras," Samaelle said. "I hear it's a thousand times—"

A quartet of black-clad teenagers passed them. A boy bumped into Samaelle hard, almost knocking her over. Madisen hooked his fingers under the boy's leather collar and pulled. The boy squawked. His dyed-black hair stuck up in rooster-tufts, and silver rings glinted in his eyebrows and nose.

"Apologize," Madisen said. Samaelle stood smiling, her arms crossed.

"Fuck that!" the goth-boy said, trying to twist out of Madisen's grip. Madisen pulled harder, and the boy gurgled as leather bit into his throat.

"Don't be a dick, Jimmy," one of the girls with him said. "This guy's cool. Check out his tux." Her green eyes glinted with good humor and provided the only touch of color in her flour-white face. She wore a silver choker, a purple plastic skirt, and at least a dozen pairs of earrings.

Something about her face tickled Madisen's mind. Why would a mortal look familiar? She made him think of television, but he'd only seen TV twice, both times certainly long before this girl's birth.

"All right," Jimmy said, standing on tiptoes to keep from strangling. "I'm sorry."

Samaelle smiled. "Not good enough. Lick my shoes and we'll call it even."

"No way! You've been walking through shit on Bourbon Street all night!" A couple of his friends laughed behind their hands. The familiar-looking girl only smiled.

Laughter makes me think of her, too, Madisen thought. Who is she?

"Jimmy just wears that collar for looks," the girl said. "He's never licked a shoe before. I tell you what." She took out two of her earrings. "I think you'll like these. You can have them if you'll accept his apology and let us leave." She held out her hand to Samaelle, who took the earrings and examined them.

"Let him go," Samaelle said. "These are nice."

Madisen let go. Jimmy scurried to stand, scowling, behind the green-eyed girl.

Samaelle held out her hand so Madisen could see. The earrings were tiny silver swords, long, thin-bladed and intricately detailed. They looked remarkably similar to Samaelle's sword.

"Jimmy made those," the girl said.

Madisen looked at the goth-boy. This rat in black was a silversmith?

"Come on, Thalia," Jimmy said, and pulled the girl by the wrist. She waved jauntily with her free hand, and they disappeared into the crowd.

Thalia. Madisen remembered her now.

"I wonder how she knew I'd like swords?" Samaelle put the earrings in. Her ears weren't pierced, but she shoved them through the lobes anyway, drawing blood.

"She knew because she saw your sword."

"Don't be dumb. Humans never see my sword unless I want them to."

"She isn't human." Madisen started through the crowd. "Let's follow them."

"I wish I understood what you were talking about sometimes," she complained.

"Don't you recognize the name?" Madisen said, walking slowly through the darkened street. Jazz music played somewhere nearby, a trumpet wailing over the distant crowd-sounds. "Thalia? Didn't you study the other pantheons?"

"Not really. I saw Gomorrah before it burned and went swimming during the Deluge. You always studied too much." She snapped her fingers along with the music. She got the rhythm all wrong.

"I'll give you a hint. That girl, Thalia, has a few sisters. Urania, Calliope, Polymnia, five others. I can't remember their names."

"Not ringing any bells," Samaelle said. She held a cup in each hand. She'd insisted on stopping for drinks, and now they'd probably never find Thalia. Madisen didn't blame her, though. Wearing human flesh meant being able to get drunk, a pleasure they seldom experienced.

"She's a Muse. Thalia is usually associated with comedy, but the Muses dabble in everything. In the beginning, they weren't even differentiated. Their individual personalities only developed over time."

"Muse." Samaelle spat, then drained one of her drinks, throwing her cup into the gutter. "Silly Greek posers. Our job's more fun."

"Agreed." Madisen put his arm around her. "But Thalia isn't allowed to inspire any more. Zeus has forbidden her to practice."

"What'd she do?"

He laughed. "She inspired performers. She inspired some of them to death. There was this television show—"

"What's television?"

Madisen gestured helplessly. "It shows pictures . . . like a play in a little box."

"I never liked plays. Never saw the point."

"Me either. Anyway, there was a television show, with an ensemble cast, some of the best comedians around, I understand. Thalia inspired a few of the actors, but she drove them too hard. They died of drug overdoses, in car crashes, maybe some suicides, I don't really remember. That wasn't all of it. She worked with stand-up comics, and authors . . . Many of them came to bad ends, burned out, killed by success. Even the ones who didn't actually die fell apart in other ways, lost their gifts, became like ghosts of themselves."

Samaelle laughed. "Sounds like she was doing our job."

"Exactly. Zeus reprimanded Thalia for driving humans to destruction. She said it wasn't her fault, that she wasn't responsible, but Zeus had just come off a bad love affair and he wasn't willing to listen. He forbade her to inspire humans any more, and she ran away."

Samaelle finished her other drink. "So she kept on inspiring humans. But why would she get a guy to make jewelry if she's the Muse of comedy?"

Madisen shrugged. "Maybe because no one would expect it. A jeweler isn't likely to become famous, so Zeus won't ever notice. I bet she's still dealing with performers, though, just not famous ones."

Samaelle stopped walking. "All very fascinating, but why are we following her? She's not even part of our pantheon. If she's disobeying authority and misbehaving, shouldn't we support her, just on principle?"

"Well . . . If we threaten to report her to Zeus, we'll have some leverage if we ever need anything from her . . ."

Samaelle put her arms around his neck and looked at him. "Oh, Maddie, more blackmail? You've got dirt on half the immortal beings in the universe, and you never use any of it. What could you possibly need from a Muse?"

"You never know," he said, embarrassed. "Don't you believe in insurance?"

"I'm the reason people need insurance." She drew a fingernail down his chest. "I've got an idea. Instead of chasing Thalia, let's find a room, and a bed, and enjoy having human bodies. We *are* on vacation."

"That sounds good," Madisen admitted. "But I hate to pass this up. How often do two fallen angels meet a Muse? It seems like we should do *something*."

"We can. Tomorrow morning we'll look for Thalia."

"Why, if not to blackmail her?"

"Maddie, I told you already, we're on vacation. We'll find her, and we'll fuck with her. We'll have fun. She can't tell anyone in her pantheon if we mess with her, because she's practicing illegally." She grinned.

Madisen grinned back. "You're the best."

"You're a close second," Samaelle replied.

"Andrew Jackson. Was he one of ours?" Samaelle squinted at the statue in Jackson Square, shielding her eyes from the morning light. The smell of fresh-cut grass and flowers filled the air here, unlike the beer-soaked atmosphere a few blocks away.

Madisen turned from his contemplation of Tarot readers and beggars. He squinted at the monument's plaque. "Hmm. Not sure. He did some impressively nasty things to the Cherokee, but he wasn't all bad. He loved his wife."

"I'll never understand His criteria for what makes a good person," Samaelle said, rolling her eyes upward.

Madisen chuckled. "Come on. Some of the shows are starting. Thalia's probably around."

Samaelle shaded her eyes. She pointed to a bearded black man in a ragged camouflage coat. He gestured violently and shouted at a trashcan.

"Is he a street performer?"

"I don't think so," Madisen said uncertainly. Angels, fallen or otherwise, weren't known for their appreciation of human art. "I think he's a paranoid-schizophrenic. That guy with the fifteen-foot-high unicycle, I'm pretty sure he's a street performer."

They joined the crowd gathering around the unicyclist. He'd set up in front of a large church, and he exhorted the crowd to move in closer, off the church steps, because otherwise the police would arrest him for obstructing the entrance.

"Sounds like our kind of guy," Samaelle said. "You really think Thalia will be here?"

"Street performers are perfect for her. They aren't famous, they leave no artifacts, and they turn into nobodies as soon as the show's over. If Thalia's working with any performers, it'll be these, because Zeus would never notice. Why else would she come to New Orleans?"

"So where is she?"

"There," Madisen said, and pointed. Thalia, still in black but without her goth friends, stood on the edge of the crowd, in the front row. The unicyclist ran a constant patter, waiting for the crowd to get bigger. The tourists were laughing already, and Madisen imagined their wallets bulging, ready to disgorge cash in exchange for a good show.

He looked around. A jazz quintet played a few benches down, and a mime performed beyond them, fencing with a nonexistent sword against an invisible opponent. Neither had a crowd comparable to the unicyclist's. "Having a Muse is good for business," Madisen said. He and Samaelle stood near the back of the crowd, where Thalia wouldn't notice them, but they had a decent view.

Thalia stepped into the cleared space and spoke to the unicyclist, then kissed him on the cheek. He grinned, tipped his ragged top hat, and blew a whistle. "Come closer! Come on!" the unicyclist called to the audience. Thalia stepped back to watch. She bounced on the balls of her feet, delighted, clearly thriving on the audience.

The performer mounted a small unicycle and pedaled, rolling to the edge of the crowd and back. He juggled a handful of oranges, then threw them into the audience. He cracked jokes and did stunts as his crowd grew larger.

"This is art?" Samaelle said. She'd once said the same thing in the Louvre.

"So it seems. I don't pretend to understand."

"Should I throw my sword into the spokes of his wheel?"

"Let's wait a while. He's just getting started."

The show went on, and the crowd swelled. The unicyclist rode back and forth on a narrow board resting on two sawhorses. He balanced on a makeshift see-saw. He told stories about being arrested, and made fun of tourists in the crowd, who laughed good-naturedly at being singled out.

After about ten minutes he called for volunteers to help him mount the fifteen-foot-high unicycle. Three men held it while he climbed, finally settling himself, arms extended for balance.

"Now?" Samaelle asked.

"Soon."

The unicyclist pointed to a small boy in the audience. "Hey, kid! See those torches? Pick them up—by the white ends, not the black ends—and throw them to me one at a time!"

The boy threw the torches underhand to the unicyclist, who caught them to "oohs" and "ahhs" from the audience. The unicyclist lit the torches and juggled them while pedaling inches from the edge of the crowd. The audience applauded wildly.

"I've got an idea," Madisen said. He knelt and touched the little boy on the shoulder. He whispered without speaking, and the boy giggled. Madisen stood up.

"What'd you do?" Samaelle asked.

"What we always do. I made a suggestion."

The boy ran into the square and shoved the unicycle. The rider shouted as he fell forward into the crowd. The torches flew from his hands. People screamed and tried to dodge out of the way. The falling unicycle didn't hit anyone, but the rider tumbled to the edge of the church steps. One arm twisted under him unnaturally, and he screamed.

"That's entertaining," Samaelle said.

"Look at Thalia." Madisen pointed.

The Muse pressed her hands to her face and shook her head, as if denying what she saw. A few people helped the cyclist get up, but Thalia didn't approach him.

Madisen and Samaelle sauntered toward her. "Hi, Thalia," Samaelle said. "That was a hell of a show. I loved the grand finale."

She looked at them, bewildered. "What? I—"

"We know who you are, Muse," Madisen said. "Do you know us?"

"Imagine me with wings," Samaelle said.

Thalia took a step backward, toward the wrought-iron fence surrounding Jackson square.

"The sword might have tipped you off," Madisen said. "Didn't you wonder why she was wearing it?"

Thalia looked at them, wide-eyed. "People do weird things in New Orleans. I don't associate swords with . . . angels?"

"You should," Samaelle said. "We're fond of them."

"We're fallen angels, actually. Not so different from you. We both put . . . ideas into people's heads."

Thalia stiffened. "You did this? Why? What have I ever done to you?"

Madisen and Samaelle exchanged glances. "You haven't done anything to us," Madisen said.

"We do things to others," Samaelle said. "Because we like to. Because it's fun."

"Certainly you can relate."

Thalia tightened her hands into fists. "I'm nothing like you. I help people, inspire them, and you . . ." She shook her head.

"Drive them to destruction. Like you do, if I recall. A matter of a few dead comedians?"

"Your kind did that," she said bitterly. "If anyone did, if they didn't do it to themselves. Zeus blamed me, but I made their lives better. Not like you."

"You talk pretty big for somebody who's been kicked out of her own has-been pantheon," Samaelle said. "Do you know how many artists we have in Hell? Do you think their painting, or singing, or whatever stupid crap they did, keeps them from the fires?"

"I'm almost certain it does," Thalia said. "Inside, where it counts, I'm sure it does."

"Don't you have some other artists to attend to, Thalia?" Madisen said casually.

Thalia crossed her arms over her chest. "What are you going to do?"

"Follow you around," Samaelle said. "Ruin some careers. Tempt a few artists to more interesting pursuits. See how long it takes you to crumble."

"Then we'll probably report you to Zeus."

"Why?" Thalia backed up against the iron fence.

"We're on vacation," Madisen said.

"It beats the hell out of sitting in a bar."

Thalia drew herself up. She barely topped five feet, but she seemed much taller for a moment. For the first time, Madisen felt uneasy. The Muses were old, maybe older than he was.

"No," Thalia said. "I won't allow it. Not this time."

"How're you going to stop us?" Samaelle said. "Inspire us to death?"

"Good idea," Thalia said.

Something hit Madisen in the back of the head, stunning him. Everything went fuzzy, and he fell to his hands and knees. While in human form, he had human vulnerabilities. When his vision cleared, he saw a silver trombone lying on the bricks, a head-shaped dent in the bell. He looked up groggily.

The white-painted mime ran toward Samaelle. She drew her sword, snarling. The mime made a sword-drawing motion in the air. Samaelle lifted her sword, startled, to parry his intangible strike. With a clang and a shower of sparks, her sword spun away. The mime extended his empty hand as if it held a foil, and a drop of blood appeared at the base of Samaelle's throat.

This can't be happening, Madisen thought, and then a clarinet bounced off his head. The members of the jazz band bore down on him. None of the tourists, walking and talking around them, seemed to notice. The protective coloration of the supernatural, Madisen thought clinically. A black man jammed a flute into Madisen's stomach like a cop wielding a nightstick. Madisen doubled over, coughing.

"We're going to get you for this, Thalia," Madisen said. He struggled to stand upright. "You'll never get away."

"Think so?" Thalia said. "This is only half what I'm going to do to you."

A caricaturist rose from a nearby table and flung sheets of paper and sharpened colored pencils at Madisen and Samaelle. The wind blew the paper into Madisen's face, blinding him.

He heard the clang of a guitar striking something solid, and the back of his head exploded into pain. His eyes filled with white light, and he fell.

Madisen opened his eyes and looked up at fluffy white clouds. His skull thundered. I see a rocking horse, he thought. And there, in that big cloud, a dragon.

He moaned and sat up, touching the back of his head. His fingers came away bloody.

Shattered instruments, paper, and pencils littered the bricks around him. He crawled toward Samaelle, who lay prone on the ground, and touched her shoulder. Someone had hit her in the forehead with a saxophone. The imprint of sax keys stood out on her skin.

Madisen blinked. Everything looked strange. Instead of seeing people and buildings as he always had, he saw their essential shapes, their underlying structures. He admired the church's spires, and noted the shifting of light and shadows on the ground. Must be the head injury, he thought.

Samaelle opened her eyes. "That bitch," she slurred. "Let's get out of this skin and go after her. She can't knock us out when we're ethereal." She stood and tottered toward her sword.

Madisen sat on the bricks, frowning. He picked up a red colored pencil and looked at it, then at Samaelle. The pencil almost exactly matched the shade of her hair. He reached for a stray sheet of paper.

Samaelle returned with her sword. "We have to move fast, before there's an ambush. She said she was going to do something else, right? What do you think she's planning?"

Madisen scribbled something with the pencil.

Samaelle looked around suspiciously, tapping her foot. "What are you doing, Maddie? We have to get going."

"Hold on," he muttered, drawing furiously. "Just a minute, I want to finish this."

"Finish what? There's no time!" Samaelle swung her sword in angry little arcs.

"Come and see," Madisen said, lifting the pencil from the page.

Samaelle knelt, frowning.

Madisen had drawn a picture of her, barely sketched in, but capturing the lines of her face and the fall of her hair. "What do you think?" Madisen said, his voice anxious, as if the answer mattered very much.

Samaelle looked at the picture. She chewed on one long red fingernail.

"It's pretty good," she said.

THE WITCH'S BICYCLE

Even her bicycle was evil.

A heavy black chain wrapped around the frame and front tire secured the bicycle to an iron lamppost in front of Antiquities and Tangibles, a cramped and jumbled antique store downtown. The bicycle seemed to strain against the chain like a half-starved greyhound, skeletal and ferocious. It was a heavy bike with wheelguards that had been new in the 1950's. The frame was dusky red, the color of rubies from a long-forgotten treasure trove. The handlebars curled like ram's horns. A headlamp on the front glittered in the afternoon sunlight, throwing bright flashes. The seat was pitted black leather, and the spokes were bright, shiny chrome. The pedals were spiked to grip the soles of shoes, and to cut anyone foolish enough to try and pedal the bicycle barefooted.

The bicycle's owner emerged from the antique store. Her hair and her dress were the same red as the bike frame, like faded silk roses, her black leather beret matched the seat, and chrome rings flashed on her fingers. Her eyes, before she put on her sunglasses, were as bright and reflective as her bicycle's headlamp. She carried a plastic bag with a real drawstring, and something inside the bag rattled and clattered. Something old and obscure, surely, as it had come from Antiquities and Tangibles, the Sargasso Sea of the antiques trade, the place where only the most marginalized and unappreciated remnants of the past fetched up.

She unlocked the chain and wrapped it around her waist like a belt, then fastened it, spinning the combination lock into nonsense numbers. She dropped her bag in the chrome basket behind the seat and mounted the bicycle. Her boots were leather, with chrome buckles. She cooed to her bicycle, and it seemed almost to steady itself, as if some gyroscopic mechanism kept it upright. As she pedaled away down the sidewalk, she sang, and the hum of the smoothly oiled bicycle chain and the rasp of the fat tires on the pavement seemed to sing with her.

She sang "What Is This Thing Called Love?"

Behind her, in the basket, the bag's contents shifted and clattered, not at all in time with the song.

Cory sat out behind the high school, throwing rocks at a sewer grate, waiting for the bus to come back. Because his school was overcrowded, there were two separate bus schedules. First load left right after school, and went fully-loaded. The second load made it back about forty minutes later, each bus picking up a dozen or so leftover students. For some reason Cory's subdivision had drawn second-load status, and now he had to suffer through this empty after-school time. He *had* to get a car next year, or at least make friends with someone who drove. The other people who rode his bus were out behind the gym smoking pot, probably. Even *they* didn't want to have anything to do with him. At least they weren't violent—just stupid. Unlike some—

"Look who's here," a smooth voice said from his left. Cory hunched his shoulders. School had only been in session for three weeks, and he'd already grown to hate that voice. He didn't even know the kid's name, the leader of the vicious little trio. He didn't have any classes with him, and in a high school of 2000 students it wasn't surprising that he never saw him during the day. But this kid—Cory thought of him as "Rocko" because he looked like a young and pugnacious version of Edward G. Robinson, though his voice was surprisingly pleasant—this kid rode second load on one of the other buses, and apparently had nothing better to do in these forty dead minutes after school than look for people to torment. His little trio—the other two Cory had dubbed "Angel" and "Curly," after Rocko's henchman from the movie *Key Largo*—usually hung around by the vending machines, harassing the freshmen who emerged from after-school band practice to get sodas or chips. Cory had run afoul of them once and gotten away with no worse than a shoving, and since then he'd spent his time reading outside or in odd corners of the school, occasionally slipping away when he heard them approaching. It could be worse, he supposed—in lots of schools there were stabbings and shootings, but as his mom reminded him, this was a good school in a good area. Which meant only the risk of being beaten up by three guys—he wasn't likely to die.

Apparently the band kids had grown wary, and the trio had gotten bored and gone searching for new meat, because here they were. Cory had been so engrossed in stone-tossing that he hadn't heard them coming.

Rocko sat down beside him and slung an arm over his shoulder. Cory shrugged him off, and Rocko laughed, that pleasant, easy laugh. "You like throwing rocks, huh? You want to have a little rock-throwing contest?"

Cory started to stand up. Rocko grabbed the arm of his jacket and pulled him back down. Cory tried to jerk his arm away, but Rocko held him tight, not even moving from his place on the curb. "Just a friendly game," he said.

Cory glanced at Rocko's buddies. Angel and Curly lounged against a science classroom, watching him, sneering. Angel was black and Curly was Hispanic. Say what you would about Rocko, he wasn't a racist. As long as you were mean-spirited and servile, there was a place for you in his gang.

"No, thanks," Cory said. "I don't feel like playing a game."

Rocko ignored him. "The way I figure it, there's nothing too hard about throwing rocks into a grate. That's not any kind of a challenge, you know? Now, if you were aiming rocks at a person, and that person was trying to get away—that'd be challenging. Don't you think?"

Cory couldn't believe he was hearing this.

"We'd need bigger rocks, though," Rocko said thoughtfully.

Cory jerked his arm away again, and this time broke free.

"Ready to start running?" Rocko asked.

"What makes you be like this?" Cory asked, frowning at Rocko's frog-like, smiling face. "Why do you do this?"

"I look at it like dogshit," Rocko said. "There's dogshit on your shoe, you scrape it off, right? I look at you, and I see dogshit, but I can't get rid of you, you just keep . . . hanging around. If I can't get rid of you, I can at least let you know you're dogshit, right? Make sure you don't forget it."

Cory just stared at him. He'd dealt with bullies in the past, and small-scale violence, but those had always been brutally stupid people, strutting for their friends. Rocko sounded so . . . *reasonable*.

"There's just this look about you," Rocko went on. "The way you walk around, all hunched up, the way you always look like you smell something bad. I see you in the halls and it *disgusts* me." He shrugged. "So I guess that's why I do this. Plus, my psychiatrist says I'm in a really explorative stage, that I'm testing my boundaries and trying to define myself."

Cory took a step backwards. Where could he possibly go? The school wasn't that big, and he had to come back here to catch the bus anyway. He couldn't outrun them if they decided to chase him.

"Anyway," Rocko said. "The place where I used to live, before I moved here, they had security guards everywhere, they had metal detectors, they had to lock down the classrooms a couple of times because of riots in the halls. Then I come to this place and there's no cops or anything, I can't believe it, I mean, I know it's the sticks, but *really*. So yeah, I guess I'm just . . . testing the boundaries." He stood up. Angel and Curly stood a little straighter when Rocko rose, like well-trained dogs. "I'm not going to *kill* you or anything," Rocko said. "But . . . you know . . . it's a long year. No telling what could happen." He glanced at Angel. "How long 'til the bus comes?"

"Fifteen minutes," Angel said. He did not have Rocko's orator's voice. His voice sounded like someone falling down a flight of stairs.

"I gotta get a fucking car," Rocko said, shaking his head. "This is just ridiculous. Another year until I turn sixteen, can you believe that?"

"You could always get a bicycle," Cory said. He wasn't sure why—it just popped out.

"What am I, ten years old?" Rocko said.

"Let's beat his ass," Curly said. "This talking's bullshit."

"Talking's not bullshit," Rocko said. "But there does come a time for talk to end. You've got ten minutes, guys. Have fun."

"We're not like him," Curly said, approaching. "We're not testing boundaries or anything."

"Nah," Angel agreed.

Rocko sat on the curb, seemingly oblivious to the impending violence, picking up rocks and examining them.

Cory couldn't do much but run. Probably a couple of teachers were still hanging around the office, and if he got really desperate he could burst into the band classroom and take refuge there until the bus came. Everyone would think he was a pussy, but he'd rather be mocked than beaten. He backed up, trying to gauge the right time to dash. He could head for the dark covered area between the gym and the science buildings, the place everybody called "the Tunnel," and then break across the courtyard and get into the main building. Maybe they wouldn't catch him.

"What's up, guys?" a girl's voice said from the direction of the Tunnel. Angel, Curly, and Cory all looked.

The girl was tall and brunette, her hair pulled back in a messy ponytail. She wore a striped field-hockey uniform, and there were bits of grass stuck to her knees. She held a hockey stick, resting it across her shoulder, and for a moment Cory thought she looked like a particularly athletic incarnation of Death, armed with some kind of wooden practice scythe. "You guys waiting for bus?" she asked, all innocence.

"We were just waiting for you, baby," Curly said, smiling widely and stepping toward her.

Cory, relieved to no longer be the focus of attention, relaxed, then immediately felt ashamed. Now they were going to give this girl shit, and he couldn't do anything about it—why should he feel better at *her* expense?

"I heard all you field hockey chicks are lesbians," Curly said, still smiling. "Wanna prove me wrong?"

She flipped her ponytail. "Oh," she said, in a bored voice. "I didn't realize you were assholes, or I wouldn't have bothered you."

Angel laughed.

She looked at him. "That was an inclusive comment."

"Bitch," Curly said. "I know—"

"Now, now," Rocko said, rising from his place on the sidewalk. "That's no way to talk to a lady."

"She shouldn't talk to me like she did," Curly said. "Nobody talks to me that way."

"Sticks and stones may break your bones," Rocko said. "And, as you might have noticed, she *does* have a stick, and you *do* have bones."

Curly snorted. "Shit. What's she going to do with that?"

The girl smiled at him. She had braces, but Cory still thought it was a beautiful smile, if a little nasty and malicious. She didn't move the stick, didn't thump it into her palm, nothing—just stood there, smiling.

"Shit," Curly said again. "Ugly bitch ain't worth the trouble." He turned his back and slouched away. Angel glanced at Rocko, then went with Curly, back toward the band practice rooms.

The girl glanced at Cory. "You're not saying much. Are you the ringmaster of this circus?"

"No," Rocko said. "That would be me. But I wish you wouldn't judge me by the company I keep. Good help's hard to find."

"So what are you doing here, then?" she asked Cory, ignoring Rocko.

"Just . . . waiting for the bus," he said.

She nodded. "Me, too. First time I've had to ride it. I used to ride home with a friend, but now practice has started . . . ." She shrugged.

Cory was never good at talking to people, especially not to girls, especially not in front of Rocko.

"He's really not worth talking to," Rocko said. "He just asks a lot of stupid—"

"I think your friends are waiting for you," she said, glancing at Rocko. "Maybe you should go check on them, make sure they don't get lost or something."

Rocko frowned, then smoothed back his dark hair. "Which bus do you ride?"

"None of your fucking business," she said.

Rocko narrowed his eyes. "Just wondered if you were on mine."

She simply looked at him.

"Fine," Rocko said. "See you around." He glanced at Cory. "And you—I'll definitely see you around." He sauntered off.

"He's a little shit, isn't he?" the girl said, watching him go. She glanced at Cory. "I'm Heather."

"Cory."

"Those guys bother you a lot?"

He shrugged, uncomfortable. "Not really. Sometimes."

"Girls mostly just talk about each other. And that can get nasty, believe me. But they don't tend to . . . hit each other so much. I feel for you."

"It's no big deal. I can handle it."

"No doubt," she said, and though he was acutely attuned to sounds of sarcasm and contempt, he didn't detect either in her voice. "Which bus do you ride?"

"228."

"Hey, me, too. Where do you live?"

"In a subdivision called Foxglove."

"Cool," she said, nodding. "My family just moved there. We're the last house on the street, down by the circle, right up against the woods. I haven't met anybody else in the neighborhood."

He shrugged, looking off toward the road, unsure whether to be nervous or pleased to hear she was his neighbor. "There isn't really anybody else our age. Some little kids is all."

"Maybe we could play basketball or something. My dad put a hoop up over the garage."

"I'm not very good at basketball."

She shrugged. "So play with me and you'll get better, right?"

"Yeah. I guess so." She was a jock. She'd stomp him at basketball. Wouldn't *that* be fun? She hadn't laughed at him yet, but she would. Everyone did eventually.

The stoners came wandering from behind the gym, and a minute later the bus appeared.

Survived another day, Cory thought. He glanced at Heather. *Got rescued by a girl.*

He got onto the bus and took his usual seat halfway back, on the passenger side. He looked out the window at the parking lot.

Heather plopped down next to him. "This seat taken?"

She wanted to sit next to him? What did that mean? "No."

"You mind if I sit with you? I mean, I know there's lots of room and all, but it gets boring sitting by yourself."

"No, it's fine."

"So what do you do for fun?" She had her hockey stick in her hand, and she thumped it against the back of the seat in front of them while she talked.

He shrugged. "I watch a lot of movies. My dad has a big library of videos."

"Cool!" She said. "I saw *The Burning Witch* last week—have you seen it?"

He shook his head. *Burning Witch* was a horror movie—from the previews it looked to be mostly about a woman who cackled and set things on fire with her mind, and then some teenagers defeated her. It looked pretty dumb. "No, I haven't. I like mostly old movies. Black and white stuff."

She frowned. "Like *It's A Wonderful Life*?"

"No . . . like *The Big Sleep* and *Lady in the Lake* and *The Thin Man* . . . " She was looking at him blankly. "Um . . . *Casablanca*? *The Maltese Falcon*?"

"Oh, yeah," she said, nodding. "Wow. You like that stuff, huh?"

She didn't seem contemptuous, exactly, just . . . surprised. "Yeah, well, my Dad really likes them, so we watch them together sometimes. He likes Humphrey Bogart and Lauren Bacall a lot. We watched a movie called *Key Largo* a couple of weeks ago. There's a guy in that movie named Rocko who looks a lot like . . . " He trailed off.

"Like who?"

He sighed. "Like that guy back at school."

"So he looks like a smiling frog?"

Cory laughed. "Yeah." He glanced at her. She was nice. Not like most of the other girls, who always found something in him to laugh at—his shoes, his hair, the way he walked, the way he talked. It didn't much matter—they always found something. Even the ones who didn't tease him just ignored him.

"I haven't seen many old movies. Maybe we could watch one sometime?"

His dad would tease him so much if he brought a girl home! He'd mean it in a good-natured way, but Cory was already wincing at the thought. Still . . . if Heather thought the movies were cool, it could be worth a little teasing.

"Sure. I'd like that." He reached out and tapped the handle of her hockey stick. "Don't they usually keep these at school?"

She rolled her eyes. "I'm supposed to practice at home, try to get 'better control' the coach says. I've got a stick of my own, but it hasn't come from California yet. My parents have so much *stuff*, it's two big truckloads. My dad's driving back with the last of it this week."

"You're from California?"

"Monterey," she said. "Lived there my whole life."

Cory grimaced. "From California to North Carolina. Seems like a step in the wrong direction."

She shrugged. "All depends on the people, right? If I can make good friends here, it'll be just as good as home was."

She flashed him that braces-and-all smile, and just then Cory would have done anything for her.

Rocko watched bus 228 pull away, his face expressionless. His two associates had drifted off, probably to smoke in the bathroom. Rocko went back outside and sat on the curb. He picked up a rock and held it up to the light, watching the bright flecks flash. He thought about dissections.

Suddenly a bicycle was before him, its rider a woman with dusky red hair and a black leather beret. She was somewhere past young, but not all the way gone into middle-age. She looked like a hippie in her long dress and tights, but her boots were a biker's, and she wore chrome rings. She looked down at him from the bike's high seat. The bicycle seemed to complement her, and he realized its color matched that of her hair.

"Rocko," she said, her voice somewhere between a purr and a rasp.

He frowned. "That's not my name, lady." He didn't like sitting here, with her peering down at him—he felt vulnerable, like a frog in a dissecting pan. He started to get up.

"Frog in a pan," she said. "Nice image, Rocko. But now you're pithed."

He froze, his ass just inches from the concrete, stopped in the act of rising. His legs began to quiver immediately from the strain of holding him up. He felt his heart beating, but he couldn't blink, couldn't move. Like a live frog pithed for dissection, his spine pierced with a metal rod, everything but the most basic physical functions suspended. His fear even had a detached quality; it was wholly intellectual, with no emotional component. He wondered clinically—and he could be very clinical—whether his glands were working, whether adrenaline was pumping into his veins. He thought not.

"Sit down," she said, and his butt hit the curb. She leaned over, the rose curtain of her hair almost touching his face. "I call you Rocko because that's what the Boy calls you."

Rocko heard the emphasis she put on the word "Boy," knew that she meant it as more than a generic term. "This is about the Boy, and the Girl, so I'll call you by the name they do."

Rocko was trying to move his arms. He wanted to lash out at her, knock her over in a tangle of legs, skirt, chrome, and chain. He thought about his psychiatrist—"testing boundaries"—he'd never had boundaries as tight as this, trapped in his own body.

"But you can have a place in this, too, Rocko. You can be the Rival. You do like her, don't you? The Girl?"

Rocko growled—or tried to. He didn't make a sound.

She laughed. "She snubbed you, didn't she? And for that dogshit, that Boy you hate without reason."

Without reason? Rocko always had reasons, and that kid, that Cory . . .

What? Well, he was a piece of shit, always had his nose in a book, he slouched around, stank of cowardice, thought he was better than everyone else . . . There. Lots of reasons. A whole truckload of reasons.

That girl, though . . . she was something else. He had no doubt she'd have used that stick today, if she'd needed to. She was pretty, but not snotty, not afraid to get sweaty and play hard. Not like Cory, who'd probably never sweated in his life.

"Yes," the woman said, nodding. "You can be the Rival. You *are* the Rival." She crooked her finger and he jerked upright. It felt like a rope wrapped around his chest, pulling him to his feet.

She's a witch, he thought, with that same, intellectual fear.

"Would you like to kill the Boy, and win the Girl?" she asked.

Kill? Rocko had a certain interest in the subject, but killing anyone would be so *messy* in the particulars. Just like beating someone up—he didn't much enjoy that, though he often desired the consequences. That was so often a problem; to achieve a certain end, he had to resort to ugly means. If only he could skip those intermediate stages, wave his hands and have someone die, or put them on the ground writhing in pain.

He looked at the woman (he had no choice, he couldn't even blink, but now he *looked*). She'd pithed him like a frog without even saying a word, and he suspected that she didn't need to hear him speak, because she could read his mind. Maybe he could learn power like that from her. The power of ends, and the circumvention of clumsy, inelegant means.

"Kill?" he said, and now his voice worked. The idea of killing lacked emotional color, too. He could kill someone easily, if he felt like this while doing it. "Sure. I could do that."

She grinned. "A will to kill is a wonderful thing. It means you always have a last resort. But you really just want the Girl, yes?"

Rocko grunted. He didn't want the girl to think he was nothing, that was for sure, and he couldn't stand to see her with a dogshit like Cory.

"So the best thing to do would be to humiliate the Boy, somehow, and let her find out about it, maybe even witness it. Then she'd know he's nothing, and that you're clever, and brave, and much more worth her attention. Yes?"

Rocko could feel her eyes boring into him from behind her black glasses. "Yeah. Yeah, that would do it."

"You and your little friends can come up with something, can't you? Something suitable?"

"Something suitable for a shit like him," Rocko said, getting an idea. Of course. Everyone had to use the bathroom sometime, didn't they? "I think so."

"Good," she said. "It's better than murder, at least for now. If you've never buried a body, you don't know how much trouble it can be."

"Cory!" his mom called. "You have a visitor!"

Cory looked up from his homework—just a worksheet on ecology, boring as mud—and frowned. Who could—

Oh. His throat tightened a little. Could it be Heather? Already? "Coming, mom!" He stopped in front of the mirror, raking his fingers through his shaggy brown hair, then gave it up as a bad job. Heather'd seen him at very nearly his worst this afternoon, and she'd seemed to like him fine then.

He hurried downstairs, into the living room.

He hardly recognized the girl he found there. Heather had been sweaty, grass-stained, red-cheeked and mussed before. But this girl—she could be one of the prettiest girls in school. She had blue ribbons braided into her hair, and wore a plain white t-shirt tucked into khaki shorts. Her sneakers were clean, too, not the scuffed ones she'd been wearing before. He could faintly see the lace of her bra under the shirt, and he looked away, blushing.

"Heather tells me you met at school today," his mom said.

"Yeah," Cory said. "She just moved to the neighborhood."

"Welcome to town, Heather," Cory's mom said. "I'll have to go meet your parents sometime."

"Sure," Heather said. "My dad's not here yet, he's driving in another truck full of stuff. He'll be around next week, though."

"I'll make a point of introducing myself," she said. "There's brownies in the kitchen, if you guys want a snack. Would you like to stay for dinner, Heather?"

She glanced at Cory. He shrugged. Heather rolled her eyes at him. "Sure. That'd be great!"

"I'll leave you two alone," Cory's mom said, glancing at Cory with a small, secret smile—a smile that meant she'd be asking him about this nice new girl later on. She went into the kitchen.

"She bakes brownies and she makes dinner?" Heather said. "What, did you win the mom lottery? We eat Chinese and pizza most of the time at my house."

"Chinese and pizza sounds pretty good to me. Mom's a research assistant for a lawyer, and she works from home about half the time. She usually makes something for dinner on the days she's home."

"How come she doesn't pick you up from school?"

He shrugged. "She says just because she's home doesn't mean she's not working."

"Well, that's too bad. It means you get to keep me company on the bus, though." She twirled around, an impromptu ballerina. "How do I look?"

Cory had never dealt with a girl his own age in such proximity before. How did you answer that? What would she think if he said she looked pretty? Would she think he liked her? Did he like her? "You look fine," he said cautiously.

"Aren't you a charmer?" she said, but it was good-natured. "I was just going to come right over, but my mom's big on making good first impressions, she said I shouldn't meet the neighbors for the first time looking all grubby. She braided my hair and made me change—she wanted me to wear a *dress*! I don't even like wearing dresses to church."

Cory wouldn't have known what to think if Heather had shown up here in a dress—he certainly would have felt uncomfortable in his own jeans and t-shirt, even if this *was* his house.

"Want to see my room?" Cory asked.

"Sure." She followed him up the stairs. "You'll have to come to my house sometime, and check out the woods out back. They're really cool."

"I go back there a lot, actually. There's some really nice, quiet places. The woods are pretty big, too, bigger than you think at first."

"Ever get lost?"

He hesitated, always unwilling to make himself sound foolish. "Yeah, once. I finally came out of the woods about a mile away on the highway, and walked back from there."

"I haven't gone far enough to get lost yet, but I'm sure I will." It sounded like she relished the idea—like it would be more of an adventure than an embarrassment. Maybe, for her, it would be. And maybe if he went exploring with her, he could learn to look at getting lost in the same way.

He showed her his new computer, and the Bogart poster he'd gotten for Christmas. She really liked his microscope, sitting dusty on a shelf—seemed a lot more interested in it than he'd ever been, truthfully. "Oh, good books!" she said, looking over his row of Charles de Lint and Orson Scott Card. She tapped a copy of *Ender's Game* with her forefinger. "I read this in school last year." She pulled down one of his *Sandman* trade paperbacks. "I've never read these. Are they any good?"

"They're awesome."

"Let me borrow them sometime? You can raid my shelves, too, if you want."

"Sounds good." So what if she liked bad movies? She had good taste in books, at least.

They talked about books for a while, then played video games. She was better than him at killing zombies, but he excelled at racing futuristic cars through decaying cityscapes.

Cory's dad got home right before dinner. He was nice to Heather—he was always nice to everyone. His parents mostly talked to Heather during dinner, asking about her old hometown, what her parents did, and so on. Cory learned a lot about her that way, and Heather seemed perfectly at ease around his parents. Dinner was chicken parmesan with salad and some kind of sun-dried tomato bread—a nicer meal than they would've had if they didn't have company over, Cory suspected.

After dinner, Cory walked with Heather out in the yard. "Sorry about that," he said. "My parents playing twenty questions with you that way."

"It's okay. They're parents, they do stuff like that. I didn't mind. As long as you can play the same game when you come to have dinner at my house."

Cory felt warm. For the first time since school had started, he began to think that this year wouldn't be horrible. It was possible Heather would meet other people, find out Cory wasn't exactly at the top of the social ladder, and drift away from him . . . but maybe she'd stick around and be his friend. That would make this year a lot better, even if they didn't have any classes together.

"Want to go down to the woods before it gets totally dark?" she asked. "There's this really cool spot by a stream, it only takes about five minutes to get there from my house . . . " Unselfconsciously, she reached out and took his hand, pulling him along. Her hand was warm, and Cory wanted to hold it forever.

Heather lived at the end of the street, and as they walked along, Cory noticed a woman riding toward them on a bicycle, moving in slow arcs, drifting from one side of the street to the other and back again, only incidentally making forward progress. She had long reddish hair, and dark glasses. She wore a long skirt, too, and Cory didn't see how she could pedal the bicycle without getting the fabric caught in the chain and the gears. The woman stared at them as she approached, slowing down. She rolled past them so slowly that it seemed like her bicycle should fall over from a lack of forward momentum. Her skirt matched the bike frame, and her boots seemed almost a part of the pedals—looking at her made Cory's

45

eyes get blurry. The impression was hard for him to define, even to himself, but he had trouble telling where the woman left off and the bicycle began, like they were a single creature made of chrome and flesh, hair and leather.

Heather's hand tightened in his, and they stood still as she rolled past them, mere feet away. She grinned, and for an instant her teeth seemed to flash like chrome. Then she pedaled on, something in a bag clattering in the basket behind the bicycle seat, like pieces of metal clanging together.

Cory and Heather stood for a moment, watching her go. "Does she live around here?" Heather asked.

"Never seen her before in my life."

"Weird," Heather said decisively, and then squeezed his hand and started walking again.

That night, Cory woke in darkness. He sat up, disoriented. Something had awakened him, but he wasn't sure what. Some noise outside, maybe? He went to the window and looked down into the backyard.

Someone was pedaling a bicycle around a circle in the grass, a girl in a nightgown. Was that . . . Heather? It looked like her, still with the blue ribbon in her braid. He frowned, wondering what she was doing down there, wondering if he should go down himself. She just kept pedaling that big old-fashioned bike, going counterclockwise around the dogwood tree in the middle of the yard.

Cory pulled on his shoes, grabbed his jacket, and slipped quietly down the stairs, frowning. Was Heather okay? Just out for a middle-of-the-night adventure?

He went out the back door, closing it quietly, then down the steps across the grass toward Heather. "Hey!" he called softly, not wanting to wake his parents.

When he got within a few feet of the perimeter of her circle, he realized the rider wasn't Heather at all. He couldn't understand how he'd thought it was—she wasn't even wearing an nightgown, and she was an adult. That's when he began to think it might be a dream.

The bicyclist skidded to a stop in front of him. He stepped away, afraid, because this was the woman he and Heather had seen earlier, the one who seemed somehow *blended in* with her bicycle.

"Hello, my darling Boy," she said, putting a funny emphasis on the last word.

"You shouldn't be here," he said. "This is private property."

"I'm here to help you. But if you want me to go . . . " She shrugged, and put her foot on the pedal.

"What do you mean?" He was cold despite his jacket, the night wind blowing straight through him. Would he be cold, if this was a dream?

"There's a boy at your school," she said. She didn't put any particular emphasis on the word "boy" that time. "You call him Rocko, yes?"

Cory nodded. It had to be a dream, but that didn't make it any more disturbing.

"He's going to do something nasty to you tomorrow afternoon, my Boy. He hates you, but that's not such a large thing—his kind is always full of hate, though he is rather more a monster than most bullies, I think. Today, though, he became *jealous* of you, too—he likes the Girl, the Girl who likes you. His jealousy is much more dangerous to you than his hatred. He'll want to do something about his jealousy, something to humiliate you."

"How do you know that? How do you know I call him Rocko?"

"Because I'm the good witch, my Boy, and I want you to defeat your Rival." She smiled, and the bag in the basket behind her shifted with a clatter.

"What's in that bag?" Cory asked.

She looked behind her, then back at him. "You'll find out soon enough. Have patience. I do. You won't need anything from that bag tomorrow. You'll just need a little bit of magic, a tiny spell . . . a *turnaround*. I'll teach you how to do it. It takes a little blood to start with, but that shouldn't be hard—I bet there will be blood tomorrow afternoon, your own blood, if you're not quick. After the blood is spilled, it's just the matter of a gesture, and a word, and certain . . . *patterns* . . . of thought. I'll show you how." She reached out toward his face, and he flinched away. "Shh, be a good Boy."

He wanted to turn and run, despite her claim to be a "good witch"—nothing about her reassured him, nothing made her seem good. He couldn't believe she had any human feeling, any more than . . . than a bicycle would.

He couldn't move, not a muscle, though, and oddly, he didn't feel afraid. He *thought* frightened thoughts, but panic didn't sing in his veins. The witch touched his face with her fingers, and with her chrome rings.

"You won't remember any of this, my Boy. Not until tomorrow, when you need to."

School the next day was the usual, everything pretty easy except for biology, where Cory struggled to understand what mitochondria did, and why on earth he should care. He'd agreed to meet Heather down by the office when she got done with classes. Earth Science was his last class, and thinking about seeing Heather again soon made it hard for him to think about "the ecology of the microcosm" that his earth science teacher kept talking about.

He didn't think about Rocko all day, until he started reading after school. He sat on a bench near the office and read *Good Omens*, thinking it'd be pretty cool if he had the kind of powers the kid, Adam, had in that book. There were bullies in that story, but they were pretty harmless—you never got the sense the kids really worried about being beat within an inch of their lives by Greasy Johnson, like Cory feared Rocko and Curly and Angel. Maybe that was because *Good Omens* took place in England—maybe people just weren't as violent on the other side of the sea.

Cory stuck the book in his bag and wandered down the hall toward the bathroom so he could pee before meeting Heather.

He stepped into the bathroom, and rough hands grabbed him, slamming him against the wall. Angel and Curly had him by the arms, and before he could even think of pulling away they stepped on his insteps, crushing his toes, pinning his feet so he couldn't kick or thrash. "Hiya," Curly said. "No girls with sticks here to save you today, huh?

"We're still not testing boundaries," Angel said. "So don't worry about that."

Rocko sauntered out of a toilet stall. "I didn't think you'd ever come to take a piss, kid," Rocko said, zipping up his pants. "I figured the place to find a shit like you would be right here, in the toilet, but then you made me wait. I'm a busy guy. It's not right, me having to wait for you."

Cory thought about the old movies he'd seen, about Bogart's effortless aplomb, the way he'd casually disarmed the gunsel from *The Maltese Falcon*. But even Bogart got beaten up sometimes, especially when two or three guys came for him at once. And Cory was no Bogart. He wanted to spit in Rocko's face . . . but what if they just planned to scare him? Wouldn't spitting make them do something much more nasty?

Curly ground his foot into Cory's instep, and Cory bit back a shout of pain. He could try to keep from blubbering like a baby, at least.

Rocko looked at his watch. "Are you meeting your girlfriend this afternoon, dogshit?"

"Leave her alone," Cory said, without thinking.

Curly and Angel laughed, one right into each of Cory's ears.

"I think he's in love," Angel said.

"I think he just wants to fuck her," Curly said sagely.

"I thought that's what *you* wanted to do," Angel said.

"True," Curly agreed.

"Does this make you feel tough, three against one?" Cory said.

"No," Angel said. "But it's more fun this way, and I usually feel pretty tough anyway. Do you think I *couldn't* kick your ass on my own?" He ground down with his foot, and Cory couldn't stop himself from yelping.

"Well, we don't want you to keep you from meeting Miss hockey-sticks-and-sunshine," Rocko said. "So we'll get this over with and then let you go." He paused. "Punch him in the bladder a couple of times, first, let's see if we can make him wet himself."

Cory clenched his teeth. Curly hit him just above the pelvic bone, and it made a sharp bolt of pain jolt through him, but he kept control of his bladder.

"That's a little too close to his dick for me, man," Angel said.

Curly scowled.

"Fair enough," Rocko said. "I guess it doesn't much matter, anyway. Bring him over." Rocko walked to the far stall, the one that was always out of order, that didn't flush properly. He pushed open the door, and a horrible stink wafted out. "We all took turns filling the pot," Rocko said. "There's some shit, and some piss, and some more shit."

Cory started to struggle then, wrenching his arms as hard as he could. Curly and Angel grunted and held on tight, dragging Cory across the floor toward the stall. Knowing he couldn't break free, Cory opened his mouth to scream—

—and Rocko shoved a wad of balled-up toilet paper in his mouth, making him gag. "Shut up," Rocko said quietly. "I can keep you from screaming—you see that, right? So no one's going to come help you. I'm going to take that toilet paper out of your mouth, and if you try to bite me, I'm going to do something a lot worse to you than I already have planned." He grinned. "I want your mouth cleared out, so you can taste my shit and piss in there, but if I have to, I'll keep you gagged. I'll just swish the next wad of paper around in the toilet bowl first. Can you be quiet?"

Terrified, helpless, Cory nodded. Rocko reached to pull out the paper.

Blood, Cory thought. The thought came with nothing else, no context, no mental referents, but he acted on it all the same, biting Rocko's finger.

Rocko jerked his hand back with a hiss, and Cory saw the flecks of bright blood on his forefinger. "You shit!" he cried. "God damn you, I'm going to *get* you for that!"

Something welled up in Cory when he saw the blood—words to be said, certain movements to be made with his fingers, and a strange twisting in his mind. He didn't know where the impulses came from, but he followed them, because he somehow knew his salvation lay that way.

Everything blurred. His vision dimmed, and he felt as if he'd been dropped down an elevator shaft, a sensation of things whipping past at high speed. *Turnaround*, he thought. An interval of time went by—he couldn't be sure how long—but when he came back to his normal awareness, things had changed.

Rocko was kneeling before the filthy toilet, his head inside the bowl, and Cory had his foot pressed down on the back of Rocko's neck. He stumbled back, horrified—what had he done? He'd only wanted to get *away!*

Curly and Angel were leaning against the wall, bleeding from split lips, looking groggy. "Fuck," Angel said, his voice slurred. "That's some kind of kung-fu shit."

Rocko lifted his head, and turned to look at Cory. The things smeared on his face made Cory gag, and it didn't help that they'd planned to shove *his* face into the toilet bowl; that didn't make it any less horrible.

"Get him!" Rocko snarled. "Get him and fucking kill him!"

"To hell with you!" Angel said. "Did you see what that motherfucker *did*? I'm not messing with him!"

Curly nodded his assent, and the two of them went stumbling out of the bathroom.

"How did you do that?" Rocko said softly, still kneeling on the floor. "You little bastard, that wasn't kung-fu, that was fucking impossible."

"Just leave me alone," Cory said, his voice hoarse. He felt horribly on edge, and he wasn't sure he'd be able to keep from crying. He backed away. "Just stay away from me, I don't want anything to do with you, leave me alone!"

He ran from the bathroom, stumbling toward the office. He slowed down and took deep breaths. Rocko wouldn't be coming after him, not right away—he had to clean his face off first. What had *happened* back there? How had he done . . . whatever he'd done?

Turnaround, he thought. The thought came in a woman's husky voice, but that didn't make any sense, either.

"Cory?" Heather said. "Are you okay?"

She came hurrying down the hallway, hockey stick in hand.

Cory shook his head. "I . . . Rocko and his friends tried to mess with me again, in the bathroom."

She scowled. "Are you okay?"

"Yeah. I got away." He didn't want to go into details, not least of all because he couldn't *remember* the details. "I'm okay."

She put her hand on his shoulder, and Cory realized he was shaking. "Take it easy. It'll be okay. Let's catch the bus."

"Yeah. Okay. It just . . . "

"It's adrenaline," she said. "You're still all jazzed-up from it. You'll feel better soon. Come on."

"You sure fucked that up, didn't you?"

Rocko jerked his head up from the sink, where he'd been washing his face for the tenth time. He looked in the mirror, but didn't see anyone behind him. He turned around, and there was the woman, the witch from yesterday. Standing—with her *bicycle*—by one of the toilet stalls.

Rocko wondered for a moment if he was going insane. Witches and their malevolent bicycles didn't usually hang out in high school bathrooms. What would his psychiatrist say if Rocko told him about *this*?

"That piece of shit had some kind of trick," Rocko said through clenched teeth.

"Looks like you're the piece of shit, now."

He took a step toward her threateningly, then stopped, remembering the pithed feeling from yesterday.

"It's not too late, though," she said. "You tried humiliation, and it failed . . . turned around on you, in fact—*you* were humiliated instead."

"So what do you suggest?" he asked, trying to stay cool. "Your last advice didn't help me much."

"As I said, the will to kill is a wonderful thing. You shouldn't do it here at school, though . . . we wouldn't want you to get expelled."

"So where?"

She shrugged. "An opportunity will present itself, Rocko. Opportunities always do."

"And what should I kill him *with*?"

"This," she said, and took the bag from the basket on her bike. She opened it so he could look inside.

"That's a pretty weird suggestion," he said after a moment.

"Not the sort of weapon a ninth grader would be expected to use, though, my little Rival. And you don't own one, and it's not something you can pick up in the hardware store, so it's unlikely to be traced back to you. As long as you keep it clean of fingerprints and ditch it after you're done."

"What do you care? What's in this for you?"

"I'm the good witch, and I'm a big believer in the power of true love. I think you and that Girl could be beautiful together, if we get the Boy out of the way."

Rocko didn't believe her for a moment, but it didn't matter. He hadn't wanted to kill Cory before, not really, but now, after what he'd done to him in the bathroom today . . . "Can you make me like I was yesterday? So that when I . . . when I do it . . . I don't feel anything?"

"Oh, my little Rival," she said. "I think that's something you can learn to do on your own. Maybe you can even learn to *enjoy* the killing."

He thought that over. She was right. And whether he enjoyed it, or felt nothing, or whatever, he could still *do* it. "I can't carry that out of here," he said, nodding toward the bag. "It's not exactly inconspicuous."

"Would you believe me if I told you it will be near to hand when you need it?"

He looked at her for a moment, then nodded. "Yeah. From you, I believe it."

Cory and Heather sat together again on the way home. "Do you have Mr. Troublestone?" she asked.

"Yeah, seventh period, for Earth Science."

"Me too, but I've got him fifth. Do you have to do that micro-ecology thing?"

"Yeah. Seems like a pretty simple report."

"Simple, but *boring*. I was thinking it would be fun to write the report about something in the real world."

"Like what?"

"Like that stream in the woods behind my house. There's flies and frogs and reeds and even little fish . . . " She shrugged. "I thought we could study that. You know how Mr. Troublestone's always talking about old-time naturalists, drawing pictures of animals and flowers and stuff. I bet if we did something like that for the stream, learned about its ecology, we'd get a good grade. And it's more fun than just reading about the stuff."

"That sounds good. You should do that."

"*We* should do it. I bet he'd let us work together, since we'd be doing more than just a report—we'd have drawings and an observation journal and stuff." She shrugged, and didn't look at him. "You know, if you want to." She kept her voice neutral.

She's afraid I'll laugh! Cory realized. *Afraid I'll make fun of her, or think she's a geek!* It was a revelation, to realize that she could fear something like that from him, and it made him like her even more. "It sounds great," he said. "I'd love to do that with you."

She grinned. "Hope you don't mind getting a little mud on your face."

"I can think of worse things."

They went down to the stream that afternoon and sat looking into the water. It would have been easier to do this project in the spring, when there'd be tadpoles and things, but they could still find interesting stuff to write about. After a while they just sat, tossing stones into the water, already easy and peaceful together.

"I had a weird dream last night," Heather said, leaning back on her elbows, looking at the leaves overhead. "About that woman we saw ride by on the bicycle yesterday. She had a measuring tape, and she kept walking around me, asking me to hold out my arms and stuff, and she took my measurements. She said she thought I'd be a good fit, and when I asked her if she was going to make a dress for me, she just laughed. She said I'd make one for her." She frowned. "No . . . she said 'You'll make a good dress for me. You'll fit like a glove.'" She shook her head. "Weird. It freaked me out a little, I don't know why. Scared me bad enough to wake me up."

Cory didn't say anything, because now he began to remember his own dream—or had it been a dream at all? "I dreamed about her, too."

Heather looked at him. "No. Really?"

"I think so," he said, nodding. "I dreamed she was riding her bicycle around and around the tree in my backyard. Only it wasn't her at first, the—the woman." He'd almost said "the witch." Had she called herself a witch, a good witch? He couldn't quite recall.

"It wasn't her? Who was it?"

"It . . . I thought it was *you*, first, and then it turned into her." Saying those words chilled him, as if he'd dropped his heart into the autumn stream running at their feet. To begin as Heather, and *turn into* that witch, what a horrible idea!

But Heather was grinning at him. "You're having dreams about me, huh?"

He blushed, then laughed, forgetting his fear. "Yeah, well, it was a *bad* dream, so don't be too flattered."

"I knew you were a charmer from the first moment I met you," she said. "I should get going—it's almost dinnertime. Want to come back here to-morrow, and start on this project for real?"

The next day was Saturday. "Sure. What time should I come over?"

"Oh, whenever. My parents usually make a big breakfast on Saturdays, but I don't know if mom will, since dad's still out of town. Come over around ten, I guess, just to be safe."

They made their brief farewells, and Cory walked farther into the woods, taking the scenic route in the general direction of his house.

Something moved in the bushes. He paused, listening. Probably it was just somebody's dog, but there were deer, sometimes, and he always en-joyed getting a glimpse of those. He looked toward the source of the sound, in a thick tangle of underbrush.

Something pushed out of the tangled vines and branches—something red, and black, and chrome.

It was the bicycle, the witch's bicycle, pushing its way through the woods. Its headlamp seemed to consider him, multi-faceted as a fly's eye.

The witch was nowhere to be seen.

Cory, frightened beyond all reason, turned and fled the woods, racing for home.

That night, as the Boy and the Girl and the Rival all slept unquietly, the witch rode her bicycle through their neighborhood. Bad dreams drifted from her like vapors, and she sang "Love is a Many Splendoured Thing," her bicycle tires humming along. The day before the transference always woke romantic thoughts in her—for without love, without the ancient dance of Boy Meets Girl, how would she keep her youth forever?

She rode her bike through the Girl's yard, her bicycle not bumping at all as it went over the grass, not slowing as it went into the trees, its headlamp dark. She had no need of the light—both she and the bicycle could see perfectly well in the dark.

She'd left off her black beret tonight, and had instead braided her hair with a bit of blue ribbon. Otherwise she looked the same as always, not yet ready to completely give up her resemblance to the bicycle in order to fully assume her resemblance to the Girl. That could wait until tomorrow, when her mind would be fully loosened.

She looked around the stream for a likely spot. The location was a good one, really—in her girlhood, when this little play had been acted out the *first* time, it had taken place in a dark wood, by a little stream not unlike this one. Her young lover (whose name she'd forgotten long ago—she just thought of him as the First Boy) had faced off against his Rival for her affection while she stood by, watching, horrified . . . and fascinated. They had both stolen their father's dueling swords, planning to fight for her like grown men. The Rival's blade had snapped against the Boy's, breaking in half. The Boy had stabbed the suddenly disarmed Rival in the heart . . . and when she saw the blood, the Girl who would become the witch understood. This murder over a Girl was not an isolated event, it was an ancient thing, enacted time and again in various guises throughout the ages. There had to be power in that, she knew, in that timeless repetition, a power that could be awakened and directed and sealed by the spilling of blood.

She took the bag from the basket and opened it. She drew out the Boy's sword and jammed it point-first into the dirt by a tree. It was a dueling epee, old but newly sharpened. It had taken her ages to find a set that looked even *close* to being right. Then she removed the Rival's sword, identical to the Boy's. She took a rasp file from her bag and sat in the dirt with the Rival's sword across her knees. She filed away at the blade halfway down its length, humming as she did so. Her bike stood nearby, seeming almost wary, standing upright even though the kickstand hadn't been put down.

She'd discovered the secret of eternal youth—one of the secrets, anyway; she supposed there must be many ways, for those willing to walk beyond the lighted paths. She'd survived so long, rejuvenating herself, by staging reenactments of that first fight, when she'd been a young thing in the first bloom of womanhood. She never let her hair turn gray, and in recent decades she rode her bicycle, to make herself seem young. She'd worked with this bicycle for so long that blood and magic had washed over it, making it into something more than a disguise and a conveyance—making it into something alive, something almost like a familiar.

She resembled the bicycle, too, dressing to match it, and that further confused the question of her identity. Tomorrow she would drink a potion to loosen her mind, to loosen the threads mooring her spirit to this body. She would put a blue ribbon in her hair, and dress herself to match the new Girl.

But that was only preliminary business, nothing more than clearing the way. The meat of her magic required other people, young people—and blood. Every few decades she found a new Boy and Girl and Rival, and put this little passion-play into motion. Making sure the Boy and Girl got together, seeing the Rival humiliated, driving him to murder. The Boy would face the Rival, and kill him, while the Girl looked on. When the blood spilled, a sacrifice to ignite the spell, the witch would *become* the new Girl, sliding easily into the young body, crowding out the resident mind—taking her place in this new variation on the old drama of love and murder. That was the power of imperative resemblance, the magic of recurring situations—she would become young, as she'd been at that first duel. Her old body would be left behind in the woods, and would cause a stir when discovered, but nothing would come of it.

The witch turned the sword over and rasped at the other side of the blade. She'd have to smear it with dirt so the marks wouldn't be noticeable. She would have a little trouble in the Girl's body, of course. She wouldn't have the girl's memories, or access to her mind—her mind would go wherever such things went when they were crowded-out, probably nowhere, into oblivion. The witch would have trouble dealing with the Girl's parents. In the past, she'd had to kill parents, but things were easier in this day and age. Now, she only had to tell someone in authority that her parents touched her inappropriately, that they invited their *friends* to touch her inappropriately. The witch could press lit cigarettes into her new young thighs, and show the burns to the teachers or the police—that should take care of any disbelief.

The witch hummed happily as she rasped, moving the file in time to her song. Finally she put the file back in her bag, satisfied. She put the filed sword into the dirt on the other side of the stream, half-hidden by a bush. She thought a duel across the water would be very picturesque. She wondered if the Girl would faint at the first sight of blood. That's what the last girl had done, and it had made the transition to her mind *much* easier. No resistance at all, just a simple expulsion.

The witch climbed onto her bicycle and rode out of the woods, into the dark. Tomorrow she would be young again. It had been too long—it had *always* been too long.

Rocko woke up Saturday morning after a round of awful dreams, in which he'd tried to stab a boy by a stream while a dark-haired girl looked on, wide-eyed and helpless. He'd felt strong in the dream, like a conqueror . . . but the next thing he knew he was dying, his blood running into the water.

He woke, shivering.

His parents weren't awake yet. Good. He slipped into the kitchen and ate a cold biscuit out of the fridge. Then he dressed, thinking about Cory, about finding the right time to strike.

When he went out the side door, he found the witch's bicycle leaning against his house. He approached it warily, but it seemed harmless and inert. He touched the curved handlebars. Just metal. He looked around for the witch, and didn't see her anywhere.

"You know the way to his house?" Rocko asked.

The bike just sat there.

Rocko took the handlebars and moved the bicycle into the yard. He climbed on and started pedaling the heavy bicycle, wondering how he would know which way to go.

The handlebars tugged under his hands, toward the left, and Rocko went with them. *Like the planchette on a ouija board*, he thought, *moving under my fingers.*

For some reason, even though he was not the type of boy to sing aloud, he found himself shouting the half-remembered words to "Love Me Tender" as he pedaled.

After about a mile, the bike started pedaling itself.

Cory walked to Heather's house with his notebook under his arm, thinking about his dream last night. He found Heather in her front yard, smacking balls with her hockey stick, driving them into one of those portable netted goals. She wore jeans and an untucked blue shirt. Her hair was mussed, and her face was red from exertion. She was altogether beautiful.

"Want to take a few swings?" she asked, seeing him.

"Maybe later."

"Any time. Want to head for the stream?" She picked up her bookbag from where it rested by a flowerbed

"Sure."

"Mom said she'll make lunch for us. She wants to meet you."

That both pleased him and made him nervous. "You told her about me?"

She laughed. "I had to tell her something when I went to your house. She made me braid my hair, remember?"

"Right, right." They ambled into the woods. She swung her hockey stick at pine cones.

"Did you have any—"

"—weird dreams last night?" she finished. "Yeah. No witch, though, just watching a couple of kids I'd never seen before try to kill each other."

"I dreamed I stabbed somebody. There was a girl there, too . . . and she came over and stared down at the kid's blood while it ran into the water. She hardly seemed to notice me, even though I tried to get her attention."

"That's so messed up," she said. "Very weird."

"I saw something yesterday . . . "

"What?"

"I thought . . . I thought I saw that woman's bicycle in the woods. Not her, just the bike, with no one riding it. But that's crazy. Right?"

"I don't know. I just wish the dreams would stop. If it keeps up, I'll be afraid to go to sleep."

They got to the stream and started talking about their project, both of them glad to have something besides bad dreams to pay attention to.

The bicycle took Rocko into a subdivision after about an hour and a half of riding. He hoped the bicycle would be around to take him *back*, because he didn't remember the way. "That sword better be here," he said to the bicycle when it began slowly coasting toward the woods at the end of the subdivision. "Not to mention that dogshit Cory."

The bicycle did not respond, but a short distance into the woods, it stopped moving, and started to fall over. Rocko stepped off and stood still, listening. He heard water, and, maybe, voices. Did Cory have friends? It didn't seem possible. But if he did . . . well, Rocko would do what he had to when the opportunity presented itself, as opportunities invariably did.

He crept through the woods, toward the voices . . . and saw Cory and Heather, right across a stream.

Heather. Shit. He hadn't expected her to be here. Still . . . maybe it was a good thing. Cory had surely told Heather how he'd made a fool of him, driven off his friends and left him face-down in a shit-filled toilet bowl. They'd probably *laughed* about it, when it should have been *Cory* she laughed at.

Well, he'd show her now, wouldn't he? Show her that he couldn't be messed with that way, not without consequences. She'd *see*.

He glanced around.

And right there, driven point-first into the soil, was the sword. He pulled it out and held it. It felt good in his hand—it felt *natural*.

No feelings, he reminded himself. *Just do what needs to be done.* He started across the creek.

"Did you hear something?" Cory asked.

"I don't—" Heather began.

The next things happened very fast.

Rocko came out of the bushes on the far side of the stream, holding something long in his right hand—was it a *sword*? He wasn't scowling, or cursing, or smiling, just hurrying toward the stream with a fixed, intent expression on his face. Cory instinctively stepped between Rocko and Heather.

"Are you crazy?" Heather shouted, falling back. Cory didn't know which of them she was talking to.

Cory retreated too, banging his elbow on a tree. He glanced that way—and saw a sword, driven point-down into the dirt by the tree trunk.

What he had to do seemed obvious. He'd done it last night in his dream, hadn't he?

He pulled the sword out of the dirt and held it before him. He'd never held a sword before, but he knew how; it felt like second nature.

Rocko stood on the other side of the stream. "This is for my humiliation," he said. He nodded toward Heather. "And for the Girl."

"You can't have her," Cory said, not sure where the words came from. "You'll have to come through me."

"So be it," Rocko said, and jumped across the stream. Cory waited in *en garde* position, his mind curiously blank. These events seemed to have little to do with him—they were almost formalities, somehow, but essential nonetheless.

Rocko raised his sword, and his face finally betrayed expression—a snarl of total, concentrated rage.

Then Heather hit Rocko with her hockey stick, snapping his sword and driving the broken pieces into his chest. A look of comical surprise crossed Rocko's face, and he looked toward Heather. She hit him in the side of the head with the flat of the stick, and he stiffened, then stumbled backwards and fell in the stream, still holding the hilt of his sword.

"Jesus," Heather said, breathing hard.

Then, off in the bushes, the witch screamed.

What had the Girl *done*? Her place was to stand to one side and watch the bloodshed, not intercede! The witch had loosened the moorings of her mind, dressed in jeans and a blue shirt to match the Girl, put a ribbon in her hair. She was ready to *become* the Girl, waiting only for the Boy to spill the Rival's blood and ignite the spell—and that had been ruined!

She ran out of the woods where she'd been watching. "Bitch!" she yelled. "You little whore, you little interfering whore!"

It might not be too late. If she could make the Rival bleed, maybe this tableau was still close enough to the original—the imperative resemblance hadn't totally broken down. She was too far away, though, she'd never get to him and kill him in time, especially with the Girl still standing there, fierce as an Amazon, her hockey stick in hand.

But her bicycle—it was closer.

Rocko sat up, groggily, and saw the witch coming, screaming. He looked at the shattered remnant of sword in his hand, and suddenly understood the essentials, if not the particulars, of the situation.

The witch had set him up. She'd meant for him to die here, and had given him a useless sword. She'd probably been behind Cory's impossible feat of strength and speed in the bathroom, too.

He would *kill* her. He struggled to his feet.

Then he saw the bicycle bearing down on him, and froze, pithed by fear.

The bicycle came out of the trees, lumbering slowly at first but then building speed. Rocko stared at the witch's bicycle as it raced toward him. Heather held her hockey stick across her chest, but she was looking at the witch, who was dressed like Heather and grinning horribly.

The riderless bicycle was going to pass by Cory. He saw its ram's-horn handlebars, only they'd twisted, so their points aimed forward, like bull's horns. They would gore Rocko easily, and his blood would pool in the stream . . .

In one smooth motion, with thoughtless ease, Cory tossed his sword point-first toward the bicycle as it passed him. His sword flew neatly into the spokes on the back tire. The rotation of the wheel slammed the sword against the frame, binding the spokes and making it impossible for the wheel to turn. The bicycle slalomed, and the witch screamed again. The bike skidded for several feet before it fell, then slid into the stream, stopping by Rocko's feet.

Rocko looked down at it, then at the witch, who stood clutching her hair and shouting incomprehensibly.

Rocko grinned. He reached down and snatched the sword from the bike's spokes. The bicycle's wheels spun, but it couldn't seem to right itself. Cory cursed softly. Rocko was going to come after him, and this time he didn't have a weapon of his own. He couldn't run, either, not if that meant leaving Heather to Rocko's mercy, and to the witch.

Rocko lifted the sword and shouted. His face held plenty of expression, now—fury, and delight.

He didn't run for Cory. He ran past Heather, straight for the witch. She hardly seemed to see him—just stared at Heather, and pulled on her hair, and wept.

Rocko plunged the sword into the witch's stomach, driving it in to the hilt, then put his hand on her chest and shoved. The witch fell over backward, her body sliding off the blade. Rocko lifted the sword high, then drove it down into her throat.

He left it there, sticking up, not unlike the way Cory had found it, sticking up from the ground. Rocko looked at Cory and Heather, his eyes glazed, breathing heavily.

"Don't come near us," Heather said, moving close to Cory, clutching her stick.

"Shit," Rocko said, his voice thick. "I'm not messing with either of you. I took care of what I needed to do." He frowned. "Almost, anyway." He approached, and Heather stepped in front of Cory—protecting him, as he'd moved to protect her.

Rocko didn't come much closer to him, though. He veered back toward the stream, and the bicycle. "*This* thing. I don't know how it works . . . but it's got a mind of its own. It might even have *her* mind." He looked at Heather. "Get that stick over here, and smash this thing up, would you? I'll get a rock."

"He's right," Cory said. "I don't know what happened, but . . . the bicycle is part of it. We have to break it."

"Don't mess with us," Heather said. "Don't mess with Cory."

Rocko shrugged. "He proved he was worth something. He saved my life." He flashed a sick grin at Cory. "If Heather hadn't ambushed me, though, and if I hadn't been stuck with a second-rate sword, I'd have finished you."

"We've seen what you can do," Heather said, looking at the witch's body, then away.

Rocko looked at the witch's body and nodded. "Yeah. I crossed a boundary there, didn't I? I wonder what my psychiatrist will say when I tell her I killed her because she was a witch?"

Cory and Heather didn't say anything. They just went to work on the bike with the stick and some rocks, shattering its headlamp first, then pounding its wheel hubs into shapelessness. Rocko bashed at the seat until it came off. Halfway through their destruction they heard shouting and footsteps.

"Who—" Cory said, alarmed.

"Grown-ups," Rocko grunted. "Those builders of boundaries. They heard all the screaming, probably. Let's finish this before they get here."

They worked faster, and when they finished, the bicycle was just bits of junk glittering in the stream.

"So much for the micro-ecology," Heather said. "The water will probably be poisoned forever."

A woman came into the clearing, followed by another woman and a man. "Heather!" the first woman shouted. "What—" She saw the witch's body. "Oh my God!" she cried, covering her mouth with both hands.

"I killed her," Rocko said, stepping forward. He looked over his shoulder at Cory, then favored Heather with a smile. He turned back to the grown-ups. "I killed her because she was a witch."

The adults looked at one another.

Heather grasped Cory's hand, hard. He squeezed hers just as tightly. This was going to be a long afternoon, and long days ahead . . . but maybe, on the other side of it, he would still be able to hold Heather's hand.

ANNABELLE'S ALPHABET

(For Adrienne)

A is for Annabelle, who turned ten today. She is on a birthday picnic with her parents, wearing what her mother calls her Alice-in-Wonderland dress, and the warm air smells of summer. Annabelle hears chimes in the wind, but her parents, arguing on a blanket, don't seem to notice. Annabelle might follow the music, later, through the yellow and blue field of wildflowers, into the woods. The chimes seem to call her name, three syllables: "Ann - a -belle." She laughs and claps her hands. Her parents murmur.

B is for Butterflies. Annabelle sees one now, yellow wings fluttering through the long grass over the hills. She chases it until it lands, then leans over to watch it resting on a blossom. Annabelle thinks it might be looking at her, but she isn't sure if butterflies have eyes.

Her father collects butterflies, pins them down and seals them under glass. She's seen him in the garage, where he keeps his collection, looking at them. Sometimes, when he doesn't know she's there, he rips off their wings, and that frightens her.

Annabelle shivers and waves her hand at the butterfly. "Go on," she whispers. "Fly away." It does.

C is for Cages. Once at another girl's birthday party Annabelle saw parakeets, yellow and blue, singing in a cage. She looked at them for a minute and decided to set them free. She tugged at the cage door, but a broad soft woman in a flowered dress stopped her. "No, dear," she said. "Don't let them out."

"I want them to fly," Annabelle said, her eyes suddenly hot and full of tears.

"No," the woman repeated, leading Annabelle back to cake and ice cream. "Their wings are clipped. They couldn't fly anyway."

"Do their wings ever grow back?" Annabelle asked, but the woman didn't answer.

D is for Dreams, of course. Annabelle dreams of green places, and she often dreams of flying, soaring over woods and water, singing as she goes. One morning, when she was five years old, she said "I flied, Mommy, last night I flied!" Her mother's eyes went wide and she made a squeaking noise, as if choking on her eggs.

"In her dreams," her father said sharply, looking up from his paper. "She means in her dreams. Everyone has that dream."

Annabelle's mother nodded and looked down at her plate.

Anabelle remembers that, even five years later. She has a very good memory, but far enough back it turns to mist and shadows and pine trees.

E is for Earthworms. Annabelle's father is a weekend fisherman, and there's a patch of black dirt behind the house where he digs for worms. Once, young and dirty-kneed, Annabelle watched him dig.

"Catypillars," she said when he pulled up a long worm, wiggling, and dropped it in the bucket.

"Not caterpillars," her father said. "Worms."

"Worms?" Annabelle said, scrunching up her face.

"Yes. Caterpillars are fuzzy, and they turn into butterflies. Worms are slimy, and they don't turn into anything. But." He raised his finger in front of Annabelle's wide gold-flecked eyes. "If you cut a worm in half, both halves go on living." He took out his pocketknife, laid a worm on a shattered piece of cinderblock, and sliced it neatly in half. There was no blood, and both halves wriggled wildly. "See?"

Annabelle looked for a moment, solemn, and then said "Put it back together, Daddy."

He frowned, picking up the two wiggling half-worms and dropping them in his bucket. "I can't, Annabelle. There's no way to put them together again."

"Oh," she said in a quiet voice. But she wondered.

F is for Fairies. Annabelle's mother is religious, and there are pictures and statues of angels all over the house, with their white wings and pale, pretty faces. When Annabelle was younger, she called them fairies. "No," her mother said sternly. "They're angels."

"But they got wings," Annabelle said.

Her mother embraced her in freckled arms. "I know, darling, but they're angels. I promise. And you're my little angel."

"I don't got wings," Annabelle said scornfully.

G is for Garden. Annabelle's mother has one, with roses and posies and tulips and other blossoms, and in the summer they buzz with bees. Once Annabelle was sent to pull weeds, but instead she took up flowers and wove them into her red hair, and made chains for her wrists. Her mother squawked and shouted when she saw, but Annabelle was serene, sitting on the lawn with her skirts spread around her. She was a flower.

H is for Hair, sunset-red on Annabelle's head. Her father's hair is sandy blonde and short, her mother's is flat brown and cut in a bob. Annabelle's hair falls in curly waves, nearly to her knees. It has never been cut.

When Annabelle's mother brushes her daughter's hair, as she does every morning, it never snags or tangles. Her mother tells herself it must be the shampoo she uses, but it certainly doesn't do that for her own hair. She chooses not to think about it. Annabelle's mother chooses not to think about a great many things.

I is for Innocence, and today as every day Annabelle is drifting farther from that state. Her father watches her sometimes as she plays, frowning, and sometimes he grins like a jack o' lantern, but he's never laid a hand on her, even to punish. Sometimes he seems nervous when he hugs her, and he never touches her back for long. Annabelle's innocence is still complete, but today she turned ten, and as she grows through double digits that innocence will disappear. For some things, some reconnections, time is growing short.

J is for Joy, and that's what Annabelle was for her parents, or was meant to be, or could have been. "She's a gift from God," Annabelle's mother said when they got their newfound daughter home, but she was hesitant, trembling. She put her hands across her belly. "We—I wanted a baby so much."

From the kitchen she heard a rasp and her young husband said "She is. You did. There's just something to take care of first." Another rasp, metal on stone, and Annabelle's mother closed her eyes. "Get it sharp," she said. "Very sharp, so it doesn't hurt much. I'll boil some water."

Somewhere in the house, far from the green places she'd known, baby Annabelle lay on her stomach and cried.

K is for Knives. Annabelle has dim memories, masquerading as nightmares. Even at ten years old, her father has to cut her food; she can't stand to touch a knife. She doesn't like meat anyway, because it reminds her too much of her own muscles, moving under the skin. She has muscles in her back that she can flex, but they don't move anything at all.

She stares at the wall as her father saws away at the food on her plate. She can't stand to look at the knife. Or at him, wielding it.

L is for Lost things. Annabelle loses things a lot, but her father almost never does; he's only once lost anything, that she can remember. Listening from the top of the stairs, Annabelle heard him shout at her mother. "They're gone! They were wrapped in cloth and locked in the chest and now they're gone! What did you do with them?"

And her mother: "Nothing. I hated them, the way you . . . brooded over them, but I wouldn't touch the things."

"Well then where did they go?"

Her mother, quietly: "Maybe they flew away."

M is for Music, and for Mystery, and this is both. Those chimes: "Ann - a - belle", ringing over the hills from the trees. They aren't birdsong, and they aren't bells, and Annabelle's parents, just a few feet away on the blanket, don't hear a thing. It is Annabelle's birthday, and she got a pink bike with a basket and a new kite to fly. The kite is in the grass, forgotten, and her bike is back at home.

Annabelle wonders if she'll be getting another gift.

N is for Normal, and some things aren't, and those things need to be cut right out. Annabelle's father knows that, and so does her mother, though it hurts her more.

Annabelle doesn't think about it. Normal is what things are, and only things that aren't what they are can be wrong.

O is for Outside, and that's Annabelle's earliest memory, of being outside, tiny in the forest, looking up at stars and pine trees. Lost. Like the baby in the rhyme, that came tumbling down when the bough broke and the cradle fell. Then came voices, and two tall people, scooping her from the forest floor, exclaiming, turning her over. Annabelle doesn't know what the memory means, but her mother sings lullabies and that's one of the voices, and her father tells stories in measured tones, and that's the other.

Sometimes Annabelle sneaks out of the house and lies down in her back yard and looks up at the sky, through the pines.

P is for Picnic, and what a wonderful idea that was. "Annabelle would love a birthday picnic," her mother said, "and it's such a pretty day. But where should we go?"

"There's a field I know, by a nice stretch of woods," her father said thoughtfully.

They packed the car and took Annabelle, and her new kite, to the field. Neither of her parents seemed to remember this place, though they'd often taken walks in the woods here, when they were younger. A strange cloud covers their memories, filling their heads. They'd last seen this field on a summer night like this one, exactly ten years before. They'd come to watch the butterflies.

This was before he started dipping the butterflies, wings and all, in chloroform. Before he locked them under glass.

Before (but only just before, a matter of minutes, perhaps) they found Annabelle.

Q is for Quiet, and Annabelle is that. Even the soughing of the wind has stopped, and her parents are murmuring, sipping lemonade. She can still hear the chimes if she holds her breath, but they're fading. Even the beating of her heart is enough to make her miss notes: "Ann- - - belle - - - a - belle." Yes, the chimes are fading, and if she intends to follow them, she must do so soon.

R is for Ripping, when the knife went dull, when things weren't quite severed and man hands pulled and blood welled up, R is for the Rasp of the knife on the whetstone, but some things are too attached to be cut neatly, no matter how sharp the blade, and they tear.

S is for Scars. Annabelle has two on her back, shiny and wide, running vertically down her shoulder blades. Her mother told her that she stumbled and fell on a board with nails in it, and that's where the scars come from. Her father told her she was scratched by a dog when she was a baby, and that's where she got them. Sometimes her muscles spasm beneath the scars. And often in the morning, after a dream of flying, her shoulders ache.

T is for Time, and Annabelle feels it shortening and shortening as the shadows lengthen and the sun slides west.

U is for Umbilicus, the first connection between mother and daughter, which leaves its mark on the child's belly forever. But Annabelle has no navel, her stomach is as smooth as the skin of a peach, unmarked and untouched. Annabelle's mother thinks sometimes of umbilical cords being cut with scissors, of that fundamental severance, which she and Annabelle never had. Instead of scissors, there was a knife, and it wasn't a cord that was cut, not the connection between mother and daughter that was severed, but a different connection altogether.

And now Annabelle is in the field on her birthday, and it seems that while some connections must remain sundered forever, others can be re-joined.

V is for Vigilant, and Annabelle's mother is that, she always keeps an eye out for her daughter. She can't have more children, that thought is always on top of her mind, and she rarely lets Annabelle out of her sight. But now her attention wanders, she even forgets Annabelle for a moment, the thoughts fly out of her head and she's back in her girlhood, laughing with her new husband. Laughing, before Annabelle, and knives, and grisly silky mementos that mysteriously disappear, just as Annabelle is now disappearing over the hills toward the forest.

W is for Worried, and Annabelle knows her parents will be, but the chiming is louder now, a part of her is calling her and that's more important than anything, and she runs across the fields into the trees, the song in her head like her own voice, her own song, calling her home, and as she runs she can almost feel herself flying.

X is for Xenophobia, the hate of the stranger, and Annabelle doesn't know that word, and neither does her mother, and while her father does know it, he would never ascribe it to himself.

Yet his daughter is a stranger, and his wife also in many ways, and himself most of all, and he hates them all, really. When he sits in the basement tearing the wings from butterflies and remembering the night they found Annabelle, hate fills him. You can't turn something into something it's not, he thinks at the picnic, looking at the fat clouds float effortlessly by. Flying.

And then his wife says "Where's Annabelle?" and things happen very fast.

Y is for Yell, which Annabelle's mother does, she stands on the blanket and shouts her daughter's name. Her husband stands, frowning, hands clenched on a napkin that he rips in half, and they both shout for their daughter, who is gone, gone, and they look for the flutter of a blue dress, for curly red hair, but there's nothing, not even in the trees, there's only

Z is for Zephyr, the gentle west wind, coming up suddenly strong over the field from the trees, blowing into the shouting faces of Annabelle's mother and father, but only the wind answers them, blowing as though buffeted by a million wings and then, like apple blossoms blowing free, like silk streamers in the air, a hundred thousand sunset red and golden butterflies burst from the trees in the forest, flying.

And after it all Annabelle knows she is not a worm, or an angel, or a flower. She is something else, something of the green, something like a butterfly that lost its wings but, after a time, regained them.

THE SCENT OF COPPER PENNIES

When she came into the coffee shop, I didn't know she was the woman who would change my life. She wore black, she had a beautiful face—that's all I noticed when she came in and walked to the counter to order a drink.

I drank Guinness for the warmth, sitting at a round table in the far corner of the coffee shop. I spent a lot of time there, but no one knew my name. Most of the people who frequented the place were hip beyond words, all tattoos and esoterica. I didn't know the bands they liked, the bars they went to, the world they inhabited.

I had a book in front of me, though it was closed for the moment, with a long coffee spoon as a bookmark. It was a collection of the year's best essays. The book had no central subject, no overriding theme—diversity was the point. I wanted to broaden my horizons, so I'd be a more interesting person. Not that I talked to many people. Sometimes I went days without speaking to anyone but co-workers and waitresses.

I got a better look at the woman as she took her drink away from the counter. My old girlfriend Charlotte had been pretty, too, but in a taller, brasher, blonder way. This woman had gray eyes, and she wore her dark hair piled atop her head. She wore knee high boots, tights, a loose skirt, and a spaghetti-strap velvet top, all black. A fringed shawl hung loosely over her shoulders. Her skin wasn't dead-white pale, and she didn't wear heavy eye-shadow or silver jewelry, none of the trappings I associated with goth types. She seemed comfortable in her clothes, as if they weren't a fashion statement but a simple fact of her being: this woman wears black.

She caught me staring and I looked away after meeting her eyes for an instant. I fidgeted with my napkin, where a splash of Guinness had soaked into the paper.

She sat down across from me, putting her cup beside my pint glass. Her drink smelled wonderful, some sort of spiced tea.

"Hello," she said. "I'm Merrilee."

I looked up. I'm a shy person, I always have been, I never know what to say. But how often had I imagined a moment like this? The way it is in the movies, when a stranger sits down at your table and introduces herself, and it's a chance for your life to take a strange turning. A chance that shouldn't be passed up, a chance at the extraordinary.

But I try not to be so obsessive.

"Mike," I said, but I've never liked the short-form. "Michael."

"We could go anywhere from here," she said, stirring her cup, scented steam rising. There was cinnamon in there, and nutmeg, and I don't know what else. I wondered how much of the delicious smell was the tea and how much was her, then felt foolish for thinking such a thing. "Two strangers," she said, "no history, no past, we've never met before. This could be a conversation, it could be an awkward silence, it could be a love affair, a friendship, a rivalry. So much possibility. Wonderful, isn't it?"

She smiled, not showing her teeth. The only makeup she wore was lipstick, just a touch of dark red. "It is," I said. "Wonderful, I mean." I wanted to say something that wasn't empty, because this was a moment teetering. It could go any way at all, she'd said as much. I was still thinking about the smell of her tea, perhaps because that was easier than thinking about her and her words ("it could be a love affair"), and when I spoke, the words had nothing to do with anything, they were just something from one of the books I had read recently. "Did you know, in voodoo, the gods don't appear as burning bushes or golden showers or swans, nothing like that. They usually manifest as smells, or sounds . . . "

"Or sensations, touches," she said, and sipped her tea. "They're more intimate gods, aren't they? They don't play well on television, they don't always make for such dramatic stories." She looked at the ceiling for a moment, at the plaster painted with clouds and fat little cherubs in a chorus-line. "But if you had to die, and be held by something, I'd rather it be the touch of feathers and the smell of cinnamon than a raging bull or a pillar of fire." She looked at me over the rim of her cup, inhaling the steam.

This was a conversation, I'd had them before, but I couldn't think of anything except her beauty and my awkwardness and the fact that I hadn't touched a woman since Charlotte, and that had been a year ago and a dozen states away.

"You want the love affair," she said. One of the dark hairs (not black, but a rich, deep brown) piled on her head came loose, falling across her forehead. "And you're an attractive person. It's not impossible. But what I like about you . . . is the way you blend in."

I looked down, sure I was being teased now, though her voice hadn't changed. "I've always been a wallflower," I said, trying to make it light.

"No, no. That's not what I mean. I mean . . . if there were vengeful ghosts, searching for you, they wouldn't see you at all, would they? They'd overlook you and go another way, down some other forking path. There's a voodoo god, the god of the crossroads. He smells of copper pennies and . . . and motor oil, I think. He's a god of choices made, and choices missed. Every moment could be anything . . . even your last one."

She'd lost me. If another woman, one less breathtaking, had sat down at my table and started saying things like this, I would have excused myself politely. Maybe I was just shallow, hoping to get laid, even if she was crazy. Being lonely can screw up your priorities. But she didn't seem like a flake, and I couldn't help thinking that the things she said made some kind of secret sense, a sense I'd appreciate if I could only penetrate the mystery.

I said "You don't blend in, though. You say that like it's an admirable thing."

She cocked her head and nodded. She drank her tea in a gulp and put the cup down. "Will you walk with me?"

I only hesitated a second before nodding.

We left together. No one called her name, which surprised me. She seemed like the type who'd get noticed in a place like this, who'd have lots of friends.

"Have you lived in Santa Cruz for long?" she asked, walking with me down Cedar Street.

I kept my hands in my pockets as I walked. "No. I just moved here a couple of months ago, on a whim, more or less. I didn't like my job, and I'd just come out of a bad relationship. So I went on the internet, applied for some jobs, and got one out here, doing graphic design."

She nodded. "That's quite a turning point."

I was beginning to see her interests, at least; the hingepoints in a life, the moments when things shift. "Yeah. I guess my life would've been a lot different if I'd stayed in North Carolina."

"You wouldn't have met me tonight, for one thing," she said, and took my arm. She was so warm and alive, she felt wonderful. I didn't even want to sleep with her, especially, though god knows I'd spent plenty of long nights fantasizing about meeting a beautiful stranger and doing just that. I only wanted to hold her, to feel her skin against mine, mingling my warmth with hers. To know for just one night, right down to my skin, that I wasn't alone.

"Have you noticed that there aren't any funeral homes here in Santa Cruz?" she said. "And no cemeteries, at least not any you can find easily. It's like that all over this part of California."

I hadn't thought about that, until she mentioned it. "That's weird. I wonder why?"

She shrugged. "Wealthy young people live here, it's a new demographic. They don't like to think about death, I guess." She shivered, though the weather was mild, and she had her shawl. "I guess no one does."

We kept walking, past an ivy-covered parking garage, past stucco walls. "You talked about blending in . . . ?" I still wasn't sure if that comment had been a dig at me or not, an ironic jab at my gray shirt, my jeans, my short hair. Mr. Nondescript, nary a tattoo nor piercing to be seen.

"There are festivals where people try to frighten away restless spirits," she said. "At least, that's the origin of the festivals. We have our version in Hallowe'en. In other cultures there's a day of the dead, and it's less about driving the spirits away, more about visiting with them, though sometimes they have to be coaxed back to the place where they belong, afterward. I wonder, sometimes, about *potential* ghosts . . . " She shook her head, as if dismissing that thought as too unimportant, or enormous, to follow. "But there are other rituals, held right after people die, to move their ghosts along. The spirits linger, you see. Some people bang drums, to frighten them away. Some people cover the mirrors, to keep the spirits from becoming entranced by their own reflections. People believe that the dead can be dangerous, though it's often unclear how, exactly. Black is the color of mourning in our country. Black, like I'm wearing. The dead don't see very well, I guess, and when you're dressed in black you blend in with the shadows, they don't notice you. If they don't notice you, maybe they won't do you harm, right? In some countries white is the color of mourning, and it's the same thing. Gray works, too. You can frighten the dead away with masks and drums, or you can try to go unnoticed . . . "

She sat down on a stone stoop in front of a closed dress shop. I joined her. She leaned against me, her head resting on my shoulder.

"You said something about potential ghosts," I prompted.

She sighed, nuzzled against me more closely. "You always had to get to the bottom of everything," she said, fondly and absently. The words chilled me for some reason, made me cold all the way through, as if my heart had been exposed to November air.

She went on. "At the University . . . or at *some* Universities . . . they study quantum mechanics. The way the universe really works, spooky contradictions, frightening paradoxes, and all. There doesn't need to be a god of the crossroads. The *universe* is the god of the crossroads."

I'd read *In Search of Schrödinger's Cat* and *Schrödinger's Kittens*, the Feynman lectures, recent articles about quantum entanglement. More broadening of my horizons. Ever since Charlotte said I was boring and narrow, right before she broke up with me, I'd been trying to expand myself. "You're talking about the many-worlds theory, right?" I said. "About the idea that everything which *can* happen, does happen . . . from an atomic level up. The universe doesn't like to make choices, so it does everything. Is that what you mean?"

"You were never good at the math," she said. "But you usually grasped the essentials." She took a deep breath, and spoke, slowly. "You used to live in Chapel Hill. One night you were supposed to go to a theater party, but at the last minute you chickened out, because you were afraid you'd be uncomfortable with so many strangers. Most actors are pretentious jerks anyway, you've always thought so. So instead you went to a bar, and met a woman named Charlotte. She spilled a drink on you, and more or less at that moment you fell in love."

I pulled away from her. "Do you know Charlotte?"

She shook her head, looking at the pavement. Tears glistened in her eyes—I could just see them in the light of a street lamp. "No, Michael. Me and Charlotte . . . we're almost mutually exclusive. If you hadn't gone to that bar, if you'd gone to that theater party instead, you might have met another wallflower there. You know, two shy people who didn't know anyone, talking together in self defense. She might have been a physics student. You might have become friends, or rivals, had a conversation . . . or a love affair." She shook now, really shivered, and more hairs came loose from the pile on top of her head, falling into her face.

She didn't look familiar. I *wanted* her to look familiar. But she didn't. She was just a beautiful stranger with a beautiful, strange story. She might have been crazy. I was too captivated to care.

"I don't know what to say," I said. "I don't know what you're saying. But, I mean, you're here, now . . . "

"No," she said, sharply. "Almost anything can happen, but not that. I fooled myself, I shouldn't have come here. You *might* have met this girl, you *might* have had a love affair, but you met Charlotte, instead, and she damaged you. She broke you in important ways."

That hurt, it stung, but it was true. "I can heal," I said, a little defensively.

She didn't look at me. She stared at the asphalt street, and spoke in a controlled monotone. "You might have met this girl, at this party . . . you might have had a love affair, moved in with her . . . you might have been out walking one night, coming back from a Chinese restaurant. She might have crossed the street, at the same time some drunk came careening around the corner . . . you might have watched that girl die, right there on the asphalt, right in front of you." I heard the strain in her voice, the tightness, how close she was to breaking.

"And maybe something happened then, in that instant before the car hit," she went on, less tense, more sad and resigned. "The smell of copper pennies and burning motor oil filled the air, a jingle of bells, many paths opening before the girl, the girl about to die. Of course she'd choose one of the paths, wouldn't she? She'd do anything, to keep from dying. So maybe the girl wouldn't have died, but only disappeared, right before your eyes. And eventually you'd convince yourself she just abandoned you, that you didn't see her disappear at all. You'd become bitter, and withdraw even more completely from the world." She laughed, harshly, the sound echoing off the empty buildings. "That's just speculation, of course. I've never been back there, to the place where the forking paths began. I'm afraid to return."

She looked at my face. "Oh, Michael. I've been so many other places. To worlds where I didn't die, where we're still together, where I like to think there's happily ever after in store for us. I'm sure in some of those worlds there is; there'd have to be, wouldn't there? But I had no place in those worlds. You already had a Merrilee there, and I couldn't take her place. Even in those happy worlds there were differences, unwanted pregnancies, different jobs, my fellowship falling through . . . They weren't the world we *would* have had, if that car hadn't come, if . . . for whatever reason . . . the god of the crossroads or the unprecedented quantum event or *whatever* happened to me *hadn't* happened. But I kept trying, kept searching. I looked for worlds where we'd never met, where I could find you, where we could start over. In most of those worlds, you met Charlotte, and usually you two broke up. So here I am. Trying again, knowing I'll fail again."

I believed her; I believed *in* her; I needed her like a religion. "It's not too late," I said. "We can—"

"You don't even know me," she said softly. "And the Merrilee I am is not the Merrilee you would've loved. I've seen too much. I'm too estranged from reality . . . or too tangled up in all the realities."

"This can be a new thing," I said. "It doesn't have to be finding something you lost, it can be *new.*"

She looked at me, her gray eyes still wet with tears, and she smiled. But it was such a sad smile. "Maybe we could. If it was that easy. But . . . I have to keep moving, Michael."

"What are you talking about? What are you looking for? You'll never find—"

She shook her head. "It's not the search—that's just how I occupy myself, how I keep the will to continue. I *have* to move on, it's necessity. I should've died when that car hit, Michael. It's not a question of fate, or destiny. There are plenty of worlds where I'm alive and well. But my death is one of the things that *had* to happen, one of the potential outcomes. Instead, I *lived.* I don't know why, but my survival left something unsatisfied in the universe. Every day I live it gets a little worse, a little more serious. I can't die at the right time, or in the right place, or in the right way, anymore. But I still have to die, and the universe is doing its best to kill me. I worry, sometimes, that I'm doing something to the world, tearing at the fabric of things . . . but then, my wandering up and down the forking paths is part of the fabric, isn't it? It's not something I chose."

"You choose to keep going," I said.

Her expression hardened, her mouth turning down. "You try doing the noble thing when the grille of a car is coming at your face, Michael. You try giving yourself up to death when there's an alternative. I don't think you could do it." She looked away, but kept talking, bitterly. "I forget that you don't know me, that you never will."

"Merrilee—"

"I wear black, to try to blend in. To make myself unobtrusive. In a way, it's a ghost that's after me. The ghost of my own death, a phantom possibility, getting realer by the moment. I can't scare it away with drums or masks, and so far I haven't been able to hide from it. Not for long, anyway. I thought I could find you, maybe bring you with me, drag you across the worlds with me . . . " She shook her head. "But you're not the one. Charlotte messed you up too much. I know. I've met other damaged Michaels, in other places. You'd never really trust me."

"Give me a chance," I said.

"Too late," she said, and stepped into the street.

I hadn't even heard the car coming. I don't know how I could have missed it. It was an old Corvair, the color of dried mustard, and it ran right through a stop sign and smashed into Merrilee as she stepped into the street.

I smelled burning motor oil, naturally enough. And pennies, old dirty copper pennies.

Somewhere across town, church bells rang the wrong time.

The Corvair swerved into the curb and stalled. An old hippie with stringy hair climbed out, eyes wild. "I hit her!" he shrieked. I couldn't tell if he was proud or appalled. "I hit her!"

I looked. Merrilee wasn't there, no body, no trace. I left the hippie lurching around the street. He peered under parked cars, looking for a body. I walked slowly home, to my rented room in a house full of strangers. I tried not to think of that house as a metaphor for my life.

Tonight I packed a bag. I'm giving myself over to the god of the crossroads. I'm going to Chapel Hill. There might be a Merrilee living there, one who's never met me, one who didn't die. I don't love Merrilee. I didn't even really know her. It's silly to think that she's destined for me. I believe there was a time, and a place, when we would have fallen in love . . . but there might not be another such time and place in this world.

Still. It's somewhere to go. It's a direction. A place to begin.

It's better than the nothing I've had so far.

THE GOD OF THE CROSSROADS

The god of the crossroads came to me
in a shabby café in Missouri, during
a time of confusion and malaise—a
personal infestation of spiritual lice,

a hundred chigger bites on the flesh
of my sense of purpose, you might say.
The god rode in the head of my coffee
server, a displaced punkette with

mismatched eyes and buzzed-black
hair and a silver ring in her left
nostril. I recognized the god's arrival
by the usual signs—the scent of copper

and vanilla in the latté steam, the jingle
of the bells hung on the door like
garlands, the revving and honking
and backfiring of cars in the street

trying to go every direction at once
and tearing themselves apart in the process.
"You're waiting again," the god said in
the punkette's sexy-raspy voice. "What

are you waiting for?"
"I can't do it all," I said, stirring
cold coffee with my forefinger. "I hate
to make decisions I can't revise

later. I used to take comfort in quantum
uncertainty and the many-worlds theory,
the idea that somewhere else, some other
me was doing *everything*." The god

snorted and said "Every other you is sitting
in this stupid coffee shop with the water-
stained walls and the rude waitstaff, or else
crouching by a rock staring at a stream, or looking

up at a flyspecked motel ceiling—and all of you
are getting yelled at by me." The god came around
the counter and thumped me in the chest. I
gasped as my heart sputtered, stuttered,

stopped

and then started again as all the engines
outside revved and the cars surged
forward. "Every road ends," the punkette
god said. "You can't linger

forever." Her mismatched eyes were one
color now, the morning blue of a sky
I once saw in Georgia, and I wondered
how many dawns and journeys I had left.
The god departed, and I whispered
my thanks to the punkette,
pushed back from the table, stood up,
and walked into the remaining

hours and miles of my life.

FABLE FROM A CAGE

Let me tell you a little fable, a story I crafted while sitting inside this dangling cage, where the rooks shit on me and steal my bread all day, and the smoke from your town fires stings my eyes all night.

Did you know the owls feed me? They bring me rats, mice, squirrels, and I eat them. That's why I haven't died yet. I'll never die, not here, wait all you like.

My fable? Yes. Oh, yes. It will, most assuredly, have a moral. Hunker down and listen for it, boys.

Once there was a thief who wandered in this country, passing from valley to valley in the night, loosening the ropes on cows and leading them away to sell in another town. He lifted bags of fruit from wagons, he picked up things that others put down. He was not a brigand, understand—he did not knock down defenseless women, he did not swagger with a looted sword on his hip, he did not terrorize the roads; indeed, he traveled *between* the roads more than on them. His crimes were all crimes of opportunity, but for an observant man, there are many opportunities for crime.

Not a brigand, no, but also nothing so grand as a burglar or a master thief. For there are men who can be like artists of the criminal trades, and this thief had known such men, but he did not compare to them. His was a lonely life, always running from one village to another, and he wondered sometimes how he had come to live in such a way—he, who had been born in the city.

Oh, yes, the city, you greedy little shits, look how your eyes widen and the drool falls from your lips. This thief had been born in the city, son of a banker, and he might have had a nice life there if he hadn't dallied with the daughter of a ship's captain . . . but that is a different story, and not a fable at all—not a moral tale, in any sense, my young ones.

So this thief—who had a fine black beard, his one vanity, a beard as fine as mine was before this month without trimming—had fallen on hard times. He was down to his last coins, and his fine clothes (lifted from a tailor's shop, and almost exactly the right size) were stained from trying to steal a pig the night before, an act below even his usual flexible standards.

He was musing on what to do next, for he had decided that three years traveling this way was more than enough, but he felt too old to apprentice himself to a trade. Indeed, he knew himself well enough to know that the moment his master smith or cooper turned his back, he would feel compelled to snatch up their tools and run away, as much from boredom as from habit.

Walking through the forest that day in a dour mood, he caught his foot on a root and went sprawling. The fall knocked the wind from him, and he lay gasping on the forest floor. Because he could not do otherwise, he stared at the dirt before him . . . and noticed a large golden bracelet in the dirt.

The thief sat up, smiling, for here was the perfect crime of opportunity, a bit of jewelry dropped by some passerby, which would not be missed, and which would enrich him. He reached down, wrapped his fingers around the gold, and tried to pick it up.

It moved a little, but something held it fast. The thief brushed the dirt away around the ring and found half of it sealed in black metal. He brushed away more dirt, curious now, and cleared a square of metal three feet to a side. The ring was no bracelet, but a handle for this trapdoor. The handle wasn't really gold, either—just brass.

The thief hesitated. He'd heard the stories, of course, of brigands with secret treasure-troves in the forest, where they kept their choicest things. Had he found such a place? And if so, did someone keep guard and watch over it?

Ah, but the opportunity. How could he walk away from such a rich possibility?

The thief wrapped his fingers tight around the ring and pulled. The door moved with surprising ease, without so much as a squeal of hinges. A great cloud of dust rose up with the trapdoor, and the thief turned his face away and coughed, his eyes watering. He let the trapdoor fall back, revealing a black square of darkness.

The thief got down on his knees and peered in, wishing for a lantern. There was no ladder and no steps—did the brigand king lower himself down with ropes suspended from the treetops?

Something shoved him from behind. The thief screamed as he fell—the brigand king had come upon him, and now he would die, sealed in with the dusty old treasures!

He hit the ground quickly, far sooner than he'd expected—and it wasn't ground at all, but a pile of soft fabric, furs and silks. A bit dusty, but more than enough to break his fall. Should he pretend to be dead? He turned over slowly, reasoning that since he'd been unable to see the bottom of the shaft from above, whoever had pushed him would be similarly blind. He peered up at the square of sky and branches, and saw no one. He sat up gingerly, but found no injuries or pains.

He sat waiting for a few moments, expecting a face to appear above, or a voice to call out, or—worst of all—for the trapdoor to swing shut, sealing him in irrevocably, leaving his spirit to guard this pile of fabrics and whatever other treasures lay in the darkness.

Something hissed, like a spitting cat, and the thief shrieked.

Then he saw light. The hiss had been the sound of an oil-soaked wick igniting.

Someone was down here with him.

He could see the lantern, a glass-sided, intricate thing, fit for a rich man's house. It sat on a marble pedestal, like the hacked-off base of a column. He saw no one near the lantern.

"I saw the trapdoor," he began. "I found it by accident, and, well—just natural curiosity, you understand—I wanted to see what was underneath. I mean no harm—"

"You're a thief," a low, neutral voice said. It came from a place in the cavern far from the lamplight.

The thief turned his head that way, startled. "Oh, no, I'm just a journeyman carpenter and—"

"A thief, and a liar." There was satisfaction in the voice now. The only ones who ever sounded satisfied about finding a thief were people who planned to kill or beat that thief very badly.

"I have need of a thief," the voice said, and then a figure stepped into the lantern-light

It was a woman.

Stop your tittering, snot-noses. This isn't a bawdy tale, you'll have to lurk under the tavern windows to hear one of those. No, she wasn't a beautiful woman. She looked like all your mothers, I'd wager, gray in her hair, lines in her face, a good sturdy build. Not a beauty. Not like that ship captain's daughter who got our thief in so much trouble. Not at all.

The woman was dressed incongruously in a fine fur coat. "You must be hungry," she said. "Would you like something to eat? I have some meat, roasting."

"I didn't mean to—to fall into your . . . home," the thief said. "If you'll show me a way out, I'll be going."

"It's not a home, thief. It's a burial chamber, like the men in the desert are reputed to build—that's the joke, I think. A cavern filled with all the things I'd need to live well, after death. Fine dishes, fine silks, lanterns, pots, tools. All I've lacked is servants." She smiled. "At least, until you arrived. And you want to leave? If I'd wanted you to get out, thief, why would I have shoved you *in*?" Her eyes were no particular color, it seemed to him, perhaps the gray of dirty wash-water, but she stared at him, not smiling at all now.

"Ah," he said. "You pushed me, you say."

"You opened the door to my prison, thief. I wanted to thank you properly, and I couldn't do that with you up there." She held up her arms, her sleeves falling away to reveal her forearms, which were covered with scars. "I have hands of air and fire. I can touch things far away."

The thief's obsession with opportunity extended to his words as well. He never knew when to keep silent, and he said "It seems to me that if you could push me *into* the hole from down here, you could have lifted that trap door yourself, and there'd be no need for thanks. Not that I don't appreciate your hospitality."

"It seems to *me* that a prison with a door that opens from the inside is no prison at all."

"Prisons are usually more secure than that," the thief agreed. He had some experience in such matters. "But they don't usually open for the casual passer-by, either."

"You are not a casual passer-by. You are the thief I've been waiting for.

No one else would even have seen the door, but you . . . you were meant to find me."

"I'm sure I don't—"

"Shut up," she said sharply, and then took a deep breath. "I offered you food, before. You smell like pigshit, but not roast pork, so I assume you had a wrestling match with dinner and dinner won. Eat with me, thief."

As he was hungry, and trapped anyway, he nodded. "I'd be most pleased."

"You have odd manners for a thief." She turned, reaching into the darkness, doing things with her hands that the thief could not see.

"I have not always claimed that occupation. There was a time when I supped at tables, not in caverns underground."

She shoved a platter toward him. Several large green leaves sat in the center, covering something. "What's this?" he said, lifting a leaf away.

The glassy eyes of a dead owl stared up at him, and the thief turned his head away in disgust. The bird's head was twisted completely around, its neck broken. "Good Lord, woman, are you mad?"

"You'd better hope I'm not mad," she said, her voice low again, and serious. "Because if I'm mad, you're going to eat that owl—beak, feathers, and all—on a madwoman's whim, and have nothing to show for it but stomach cramps and shit that cuts you."

She was serious, the thief could tell. "And if you're not mad?"

"Then after you eat that owl we'll get out of this hole, thief, and we will steal something grand."

"I can't," he said, looking at the dead bird. It was *huge*—even plucked and beheaded and cooked he couldn't have eaten it all. "I'm sorry, I don't know why you ask this of me, but I can't."

Something tightened around his throat, like blunt, flat fingers, cutting off his air. He choked and clawed at his throat, but his fingers touched only his own skin.

"Eat it, or die," she said.

He gasped his agreement—he had little choice. The invisible fingers loosened, and the thief rubbed his throat. "Can I have a knife at least?" he asked, dismayed by the roughness of his voice.

"Of course," she said, and tossed a blade onto the furs beside him. He'd expected a jeweled dagger, but this was a working-man's knife, serrated on one side, sharp on the other, with a stained leather grip. He looked at the owl, at the knife, at the woman. "Aren't you afraid I could kill you with this, faster than you could stop me, hands of air or not?"

"Not at all," she said.

He winced, nodded, and looked at the owl.

"It's fresh," she said, her voice surprisingly kind. "As fresh as it can be. I caught it before I was trapped here, a long time ago, intending to use it myself. I've spent considerable effort to preserve it. You don't have to eat the entrails. They'd make you sick, and anyway, I have other uses for them. And you can have lots of water, while you eat." She passed him a fine porcelain pitcher, and he dipped his fingers in to feel cold water. "We're not barbarians here."

Yes, he ate the owl, the whole thing—eyes, claws, beak, feathers. She let him grind up the talons with a stone and mix them in with water because he feared they'd cut his throat going down, otherwise. He didn't vomit, because she told him that if he did, he would have to eat what he threw up, every foul speck.

Oh, you boys love this one, don't you? You'll be telling it to your friends for months. The more disgusting it becomes, the more horrible, the more you'll eat it up. You shits.

Be gladdened, then. It gets worse.

She refilled the pitcher from the spring twice, and he drank it all. His stomach clenched, and it took all his concentration not to vomit. He'd never tasted anything so foul, never endured anything so horrible.

The woman spread the owl's gray, flecked entrails on a square silver tray. She prodded them, smiling and nodding as the thief fought his urge to gag.

"Eat a dead owl for breakfast," the woman said, laughing softly, "and nothing worse will happen to you all day."

"Now will you show me the way out?" the thief asked through clenched teeth, arms wrapped around his belly.

"No, dear. Now you'll sleep, and then *you'll* show *me* the way out."

The thief did not believe he'd ever be able sleep, not with that pain in his belly, but the woman offered him a cup, and he drank something sweet and heady from it, and fell into sleep.

He dreamed of flying, and swooping down from the night, and listening. The world was a teeming place of flitting movements, small sounds fraught with significance, strange odors. Eating was everything. Blood was everything. Flying was not the way humans imagined it, a consuming thrill of freedom, a transcendent experience.

Flying was just the fastest way to get to the blood.

The thief woke, opening his eyes to sunlight and trees. No furs beneath him—only soil, and a root digging into the small of his back. He would have believed it all a dream, if not for the rough, thick taste of feathers still on his tongue. Not even two pitchers of water had been enough to wash that away.

"You see, you *did* show me the way out," the woman. "You flew, and took me with you."

He turned his head slowly. His stomach didn't hurt so much now, but his limbs felt stretched, and his head hurt. The woman sat cross-legged in the dirt, her sleeves pushed back, the scars on her arms horribly white in the sun.

"We're free," he said.

"I'm free, my darling," she said. "You belong to me for a while yet. But I'll make it worth your while. You used to be the lowest of the low, but soon you'll be a master thief." She touched his forehead, and he flinched away at first, but her fingers seemed to soothe the pounding in his skull, so he let her go on.

When she drew her hand away, he saw her scars again. "What happened to your arms?" he asked, and then regretted it instantly. What madness, to remind a woman—a creature!—like this of an old injury, and old pain!

She didn't get angry. She just said "A knife happened," and stood up. "Let's go, thief."

"You call me thief. It's a good enough name. But what do I call you?"

"Call me Mistress, call me wench, I don't care. Come *on*."

He got to his feet. "What really happened? How did we get out?"

"You consumed the owl, and partook of its spirit. Part of its power became yours, and you flew from the pit. You carried me with you."

"That's unbelievable. I've heard stories, but . . . "

"I'm what the stories are made of," she said. She set off into the forest, walking with long strides.

"I guess the owl energy is all used up now," he said, a bit wistfully, following her.

She laughed. "It's not like a skin of wine. It's the creature's *soul*, and you consumed it. Its power is in you forever, for as long as your own soul endures." She glanced at him over her shoulder. "That doesn't mean you know how to use it, though. You took on the properties of the beast and then you fainted. I'll expect better than that when we get where we're going."

"Which is where?"

She said the name of the thief's home city.

He stopped short. "I can't go there! I've been exiled from that place!"

"Some say Fate can be bargained with, when the wind is right. But I'm not Fate, and you won't change my mind."

"We won't make it before the snow," he protested.

"Not by walking," she agreed. "That's why we'll have to fly part of the way."

She didn't demand that they fly right away, just that they walk. He squatted behind a rock about noon, but saw no feathers in his shit.

He tried to make conversation. "How did you wind up in that hole?"

"I thought there was something inside it that I wanted. So I went in after it, and then someone shut the door on me."

"What were you trying to find?"

"The same thing we're going to steal, thief, so you'll know soon enough."

They reached a village just before dusk. She led him through the rutted streets to a thatched building, an inn. The sign read "Goats and Compasses" and depicted a ram's head and a compass rose. The woman nodded toward the building. "You should eat, and I should get used to people again. Let's go inside."

"I'm almost out of money," he said. "I can't afford a night in an inn."

"I suppose you didn't notice that you were in a cavern of *treasures* last night, did you? I have coins. Old coins, from kingdoms long gone, but they'll still recognize silver, I wager."

She started for the door, then paused, looking above the lintel. "Oh, what's this?"

The thief peered upward. "Just a horseshoe nailed over the door. For good luck."

She laughed. "What good do they think that will do? Did you know that, in the olden days, a king passing judgement would make the petitioner pass through an iron gate, to prove he wasn't enchanted, or one of the Fair Folk? People believed that a fairy creature would scream and burn at the mere proximity of iron, and they hung up horseshoes over their doors to keep such creatures from passing freely." She smiled at the thief, looking not at all motherly. "It's good to see that human foolishness endures." She strode through the door.

The thief followed, shaken. He'd been denying the obvious, trying to convince himself the woman was just a witch or a madwoman touched by the gods, but now he began to wonder if she was human at all, or actually something from the twilight realms. He'd believed that the Fair Folk would recoil from the sight of iron, if such creatures existed at all. Apparently they were sturdier than he'd supposed.

He wondered at the scars on her arms, though. A knife, she'd said, but what kind of a knife could harm the likes of her, with her hands of air and fire? One with an iron blade? Perhaps the presence of iron alone couldn't harm one of the Fair Folk . . . but it could be that their bodies were vulnerable to iron's touch.

He would have to keep that possibility in mind.

What's that, snot-nose? Your father's a smith, and he told you that devils and monsters and Fair Folk flee from the sight of iron?

Well, that's as may be. This is a fable, not a true history, and fables have all manner of fantastic things in them, don't they?

And you, what is it? Oh. You thought fables all had talking animals. Well, mayhap the owl spoke before our thief ate it, hmm? Could well be.

Do you care to hear about their evening in the inn, and the music they heard, and the strange way the woman had of laughing at people and the way they dressed? Or do you wish to move ahead, on to something bloodier?

I thought so. I know boys. I used to be one.

They shared a room. The thief took the bed gratefully, though he suspected the woman was not being kind—she would not sleep at all, he supposed. She sat on the floor with a lantern by her knees, shaking bits of bone and brass onto a cloth and studying the patterns they made. Sometimes she frowned. Sometimes—and this was worse—she giggled.

After what felt like only a few moments of sleep, the thief awoke to a great pounding on the door, and someone shouting. "This is the innkeeper! Open the door!"

The woman stood by the window, her mouth turned down. The thief looked at her. "Should we go out the window?" he said, knowing the sound of trouble when he heard it.

"No. I'm curious to see what he wants. Open the door."

The thief pulled his shirt on. The door shuddered in its frame. The innkeeper was hitting it with something heavier than his fist. "Don't knock your own door down!" the thief yelled. "I'm coming."

He unhooked the lock and pulled the door open. The innkeeper stood in the doorway, his face red with fury or exertion, and he held an iron-headed cudgel in one hand.

"What is it, my good man?" the thief asked.

"This money," he said, and flung a handful of coins at the thief's chest. "It's nothing but painted bits of wood! I don't know how my wife mistook it for the real thing in the first place, but I'm no so easily fooled. You owe—"

"Painted *wood*?" the woman said sharply. "It's not real?"

The thief stood aside, more than willing to let her take over. She went to the door. "I'm . . . sorry for the mistake. Here . . . " She opened her coin pouch and shook the contents into her palm. She looked down at the coins in her hand and made a small sound of dismay.

"More painted wood," the innkeeper said. "That won't buy you much, I'm afraid, not even mercy. *You* can leave, old woman. But I'm going to have your son lashed with a horsewhip. It's been a while since the mayor worked his arm."

"I have money," the thief said, reluctant to part with his few coins—which wouldn't cover the room and their meals anyway—but even more eager to avoid a flogging.

"That bastard," the woman said, still looking at the coins, oblivious. "It wasn't even a real treasure trove, just enchanted junk. I wonder what I was *really* resting on all those years, that I thought was a pile of furs?"

"Don't talk about enchantment," the innkeeper said, fear showing beneath his anger. He lifted his cudgel. "I won't have talk of witchery here."

"You may not forbid me anything," she said, looking into his face. "Stand aside, and we'll be on our way."

He slapped the head of the cudgel into his hand. The thief saw how her gaze followed the movement. She feared the weapon.

"Stand aside, or you'll be a puddle of blood in a moment."

He laughed aloud. "You should be whipped, too, woman. I'll see to it."

"Oh, will you?"

His arm, the one holding the cudgel, bent backward. He cried out and then his forearm bent sharply in an impossible direction, and the bone cracked. The cudgel fell from his hand, and the woman jumped back when it hit the floor.

The man opened his mouth as if to scream, but no sound emerged. His other arm jerked, and then his left leg, and he fell to the floor. The woman's hands of air and fire were at work again.

The thief stood with his money pouch in hand, afraid to move. The woman glanced at him. "Come on, thief. Follow your calling. See if he has a purse. We're not as well off as I'd supposed before. We'd best replenish our coffers."

The thief did as he was told, though he found the man's silent thrashing pitiful and disturbing. He fumbled at the man's belt and found a small purse that jingled. He snatched it away, breaking the leather thong.

The man slid into the room on his face, dragged by invisible hands. The door swung partway shut, but the cudgel was in the way, and held the door ajar. "Move that club!" the woman said. "Now!"

The thief did so, nudging it out of the way with his foot. The door slammed shut. He looked down at the weapon. Perhaps the old stories had a grain of truth to them after all. Perhaps the Fair Folk *couldn't* touch iron—at least, not with their hands of air and fire. They could move doors, beds, people, but nothing made of iron.

The trapdoor over the cavern had been made of iron, he recalled. And probably the walls of the cave were full of it as well. Whoever had imprisoned this woman had done his work well, until the thief came along and ruined it.

He heard a horrible, wet noise from behind him. He didn't look. "What are you doing?" he asked.

"Turning him into a puddle of blood, like I promised," she said. She did not sound angry, or pleased, just . . . intent. She was a woman doing a difficult job well.

The thief kept his face turned to the wall.

Long minutes later, she said "I don't suppose it's worthwhile to eat him. His spirit can't have much of use. Stupidity and miserliness and little else."

"Can we go, now?" the thief asked, shuddering. He would not eat human flesh. Never that, no matter what she said, no matter if it gave him the strength of a giant or the mind of a scholar or the power of a king. Never that.

"We can go if you're ready to fly. I'd prefer if you did it without fainting this time."

"All right. I'll try."

They slipped out of the inn quietly, going down the back stairs. To avoid exiting through front, they went into the kitchen. They could escape through the back door.

A little boy, shirtless, no more than ten, stood by a long table, munching on a piece of bread. The thief and the woman stopped short. The boy swallowed silently, then narrowed his eyes. When his expression soured, it became obvious that he was the innkeeper's son—their features were nearly identical. "Father!" he shouted, startling the thief. "Father, people's in the kitchen, trying to leave without paying!"

"Shut up, boy," the woman said, and stepped forward, raising her scarred hands.

"No!" the thief said. "Let's just go, we'll fly, come on! He's only a boy."

The woman glared at the boy and hissed. The boy's head rocked as if he'd been slapped.

The thief grabbed the woman's arm—it felt like flesh, ordinary flesh, but what did he know?—and pulled her toward the door.

They emerged into the wide space between the inn and the stables. "We need open air," the woman said. "Too many eaves here." She started toward the back of the inn, and the thief followed. In the open space out back, the woman turned on him. "Now fly, you bastard. South."

"I—I don't know how—"

"You know," she said. "You remember it in your bones and in your bowels. What's flying? Why do you fly?"

He struggled to put the concept into words. "To get to the blood," he said, remembering his dream, remembering the strange experience of viewing the world through an owl's senses. "I fly to get to the blood."

"You *remember*," she said, "you *imagine*, and that is but one short step from the act itself."

"Yes." He stared past her, into the sky. Sky above, blood below. Yes.

He heard footsteps and a shout. Dimly, with a bird's disinterest for things scurrying on the ground, he saw the innkeeper's son, still holding his chunk of bread. The boy yelled something the thief couldn't understand.

The thief wondered if the boy was blood, and decided not. Too big.

Since there was nothing to eat here, the thief flew away. He felt something—a presence next to him, or on him, or beside him—but that seemed only right and natural, and he thought of it no more.

He flew South, towards blood.

After a long time, the thief stood swaying in a field, the taste of something nasty in his mouth. He spat out bits of fur.

The woman stood beside him. She patted him on the back. "You swooped down and snatched up a mouse. Sorry. I couldn't stop you."

He spat again, and gagged.

"Oh, stop that. You ate a whole dead owl, surely you can stand the taste of one little mouse. The essence might help you be stealthier, too."

"I wish I'd never fallen down your god-rotted hole," he said, spitting again.

"That's only because you haven't found untold wealth yet. Come, we're near the city of your disgrace. It's been a long time since I've been there. I wonder how it's changed?" She glanced at him. "Do you want to see your parents or . . . anything? You humans have strange ideas about such things. You've been good, I'm willing to indulge you." She walked through the moonlit pasture, beckoning him to follow.

He didn't look at her. This was the first time she'd openly admitted that she wasn't human. "No. They . . . they agreed with the judgment passed down by the mayor. They agreed that I should be exiled. They're very strict, very traditional. They forget what it's like to be young and hot-blooded . . . "

"Young and hot-blooded." She shook her head. "Your kind mystify me. I've always been as old as I am now."

He sighed. "Can't you even pretend to be a normal woman?"

"Once we're inside the city walls, certainly. If that proves advantageous. But here, between us . . . what's the point?"

"What's going to become of me, when all this is done?" Humans never got the good end of a bargain with the Fair Folk in the stories, and he hadn't even struck a bargain with this one, just been coerced along.

"I think I'll keep you for a while. You are a useful set of hands, and you have some spine, though it's buried deeply. We've had a rough time of it these past two days, I know, but things will get better, once I take care of this little errand." She shook her head. "I left the Isle of my people a very long time ago, to fetch this item. I never imagined it would take so long. It's even possible that my Queen grows impatient, and her patience is like that of a mountain."

"What are we stealing? Why do you insist on keeping it secret?"

"Just contrariness. Why do you want to know so badly?"

"If I'm supposed to *steal* something, it would be helpful to know what it is, so that I can make plans!"

"You never make plans anyway," she said, waving his objections away. "You wait for a clear opportunity, and you seize it. In this case, I'm going to prepare the opportunity for you. All you have to do is grab what I tell you to grab and then follow me."

The thief was unhappy with that, but he could do little about it. So he followed the woman as they neared the city of his birth, a walled city on the coast. As they neared the gates (which were just opening as dawn approached), the thief noticed something strange. Several wooden cross-pieces had been erected outside the wall, and a metal cage hung from each beam. "What are those for?" the thief asked.

"I don't know. It's your city."

"They didn't have these last time I was here."

A man sat in one of the cages, his legs crossed beneath him. The bottom of the cage hung at roughly eye-level. The cage was floored with wood, and the prisoner sat cross-legged, staring blankly toward the city.

"What's this?" the thief called to him. "What's the meaning of this cage?"

The man looked at him for a moment, then turned his face away, and wept.

"Imprisoned in an iron cage," the woman said, horrified. "I wonder if he's only meant to hang there for a short time, or if they'll leave him until he dies?"

The thief only shook his head.

"You humans. Your ingenuity never fails to amaze me."

You look like you're about to piss yourself, smith's son. What is it?

Yes, I know every town you've ever heard of has punishment cages, like this cursed one I'm inside, like the ones the thief saw, yes. What of it?

He'd never seen one before because this fable takes place in the past, in a time before any of you were born, when your parents, if they lived at all, were mere children themselves. The cages were a new thing, then.

Ask your mothers and fathers if you don't believe me, or your grand-parents. I wager they'll tell you they used to live in pleasanter times, that people haven't always been so treacherous and cruel, and that there was no need for these cages, long ago.

They're wrong, though, my boys. People have always been as they are now, throughout all time.

I know, you're impatient. We're almost done. I'll pass by their arrival, the way they came through the gates unnoticed, the thief surprised and a little dismayed to find that his exile was of so little importance that the guards didn't even recognize him. He knew there were those in the city who *would* know his face, though, even with his black beard, and so he walked with his head down. The woman walked the streets with great assurance, and the thief's heart sank as it became clear that she intended to begin this grand theft of hers right now, in daylight.

And then they reached the destination, and it was a house the thief knew.

"No," the thief said, stopping short on the cobbles. "Not that house."

"None other," the woman said. "Do you know it? Is it the home of a childhood friend, perhaps?" She half-smiled, and the thief wondered how much she knew about him, wondered if she could see his dreams, or hear his memories and thoughts.

"It is the captain's house. The house of the man who had me exiled."

"Well," the woman said, pleased. "I told you it was destiny, didn't I? You're familiar with his house, then, the arrangement of rooms?"

"Yes," the thief said, because she would know if he lied. "Yes, I've been inside many times. What can he have that you want?"

"Something his father stole . . . or his father's father, or perhaps the one before that. Who knows? I can't keep up with your teeming generations, thief. Some ancestor of his landed on the Isle of my homeland and, through blind luck and stupid audacity, made off with something that belongs to my Queen. When I came to steal it back . . . I found that I could not do so alone, that I needed a human agent. Before I could get help, I was tricked into the prison where you found me."

"How did you wind up in a place so distant from here?"

"That's a long story," she said darkly. "And one I have little interest in telling you. I imagine the one who holds that treasure now will be less cautious, less resourceful, than his forefather."

The thief knew the captain, and he doubted her assessment. The captain was a formidable man. "How do you know he even has the treasure? Fortunes change over generations."

"It's in the house," she said. "The owl's guts told me that much."

"Ah. What do we do now?"

"We break in, and murder everyone in the house, and you scoop up the treasure when I point it out to you. Easy enough, yes?"

The thief stared at her. "Murder?"

"Yes," she said placidly. "I am to kill the thief—or his descendent, as that's the best I can do—and all who serve him, and all who dwell in his house."

"But . . . his daughter . . ."

"Ah, yes. The root of your exile. You'd best hope she's married, and living in another man's house, hadn't you?" She raised her eyebrow. "But I suppose her value as a wife might have been . . . diminished . . . by the cause of your exile? Unless human customs have changed greatly while I've been underground."

"I won't help you if you kill her," the thief said.

"We'll see," she said.

They proceeded up the walk to the captain's front door. The woman pounded on the wood with her fist, then frowned. "Look, the doorknob's made of iron," she said. She peered at the doorjamb. "And there's iron hammered onto the frame, here. That wasn't here the first time I arrived. It appears I taught the old man caution, though as usual they misunderstand the relationship my kind has with iron."

"I knew a man once," the thief said slowly, "who couldn't eat shrimp or lobsters. If he did, his skin puffed up and turned red and split. Is it something like that, that iron does to you?"

Before she could answer, the door opened. The thief tensed, expecting to see the captain's face, expecting to be shouted at and struck.

Instead, it was the captain's daughter, a bit older of course but still lovely, her hair falling in fine curls around her face. Seeing her brought forth a welter of emotions—shame at what he'd done to her life, wistfulness for those sweet, exciting days with her, sadness at what had become of his life, resentment of her as the fundamental cause of his current situation.

"Yes?" she said. "Can I—" Her eyes widened as she recognized the thief. "You," she said, and for a moment he thought *she* would strike him—he'd chosen exile over marriage to her, which certainly gave her cause for anger. But she only said "You have to go! What if my father sees you?"

"My nephew has come to beg your father's forgiveness," the woman said.

The thief stared at her—fortunately, the captain's daughter did, too, and so she didn't notice his expression. "What? I don't—"

"He's my grand-nephew, in truth, and after his . . . unfortunate experiences here . . . he came to live with me. He has made quite a life for himself, down the coast, and he has always regretted what happened. He'd like to speak to your father, to offer his apologies, and . . . if possible . . . find out what he has to do to make things right." Then, as if the question had just occurred to her, the woman said "Have you married, child?"

The captain's daughter looked at her, then at the thief, and shook her head. "No. I never have."

"Then we've come in time," the woman said. "May we come in?"

The captain's daughter stepped aside. The woman glanced at the thief, grinning with her eyes, and stepped through the door. The thief followed.

The daughter led them down the hall, glancing over her shoulder at the thief all the while, worry and confusion showing in her face. The thief avoided her gaze, glad the woman hadn't killed her straight out, but troubled by this pretense. There could be no neat way out of this. There would be a theft here, at the very least, and if he knew this woman at all, there would also be blood.

Perhaps I can intercede to save her life, he thought, looking at the curls falling down her back.

But that was a foolish thought. To avoid thinking, the thief looked around the house. It hadn't changed much. The walls were hung with brass nautical implements and lined with shelves and cabinets, which held strange curios from other lands—figurines, bits of statuary, slivers of petrified wood, crystal formations.

The daughter led them to a sitting room. "Father is in his office. I'll . . . I suppose I'll go and get him. You can wait here."

After she left, the woman said "Do they have servants?"

The thief jumped. "N-no, they didn't, anyway. A woman came in the evenings to cook for them, but that was all. The mother and daughter kept the house in order otherwise.

"So just the parents and the girl to contend with. Good."

"Why did you tell her all of that, about my coming to make things right?"

"I was going to twist her head off, thief, but I decided to honor your wishes, for the time being, at least. I told you you'd been good. I'm feeling indulgent."

"You don't—"

Someone shouted elsewhere in the house, and something crashed, like furniture falling over. Boots pounded down the hall.

"I think Papa's coming," the woman said.

The captain entered the room, stopping just inside the door. He ignored the woman entirely, staring at the thief. "You," he said. "I didn't believe her. I didn't think you were *this* sort of a fool." Daintier footsteps followed, and the daughter and her mother appeared behind the captain, each laying a restraining hand on his arm. He shook them off and stalked into the room. He was not a big man, but strong, his muscles standing out like ropes.

The woman raised her arms, and the captain stopped in mid-stride, his eyes bulging.

"Now that you've calmed down, perhaps we can talk," the woman said. The daughter and the captain's wife stood unmoving, too, their eyes wide. "You have something that belongs to my mistress—a jewel, a green jewel. One of your grand-sires stole it, and I've come to take it back." She stood and approached the captain. She brushed back her sleeve and turned her arm, showing him the scars. "That old thief cut me, too, and trapped me. You look very much like him, and if you don't cooperate, I might forget the distinction between you and your ancestor. We wouldn't want *that*."

The captain twitched a little around the mouth. The woman stepped close to him and touched her finger to his chin. His mouth dropped open. He made a low, moaning sound.

"You don't want that old jewel anyway, do you?" she asked softly.

"No."

"So where is it?"

"My office."

She turned and looked at the thief. "Let's go fetch it, then."

The thief nodded, queasy. He'd thought he hated the captain, but seeing him like this, afraid and paralyzed, made him sick, not satisfied.

"This is a good opportunity for you," the woman said. "We've got him right where we want him. You can make any . . . demands . . . that you like. I'll see that he agrees." She looked, pointedly, at the captain's daughter.

The thief looked at her, the woman he'd loved once, or believed he'd loved. At her body, still beautiful, which had once moved under him and still moved in his dreams. He could have her, he knew. Take her with him. The woman could even make her . . . love him. If he wanted that.

But he hadn't wanted her enough to stay and marry her the first time, had he? And he shouldn't do so now. She deserved better.

Slowly, the thief shook his head. "I want nothing from this house."

The woman curled her lip. "You think you're being noble, I suppose. She might have had a pleasant life, with you. I could have made her forget this nonsense." She clapped her hands together, as if brushing off dust. "Very well. Let's go." She lifted her hand, and the daughter and her mother fell, to lie stiffly on the carpet like tumbled statues. The thief winced, but he could do nothing to help them. He'd done all he could.

They went to the captain's office. The woman stepped inside, assessed the room—shelves of books, a large desk, lamps, chairs—and walked straight to a glassed-in case. "There," she said. "The jewel."

The thief looked into the case, and saw no jewel. Only a large dark sphere of . . .

Ah. It was an intricate, spherical metal cage, a thing of curves and layers. A journeyman smith's useless piece of finery, perhaps. An iron ball of filigree, as big as two fists held together, with a tiny green jewel set deep in the center.

"You can't even touch it," the thief said.

"Why else do you think I brought you?"

The thief nodded. He took a heavy piece of quartz from the captain's desk and shattered the glass, then reached inside and grasped the iron cage. "It's cold!" he gasped.

"I imagine," the woman said. "Though it would burn me. That jewel is from my Queen's crown, and it carries a little bit of her royalty still—like a scent that lingers on a pillow. To have even the Queen's decoration trapped in a cage of iron . . . " She shook her head. "The antipathy is strong, and it makes the iron cold."

"What do we do now?" the thief asked, his fingers growing numb. "Where . . . where do we go?" For he was thinking of the far Isle of the Fair Folk, and of the wonders and horrors he would see there, of the madness and forgetfulness that would surely overcome him on those shores.

"Back to the hole in the ground," she said. "There are smith's tools there, among all the other things. And as iron cannot be enchanted, I know those tools are real, and not bits of wood or offal made to look like coins and furs."

"You want me to break this cage, and free the jewel," he said. "I've never used smith's tools."

"If you can't figure it out, my thief, we'll just find a blacksmith and let you eat him whole, hands and ankles, heart and eyeballs. Then you'll know how to wield a hammer. Do you prefer that course?"

"I . . . think I can learn enough on my own to break this cage."

"Acts of destruction *are* the easiest to learn, aren't they, thief?"

They went down the hall.

"What will become of the captain and his family?" the thief asked. "Will you spare them?"

"Would you like to consume the daughter, eat every bit of her, and keep a little of her with you always in that fashion?"

"Gods! No, monster, I would not!"

"Very well. Then her soul will be consigned to wherever such things go. I'm going to kill them all, thief."

"You horrible—"

"Clutch that ball tightly, my dear," she said. "And go to *sleep*."

The thief did.

He woke, groggy, lying on a pile of musty furs.

"My sleepy thief. I hit you with that enchantment hard. I'm sorry."

He sat up in the dimness and screamed as every part of his body exploded into pins and needles as his sleeping limbs woke.

Only his hands, still clasping the metal ball, were awake. The proximity to the iron had kept her enchantment from making his hands fall asleep.

"That's right, move around," the woman said. "Work out the stiffness."

"We're back?" he croaked, his throat dry. "Underground?"

"You walked the whole way, though it's a jerky, stiff-legged walk, and it tired me out to drive you that way. I thought you'd wake up sooner, but I was a little . . . annoyed . . . when I put you under. You really shouldn't speak to me harshly, thief. I had you drag away the old metal trap door and build a wooden one to replace it, and there's a ladder now. Otherwise, yes, this is our familiar abode."

"The girl, the captain's daughter—"

"A puddle," she said, waving her hand. "A pool of nothing much. When your arms are well awake, the smith's tools are there, and I've got a fire going. We'll figure out how to break that ball."

"Why did you kill them?" The thief squeezed the cold iron ball.

"Because of the hurt their ancestor gave me. He was beyond my reach, so I contented myself with the descendents."

"You're inhuman."

"You state the obvious."

"I need water," he said suddenly.

"I imagine."

"The pitcher is . . . ?"

"Over there," she said, and stretched out her arm to point.

The thief saw his opportunity. He hurled the ball as hard as he could toward her midsection.

She grunted as the ball struck her, then screamed. Smoke rose from her dress as it caught fire. In the dimness, the thief could hardly see what had happened, but it seemed that the iron ball had buried itself into her stomach.

"You shit-eating bastard," she shrieked. She reached down as if to pull the ball away, but screamed and pulled her hands back when she touched it.

Insubstantial hands gripped the thief's throat, and he grunted and started toward the fire and the smith's tools. The hands fluttered, faded, returned. She'd been tired anyway, she said, and now she was grievously wounded. Her hands of air and fire were tired. Still, his vision dimmed and he fell to his knees near the anvil. He reached out and gripped a pair of iron pincers. He struggled to lift the heavy tool, but managed to press it to his throat.

The woman screamed anew, and the invisible hands withdrew.

The thief laboriously gained his feet and stepped toward her. The ball of iron was almost invisible now, burning its way deeply into her guts.

"We could have had such fun," she said, coughing up smoke. "You would have lived forever, if you'd just agreed to serve me."

"I think I might have figured out a way to do that anyway," the thief said. He struck her in the face with the iron pincers.

It took him almost a full week to eat her body. She had no organs or bones, just soft, spongy meat throughout, which both relieved and disturbed him. Her flesh tasted like nothing at all, but it still repulsed him to cut and consume her.

The stories said that the Fair Folk had no souls, and so he wondered whether eating her would have any effect—what good was ingesting the spirit of a soulless thing?

But the night he finished her, he had strange dreams. And when he climbed the ladder and emerged into the dark forest, he discovered that he had hands of air and fire, and could move things with a thought, and feel them from far away.

As the years passed, he found that he did not age as men did, nor did he take wounds.

And so he felt satisfied, at last, that he was a master thief.

That's my story, boys. And now the sun's near gone, and you should go home, yes?

Ah, the questions, the questions. What became of the thief? Well. Long after he ate the woman who was not a woman, after many years of wandering, he began to ponder his weakness. Because you see, along with his hands of air-and-fire and his long life, he'd also acquired the woman's weakness. He could no longer touch iron—the metal grew cold if he even put his hand near it, and he knew it would burn him if he touched it.

But he thought to himself, *Am I not, at bottom, a man? Could I not, perhaps, overcome this weakness, if I only had the right meal?*

The thief thought back to the woman's suggestion that he could eat a smith to gain familiarity with tools. And the thief thought, *Yes—perhaps I'll eat a smith, and gain his ease with iron, and the metal will vex me no more.* For it is amazing how many things in this world are made of iron, boys, not least of all this cage. The thief had never eaten a man—he'd kept that vow all those years, because the woman did not count as a human, you see—but he thought the time had come to forget silly vows, just as he'd forgotten the face of the captain's daughter.

So the thief came to a village, and took a room in an inn, which had a ram's head on its sign, as many of them do. And the next day he went to the smith's. He was uncomfortable around the horseshoes and the anvil and the hammers but managed to put on a peaceful face. He hailed the smith, intending to inquire after a bit of work and then kill him and spirit his body away for a leisurely meal.

The smith looked familiar, and from the way his eyes went wide, the thief knew he recognized him, too.

Ah, boys—your own eyes are wide. Is this a familiar story?

The smith looked just like the old keeper of the inn, the one the woman had killed that first night the thief traveled with her. Casting back, far back in his memory, the thief thought that this, perhaps, was that same village, grown a little larger, but still the same. He realized the smith was the inn-keeper's son all grown-up, that with his father dead he'd had to apprentice to a trade other than inn-keeping.

The son recognized the thief, and in his face it was clear that he remembered the witchery, remembered the murder and seeing the thief fly away.

The thief threw out his hands of air and fire, but the smith had iron all around him, and a hammer in his hand, and the invisible hands rebounded from those things.

The smith struck our thief with a hammer, and knocked him down, and the thief woke in a cage—yes, like this one, very like—with a grievous burn on his face from the hammer's iron. The thief tried to escape, but he could not open the cage himself, because his hands could not touch the iron bars, neither his real hands nor his *other* ones.

And now, my boys—the moral.

I fear I have misled you. There is no moral. Because a moral comes at the end of the tale. If I stayed in this cage, and died, there might be some lesson to be learned from my long life. But my life hasn't ended yet, and so it's a poor time for accounting, before the ledger's even closed.

Because I can still grab you, brats, despite this metal all around. I can reach my hands of air and fire through these bars and grasp you lightly by the necks, as I've done now. And you, smith's son . . . you'll go, and take—and *steal*—your father's smallest hammer and chisel, and come back here in the dark, and break this cage open. If you don't, I'll squeeze your friends until they're blue, and then black. And if you serve me . . . perhaps I'll teach you secrets, and show you wonders.

You only look afraid, now, but you'll learn to look happy, and hopeful, and bright, in time.

And after you release me, perhaps we can find something good to eat, yes?

BLEEDING WEST

Kentucky Tom Granger stood in the dust-beaten main street of a town called Tolerance and faced the Spirit of the bleeding west. Wooden buildings lined the hardpacked street, discolored to gray uniformity by the sand-laden desert winds. Tom had crossed the Arizona border to reach the town, but Tolerance was not in Arizona, or any other state, either. Tolerance was simply in the west.

The seventeen badges pinned on Tom's ragged shirt glittered in the high sunlight, one for each lawman he'd killed since coming west. An ancient razor-strop hung around his neck like an untied scarf. His twice-great-grandfather had fought with the Kentucky volunteers in the War of 1812 and helped skin Tecumseh, the Indian chief who fought with the British, in 1814. The dangling strop, made from the flesh of Tecumseh's back, constituted the Granger family's sole heirloom.

Tom wore a pair of Colt .45 Peacemakers with plain wooden grips. He didn't go in for ivory inlays or engraved initials. Tom's guns were killing tools, and in their simple utility he found a powerful symbol of a lost time.

The Spirit of the bleeding west stood under the high noon sun, nevertheless casting an impossible shadow that stretched all the way to Tom's feet. The Spirit didn't move, and Tom couldn't make out anything but its huge hat, and its hands hanging motionless above its gun butts. Tom coughed, then pulled his bandanna over his nose. He'd grown accustomed to dust over the years, but the dust in Tolerance seemed thicker, dryer, and more abrasive. This dust could get into his lungs and slice like diamond chips until he spat blood.

Tom drew a deep breath through his bandanna. "I want to ride with you!" he shouted.

The Spirit, a faceless silhouette, did not react.

A wet, gurgling laugh came from Tom's right. He turned, drawing his gun, and saw a man leaning against a hitching post in front of the Trail Blossom saloon. A dead horse lay beside him in a broken-legged pile, still tied up. The man (or *thing*, Tom thought, gripping his guns more tightly) wore a black banker's suit and a bowler hat. His gray skin glistened, and while his green eyes had no pupils, Tom could see the amusement there.

Tom lowered his gun. "What's so funny?"

"Oh, nothing," the thing in the suit said. "Just thinking how one man's hell is another man's heaven." He cocked his head. "Come on in, stranger. I'll buy you some firewater."

"You'd better not be laughing at me," Tom said. He glanced up the broad street. The Spirit of the bleeding west had moved on, but it wouldn't go far.

"Stranger," the thing said seriously, "in Tolerance, I'll do anything for a laugh."

Broken glass crunched under Tom's feet when he entered the Trail Blossom. Overturned tables and chairs littered the sawdust-covered floor. A few men sat in the back, playing cards, and they looked up with sharp-eyed curiosity when Tom and the thing came in. A blonde woman dressed in red (and little enough of it) sat at a busted piano, tinkling keys at the high end of the register. The bar was as utilitarian as Tom's guns. People came here to drink, screw, and gamble, and the place made no pretense to any other purpose.

The thing in the suit lifted a fallen table with one hand and set it upright, then placed a pair of chairs beside it. "Have a seat, stranger. Want a drink?"

"No." Tom sat down, sizing up the heavyset bald bartender and the five card-players in the back.

"No?" The thing sounded surprised. "I don't think I've ever offered to buy a man a drink before and been turned down."

Tom tipped back in his chair. "They say the drunker Doc Holliday got, the faster he drew. I'm no Holliday. When I get drunk, I can't shoot straight, and there might be shooting today."

"Suit yourself," the thing said, and went to the bar. He returned with a shot glass and a thick deck of oversized cards. He sat and shuffled the cards deftly. He had seven fingers on each hand, and delicate webbing between them. "I'm Cosmocrator," he said. "Call me Cos."

"Tom." He looked at the cards distrustfully. He'd met a fortune teller in Missouri who read his future with cards like those, and she'd predicted his death in a dry gutter. "Those aren't Tarot cards, are they?" Tom rubbed his single Texas Ranger's star with his thumb.

"No, no. Just a homemade deck. Cards are rare here, valuable as gold. I used to have Tarot cards, but when I came to Tolerance, the pictures changed." Cos made a sour face. "Death became a big cowboy with a straw in his teeth. The Hanged Man hung by his neck instead of his feet, and the Lovers . . . " Cos shivered. "The Lovers wandered in the desert, raving, and they'd gouged out their own eyes. I don't like to look at them anymore."

Tom took that in thoughtfully. He was not as dumb as most people thought—perhaps not as dumb as his profession demanded. "Then it's true. This place, Tolerance, stands outside the rest of the world, and the Spirit of the bleeding west still rules."

Cos riffled the cards. "The Spirit lives here. Deserts are hard places, stranger."

"Not anymore," Tom said bitterly. "The frontier's gone. The gangs are all broken up, the boomtowns are busted, and even the law's gotten fat and lazy." He touched the Ranger's star and remembered one lawman with a scar on his cheek who hadn't been fat or lazy, not a bit. He'd almost been too fast for Tom.

"Oh, I don't know," Cos said, grinning. His teeth looked like shards of broken seashell, poking up crookedly from bloodless gums. "There's a sense in which all deserts are one desert. Not in the particulars, maybe . . . but they have the same nature. Merciless. A proving ground. Isn't that why you came?"

"I expected a different place," Tom said. "You can't ride anywhere without tripping over fences and families these days."

"You expected the James gang," Cos said sympathetically. "Stagecoach robberies. Tombstone at its peak. Sharpshooters. Men calling each other out. Right?"

Tom nodded. "But Doc Holliday's dead of tuberculosis, Frank James is shot in the back, and Wyatt Earp's retired, for good this time." He took the strop from around his neck and stretched it between his hands. "I came west too late."

"So you looked for Tolerance. To find what the west lost."

"The spirit," Tom agreed.

"He lives here," Cos repeated. "Same as the djinns in any desert. First cousin to Shaitan from Arabia, only different in the details. The hat. The gun." Cos smirked. "The sexual diseases."

"I don't know what you're talking about."

Cos sipped his whiskey, not even throwing back the shot like a real man would. "I don't expect you do."

"What are *you* doing here?" Tom nodded at the poker players. "Those boys are human, at least, men and gamblers and likely fighters. What made you seek out Tolerance?"

Cos laced his hands over his gut. "I'm not from the west. I come from the east, the *far* east, a different place, ruled by different spirits . . . including the big one who made the earth. In the early days, I was given dominion over the tenth part of the waters. But then came a conflict . . . a *showdown*, you might say . . . and I sided with the upstart, a djinn named Shaitan."

Tom nodded. He didn't know if he believed Cos, but the story sounded almost familiar, in a sideways sort of way.

Cos shrugged. "The big spirit didn't like that, and as punishment, I'm forced to wander the earth's deserts, and never touch water again." He wiggled his webbed fingers. "The big spirit has a pretty uncomplicated sense of justice." He looked at the ceiling. "Speaking of which, there's some justice coming soon in this town. Or Law, at least, which is the next worst thing."

Tom caressed his badges. "I've dealt with the law before."

"Not like this." Cos turned over a suicide king. Instead of a sword, the king held a gun with an absurdly long barrel. "You've fought agents of the Law. This is the Law himself, the Law*man*, and the ghosts of all your victims ride with him." Cos turned over a red ace and whistled. "He won't be interested in you, though. He'll go after the Spirit, and kill him, and Tolerance will turn into another ghost town, and the bleeding west with it."

"Not if I can help it," Tom said. "He'll have to climb over me to get to the Spirit."

"Well, hell, of course," Cos said without looking up from his cards. "It wouldn't be the west without a showdown."

A high wind rattled the windows. The gamblers in the back of the room exchanged nervous glances. One with long sideburns said "I call" in a reedy voice. The men showed their cards, and the winner raked in the pot without anyone fussing or complaining. They looked at the saloon's batwing doors nervously, though Tom didn't see anything out of the ordinary. The saloon girl stopped tinkling the piano.

"Last call!" the bartender yelled.

"What the hell?" Tom said. "It's high noon!"

"It's always high noon in Tolerance," Cos said. "At least, it always has been. I think night could be falling."

The gamblers put on their dusters and hurried out. The saloon girl followed. Cos smirked at them. The beefy bartender came over, twisting a rag between his hands. He nodded to Tom, then put a hand on Cosmocrator's shoulder. "You leaving, old son?" Sweat beaded on his bald head and ran down his nose. "He's coming. Can't you hear the wind?"

Cos flipped another card lazily. "Why should I leave? I've already been sentenced by a higher law than his. I might stay to see how it plays out."

The bartender looked at Tom, his bloodshot eyes panicked as a broken-legged horse's. "You'd better saddle up, stranger. The Lawman's on his way. Tolerance won't be a haven for the likes of us anymore."

Tom tipped forward in his chair. The legs thumped hard on the board floor. "You're leaving?" he said, his voice low and smooth as a viper's crawl. "All of you?"

The bartender smiled nervously, laughed a little. "It's death to stay. Death and, hell, justice. It's been a good place, but we knew the end was coming . . . " He shrugged. Cos watched the exchange with appraising green eyes.

"It's a war," Tom said. "A war to save the last bastion of the old west from the rule-makers and the fence-builders." He stood up fast and kicked his chair away. The bartender flinched at the noise. "If you leave, instead of fighting, you're no better than any other deserter."

The bartender frowned and spat. "Stay and die if you want. I'm leaving." He started toward the door.

"We shoot deserters where I come from," Tom said quietly, and drew. He didn't give the bartender a chance to argue or change his mind. People who fought under threat of murder didn't fight their best.

Tom shot the bartender in his startled face, and winced at the loud report.

Cosmocrator raised his glass, looking at the dead bartender. "Rest well, partner," he said.

"I'll get the others," Tom said, not pleased by the prospect of gunning down the gamblers and anyone else who tried to run, but determined to do so. He stepped into the dusty street.

The gamblers from the Trail Blossom lay in a neat row in the center of the street, shoulder touching shoulder, the soles of their boots facing Tom. The saloon girl lay there, too, her red dress already dulled by the blowing dust.

"Yellow," a voice said, and Tom froze. He'd heard that voice in his dreams, hard as a gun barrel, cold as a winter night on Boot Hill. The voice of the west. "Yellow, every one." Tom turned his head and saw other dead men and women lying farther down the street, and doubtless dead people filled the cross-streets, too.

"I'm not yellow," Tom said. He swallowed. "Sir."

"Look at me."

Tom looked at the Spirit of the bleeding west. It sat mounted, in a cracked saddle, and Tom guessed it would stand at least seven feet tall. Built like a normal man, but bigger in every proportion. Tom felt no surprise when he saw it had no face, just a tattered hat throwing more shadow than it should have. A straw dangled, clenched in unseen teeth. The Spirit wore chaps of a strange, too-pale leather, and its huge guns matched Kentucky Tom's exactly, except they were a little bigger. The Spirit sat astride a black horse-shape, a mount composed of coal dust, mud, barbed-wire, and rocks, with shiny bullets for eyes. The Spirit, or its mount, smelled of gunsmoke and blood. "Nice badges."

"I earned every one," Tom said, looking into its dark non-face.

"Saddle up," the Spirit said. "Ride with me."

Tom's horse had died days before, ridden beyond exhaustion and abandoned in the desert. "I don't—"

The dead horse tied to the hitching post stirred, then pulled itself laboriously upright. A broken bone stuck out of its right foreleg. It turned its sightless head to Tom and whinnied. Tom felt a shudder of revulsion, and suppressed it. He put his hand on the saddle horn and swung onto the horse's back. The horse sagged under his weight, and Tom had a horrifying vision of breaking its spine and falling right through its rotten body, but the horse stood firm.

The Spirit cocked its head. "Lawman's coming," it remarked. The wind screamed, and the wooden buildings creaked dangerously. "Let's go kill him."

The Spirit whipped the mount's reins and galloped toward the outskirts of town, leaping over the stacked dead, and Kentucky Tom Granger followed.

Tom reined in his horse under a wooden arch with a steer skull nailed to the crossbeam. The Spirit stopped a little farther on, its mount walking back and forth beyond the edge of town. Tom had entered Tolerance through that same arch this morning, and didn't want to leave again unless he had to.

"Your horse is dead, Tom," Cos said.

Tom jerked, and his horse danced a few feet sideways. Cos leaned against a rain barrel. Poor old cuss, Tom thought. He stays close to water as best he can. "I noticed."

"See that dust storm?"

Tom looked toward the horizon, where a hazy curtain hung. "Yep."

"That's the Lawman and his ghost-posse. Better shine up your badges if you want to scare them. I hear the Earps are riding with him."

Tom frowned. "Morgan? He's the only one who died."

"Virgil, too . . . or at least part of him. His ruined arm, maybe. And Wyatt."

"But Wyatt's not dead!" Tom protested.

Cos rolled a cigarette, his seven fingers flying. "No, but he isn't a marshal any more. His career as a peacekeeper is dead . . . and the ghost of that career is on its way. Ghosts ride with the Lawman, but so do memories, and fragments. They're drawn to him, to his big shiny badge, like moths to a candle." Cos licked his cigarette closed and tossed it to Tom, who caught it without thinking. "The condemned man gets a last smoke," Cos said.

"I can't decide if I like you," Tom said, tucking the cigarette into his shirt pocket. "But I thank you. I'll smoke it after we kill the Lawman."

Cos nodded. "I don't know if I like you, either. I'm going back to the Trail Blossom. I'll leave town when the buildings blow over . . . or I'll wait to congratulate you." He walked over and stuck out his hand. Tom leaned from horseback and shook with him, once. His fingers came away moist. Cos walked back toward the center of town, whistling.

"Tom!" the Spirit said, and Tom kicked his horse forward without even thinking, drawing up along side the towering Spirit.

Figures resolved out of the dust, one clearly in the lead, leaning forward in his saddle. Riding a white horse, Tom thought. Figures.

"Stand true, partner," the Spirit drawled.

The Lawman stopped in a cloud of dust. His posse hung back. Tom's head hurt when he tried to count them. He saw Wyatt Earp, mustache drooping, and Texas John Slaughter, and a few other faces familiar from pictures. Faces familiar from life, too, several belonging to men Tom had killed. None of them wore badges. Some lacked arms, or legs, or eyes, and all of them flickered, as if they had no substance of their own, only bodies drawn from dust and animated by justice.

The Lawman was solid, though, built on the same larger-than-life scale as the Spirit. His clear blue eyes regarded the Spirit coldly. Not a speck of dirt marred his clothes, and his blond hair looked perfectly combed. The gold star pinned on his vest shone like the sun. He chilled Tom's blood, then boiled it. That's the one, Tom thought. The one who broke the west, come to finish the job.

"No place for the law here," the Spirit said.

"The Law makes its own place," the Lawman said. "We're taking you in, or taking you down. Your choice."

The Spirit didn't reply, but for a moment, Tom saw *through* its dirty cowboy gear, to something fundamental. Something red, made of leaping flames. Something with scorpions for fingers and a face made of smoke. Tom felt chilled, and remembered Cosmocrator saying *I sided with a djinn named Shaitan.*

But Kentucky Tom Granger had cast his lot, and he wouldn't change his bet at the last minute.

Tom threw back his coat to show off his badges. He didn't know why, exactly; just seemed like it might piss the Lawman off. The Lawman didn't appear to notice, only kept staring at the Spirit, as if they were having a showdown Tom couldn't understand.

The posse, however, became agitated. They looked at one another, and at the Lawman, and back at Tom. A few of them nudged their horses forward, uncertainly.

Tom laughed out loud, and the Lawman jerked in his saddle, noticing him for the first time. Men like that hate the sound of laughing, Tom thought, and laughed harder. He touched his Texas Ranger's badge. "Come on, boys!" he shouted. "You're backing the wrong man!" A few of the ghosts and fragments moved away from the rest, hesitating. He didn't expect the ghosts to believe him, but he'd certainly confused them. If the

Lawman's shiny badge attracted them, then Tom's could, too. "Sure, he's got a Godalmighty big badge, but I've got *lots* of badges! I'm the Lawman here!"

Now the Spirit laughed, a dirty chuckle. A laugh with the pox, Tom thought, which made him laugh all the harder.

The Lawman growled and went for his gun, a shiny Colt with gold and ivory grips. Tom knew he couldn't outdraw him. He didn't try. He whipped the razor-strop from around his neck and smacked the Lawman's oversized hand with it. Tom shouldn't have been fast enough, but he was. Maybe the strop's bloody origin gave it power, or maybe the Spirit lent Tom some extra speed. Either way, the Lawman's shot, aimed for Tom's chest, went wild. The Lawman dropped his gun and yelped. Just like whipping a kid with a belt, Tom thought, pleased.

The Lawman stared at Tom, stunned, and then looked at his bleeding hand.

"About to shoot me in cold blood!" Tom shouted. "Didn't even give me a chance to surrender! What kind of Lawman is that?"

Several of the posse turned their horses and galloped away, dissolving to dust before they got far. A few others moved forward, as if planning to stand with Tom.

"Enough of this shit." The Lawman dipped for his other gun.

The Spirit drew first.

Tom saw the bullet fly, really *saw* it, moving slow as a gliding hawk. The bullet writhed like a scorpion, a stinger lashing from one end, venomous fangs sliding out of the other. The living bullet smashed into the Lawman's startled face.

The Lawman's hat fell off. A moment later, he tumbled from his horse. The Lawman's hand twitched as if still reaching for his gun.

"Cheap shot," the Spirit said. "I had to take it."

The remaining members of the posse (among them the scarred Texas Ranger Tom had barely killed outside Amarillo) opened fire on the Spirit. Tom's horse screamed and buckled under him, and Tom fell to the dirt, hard. He cracked his head on the hardpacked ground, and all the wind whooshed out of him. I'm hit, I'm hit, he thought wildly, but nothing hurt except his back and his head.

The Spirit fell, too, along with its barbed-wire-and-mud horse. The bullets pounded into the Spirit, making its huge body jerk like a strip of bacon frying, but none of the bullets hit Tom. The posse didn't aim for him, or else their ghost bullets were fit only for killing a djinn.

The posse blew away, dissolving to dust, their pistol shots fading, eventually sounding like nothing more than distant echoes.

Tom's looked at the Spirit's unmoving body, then lowered his pounding head. *Goddamn*, he thought, and passed out.

Tom opened his eyes and saw Cosmocrator's face, thin lips, scummy green eyes, and gleaming seashell teeth. "You alive?" Cos said. "Guess so. I wanted to bring you some water, but . . . " He shrugged. "Shit. You know." He shook a bottle of whiskey over Tom's face. "Want to drink this now?"

"Sure," Tom croaked, and sat up. He drank from the bottle, the whiskey burning his throat but exploding to warmth in his belly.

"They killed the Spirit," Cos said.

Tom looked at the pile of mud and filthy clothes, all that remained of the Spirit of the bleeding west. "But we got the Lawman."

Cos laughed, a little nervously. "Tolerance is still here. The buildings didn't fall down. I guess . . . " He swallowed. "I guess you're the big gun around here now." Cos looked over his shoulder. "There's people riding around outside town . . . or maybe ghosts. I got a good look at one, he had a white scar on his cheek." Cos drew a finger down his face to illustrate.

Tom put the bottle aside and crawled to where the Lawman had fallen. The body was gone, but his gold star still glittered in the sand. Tom picked it up. The badge felt warm in his hand.

Tom pinned it to his vest, right above the Ranger's badge. He fished the cigarette out of his shirt pocket and stuck it in his mouth. "Bring 'em on," he said. He clapped Cosmocrator on the shoulder. "Like you said. It wouldn't be the west without a showdown."

Sharing the bottle, they walked back to the Trail Blossom.

BEHEMOTH

I answered the doorbell. A punk stood on my front porch, silver fish-hooks glinting in his nose and earlobes. He wore colored contact lenses, one eye yellow as piss, the other black. Dirt caked his undershirt and torn corduroys.

"Selling girl scout cookies?" I asked, trying to smile, hoping he didn't want to kill me for my pension check.

He shifted from foot to foot nervously, and I wondered what drugs he'd taken that day. Something that made him jittery. "Are you Adonis Sinclair?" he asked.

I looked at him, thinking: It can't be. "Harry. Harry Sinclair. I go by my middle name. Mom had high hopes for my looks."

He didn't smile. "You have to come with us, Mr. Sinclair."

I looked past him to the street and saw a beat-to-shit gray sedan idling on the curb, spattered with mud up to the windows. "Why's that?"

He answered with a question, his voice hoarse. "Did you really do it? Find him, all those years ago, and start the Order?"

"The Order?"

"The Order of Watchful Vigilance."

I didn't laugh, though I wanted to. It's impolite to laugh at someone's religion. Dean came up with that name, I thought. "I guess I did. I never called it that, and neither did Dean, when I knew him, but I imagine we're talking about the same thing."

"Dean didn't think we'd find you," the boy said.

"He's still around, then." I hadn't seen Dean in almost fifty years. "I'm glad to hear that. We were best friends, a long time ago."

"We need you to come, Mr. Sinclair."

I leaned against the doorjamb. I didn't want him to see me shaking. "I'm old, son. I'm not inclined to take any long trips."

"He's moving," the boy whispered.

I shrugged. "He moves. Not often, but sometimes."

The boy shook his head. "No, he's *moving*. Walking around. And he asked for you, Mr. Sinclair. How do you think we found you? He told us where you were. Showed us in a vision."

"Moving." I licked my lips. It's hard to believe, I know, but I hadn't thought about Behemoth in years. Hadn't seen him, either, not since the last time I saw Dean. "Did he say where he planned on going?"

The boy squirmed. "In the dream we saw something. Like a snake, but bigger. And beautiful." He swallowed. "And dying, scales flaking off into the water, showing bone."

"Oh, shit," I said. "Let's go."

Me and Dean found Behemoth when we were ten and eleven years old, respectively. We lived in a little nothing Georgia town called Pomegranate Grove. We spent a lot of time raising hell in the woods outside town, whooping like Indians, playing at war, creeping through the brambles like jungle explorers. We never discovered the limits of the woods, but they extended farther than they should have. I'm not talking about any funny business with time and space, just that people owned title to wooded land they should have cleared, good land they could have used for farming or development, but instead left wild. Behemoth's woods are special, maybe even sacred, and people just . . . overlook the real estate possibilities, I guess. I got curious a few dozen years back, after I received a barely legible postcard from Dean about the new acolytes, and tracked down some satellite photos of Georgia.

That huge swath of untouched forest shows up perfectly clear on satellite photos, and it's even bigger than I imagined. I don't remember the exact dimensions, but it's big enough for a dozen people and Behemoth to live in, undiscovered, forever. I doubt anyone will clear the forest, not as long as the (potentially) largest land animal in the history of the world resides there.

Me and Dean finally convinced our parents to let us go camping for three days. Our Dads gave permission, despite our Moms' protests. Both our fathers loved the woods. They went deer hunting together, and they taught us a fair bit of woodcraft. Two days into our trip, deeper in the woods than we (and probably any human) had ever penetrated, we found Behemoth.

We made camp against his side. Behemoth hadn't moved in decades, maybe centuries, and moss and lichen grew all over his body. His side looked like a gray mound of rock, and that evening I leaned back against him. Behemoth breathes about twelve times a day, and his heart beats even less frequently, so I didn't notice any unusual vibrations. We probably never would have realized what we'd found if Dean hadn't tried to carve his initials into the "rock" with his pocketknife.

He didn't make a mark, and he scratched harder, and still no mark, so he held the blade like an icepick and jammed it in. Even back then Dean never gave up, no matter how trivial the challenge before him.

Behemoth didn't roar or jump or anything like that. If he had, we would have run, and things would have been different for me and Dean. Instead, Behemoth simply rose on his elephant legs and bear's-paw feet and swung his ivy-covered crocodile head toward us.

I froze, because that's what you're supposed to do when a rhinoceros gets angry at you, and I wanted to believe Behemoth was a rhinoceros, or something similar.

Dean, on the other hand, screamed and fell over.

Behemoth spoke to us, but not with words. He spoke into our minds, with pictures and blurry strange imaginings that somehow conveyed this: Be peaceful. Don't fear. Don't run.

My heartbeat slowed. Dean picked up his knife, looked at it, looked at Behemoth (even then, at his smallest, twelve feet high and twenty feet long), and folded the blade shut.

"Hi there," I said. "I'm Harry."

Adonis, Behemoth thought. I saw an image from the myth, the part where the boar gores Adonis, fatally wounding him. Red flowers sprang from the spilled blood.

Okay, I thought. I'll be Adonis, much as I hated the name. The 600-pound gorilla can call me whatever he wants.

"I'm Dean Mather," Dean said. Behemoth thought of a man in pilgrim garb, and women hanging from a gallows. Years later I realized he was thinking of Cotton Mather, the witch-hunter. Behemoth has a peculiar sort of awareness.

He didn't send Dean the image of the witch hunter, and I knew he didn't show him the next image, either: Dean as a frolicking, bumbling jester, wearing cap-and-bells and ugly yellow leggings. Understand, Behemoth's thought wasn't *cruel*—I even sensed affection in the image, but also brutal dismissal. You can laugh at the clown, and even like him, but you don't trust him with anything important. You don't love him.

Sit down boys, Behemoth suggested, showing an image of us around a small fire, with me and Dean laughing.

Sit down, he said without words, and I'll tell you about an apocalypse deferred, and about the only one I love in all the world.

The acolytes drove all night and into the next day, down new interstates toward the old town of Pomegranate Grove, Georgia. I didn't have to notify anyone about my trip. I'd been moldering in retirement for five years, and there hadn't been any family for a long time. Not since I lost my wife, two years after we got married. She didn't die—I just lost her. Lost. I make it sound like a set of keys that got misplaced. It would be truer to say that I threw her away, like someone might accidentally toss a winning lottery ticket into the trash.

The punk drove for a while, then the dreadlocked hippie. He offered me some marijuana, but I turned him down. I've never tried the stuff. I had a steady job during the Summer of Love, and even then I was too old to be trusted. The willowy-pretty girl in the back seat with me never spoke, not once, but she looked at me with flat-out adoration. If I'd been even thirty years younger, and the type to take advantage . . . Well, I wasn't, on either count, so I didn't think about it. At my age, that's not as difficult as it used to be. The car slowly filled with the reek of pot, too many bodies, and bad fast food.

We reached Pomegranate Grove at first light. My kidneys throbbed like rotten teeth. The kids stopped to let me pee every couple hours, but the nonstop driving played hell with my body. It interrupted my sleep cycle, too. I snapped at the kids and sat sullenly as the pines and fields flowed by. Just inside the Georgia border, it hit me. We were going to see Behemoth, the friend I had abandoned for a woman, but who still loved me enough to call me back in his time of need. That thought sobered me some, and broke my bad temper. I didn't feel any better, really, but I realized how petty it was to bitch at these kids when Behemoth certainly felt much, much worse.

We passed through Pomegranate Grove, past different stores on the same old streets, and then drove into the woods.

Right into them. I screamed and put my arms over my face, sure we'd hit a tree, and the girl patted me on the leg reassuringly. I uncovered my face and looked. A path opened before us, as smooth as any well-graded dirt road can be, winding ever deeper into the trees. I wondered if the road always existed, and people simply overlooked it, or if Behemoth created the road when we needed it.

We drove into a large clearing, a space filled mostly with Behemoth's reclining body.

I got out of the car and took a hesitant step forward. I'd forgotten the smells. Mainly the pine of the woods, but under it all the earthy scent of Behemoth himself, a smell like wet red clay. Behemoth looked smaller than I remembered, and I wondered if I suffered from an enlarged perception of the past, or if he had actually lost stature over the years.

"Behemoth," I said. His head, part crocodile, part elephant, part the rest of the menagerie, swung toward me.

Adonis, he said, again with the image of the beautiful youth facing off against the boar.

I thought about Aphrodite, the goddess of beauty, and how she'd loved Adonis. She never truly loved anyone else.

You came, Behemoth said.

"Of course I did," I said aloud. Several acolytes stood around, watching. I didn't see Dean anywhere. When you live with your God physically on a daily basis, I guess you get used to it. It must be a thrill to meet the long-lost co-founder of the Order. People need someone to idealize. "They said you needed me. They said . . . something about a beautiful snake."

Yes, Behemoth said, and showed me the same vision he'd given his followers, a golden serpent writhing in shallow, frothing water under a steel gray sky. Shining scales fell from her head like shingles torn from a shack roof in a hurricane. The acolytes had never heard Behemoth's whole story, so they hadn't understood him properly. I did.

Behemoth said: Leviathan is dying.

That first night with Behemoth me and Dean made a fire and ate beef jerky. Dean offered some to Behemoth, and he politely refused. Behemoth eats a little grass once in a while, but that's all.

Behemoth told his story in pictures, and sometimes the images still show up in my nightmares. Tree branches hung with streamers of torn flesh. The moon cracking like an egg, spilling blood into the sky. Great black dogs, big as mountains, charging across the clouds, lips peeled back and snarling.

Behemoth showed us images of an overdue apocalypse. He told us the end hadn't come on schedule, and Behemoth's life couldn't proceed until it did. He had a role in the end days as the chief monster of the earth, leveling mountains, destroying cities, and ravaging the land.

At the time I wondered how he could manage that much devastation, but later I discovered that his body could change, especially when he wanted to go somewhere quickly. He didn't hate mankind, but he would destroy us, acting as an instrument of the powers-that-be, whom Behemoth had never met. He came into existence with the knowledge of his role, his strength, and his single limitation: He is a creature of the land, and cannot touch water.

Behemoth knew about Leviathan from the first, too.

Leviathan, his female counterpart, lived in the sea. She could never touch land.

In the last days Leviathan would destroy all trace of man on the oceans and devastate the coastal cities. Behemoth looked forward to those days, not because he particularly cared about destroying the world, but because at the end of the world he could finally join Leviathan.

He loved Leviathan more than I can even imagine loving. I cannot describe the visions he gave us to convey that emotion. He knew what Leviathan looked like, though he'd never seen her with his eyes, and he showed us. Despite her fearsome serpentine shape Dean and I fell in love with her, too. Behemoth perceived her as the most lovely creature in the world, and we saw her as he did.

They couldn't be together until the last days, when blood would saturate the soil and fill the seas. Either one could travel in blood. That was their mutual medium.

Behemoth had waited more patiently than any bridegroom anticipating his wedding night, but the end hadn't come. Behemoth began to despair that it never would.

After his story he went back to sleep. Me and Dean sat quietly, looking at his moss-covered body and talking about what we'd heard. Maybe back then I saw the fanatic zeal in Dean's eyes, burning brighter than our campfire, but probably not. Kids don't think about things like that, or at least the kid I was didn't.

We settled down to sleep in the cloudy dawn. Dean unrolled his sleeping bag on the far side of the fire from Behemoth, keeping a respectful distance. I thought nothing of throwing my blanket right up against him, sleeping with my back to his bulk. I didn't worry that he would turn over on me. Creatures with moss growing on their bodies, I reasoned, couldn't be restless sleepers.

We had to go home the next day, but a week later, we came back to see Behemoth again.

I touched Behemoth's crocodile head, rubbing the tough, bumpy skin between his eyes. "What happened to Leviathan?" I said. The acolytes gathered around me in a semicircle, and I glared at them in irritation. Why did they have to crowd us that way?

But they'd stayed with Behemoth for years, ready to tend his needs, while I'd left. They'd fulfilled their duty by coming to get me when Behemoth asked. What right did I have to begrudge their presence? I hadn't bothered to visit Behemoth in decades.

Behemoth showed me visions of Leviathan, miles of vast undulating scales, trying to crawl onto some desolate beach. Wherever her belly touched, her flesh tore open, and she slithered back into the sea, which clouded with blood. She swam away, slowly, and found another beach, where she repeated the process.

She wants to build a path to me with her own blood, Behemoth said. But she can't bear the pain for very long, and anyway, she will empty herself before she succeeds.

Leviathan couldn't bear to live without him any longer. I tried to imagine her loneliness, trapped in the sea's cold, gray infinity. At least Behemoth had me and Dean.

Well, me for a little while, until I left with Belinda. Mostly he had Dean.

I caught an undercurrent in Behemoth's thoughts, a brief image of Behemoth himself splashing into the water after Leviathan. His skin sizzled and boiled off, and I felt his shame radiating like heat. If Leviathan gambled with her life to try and reach him, why didn't he do the same? Didn't he love her as much?

"Of course you do," I said, smoothing his head. "I know how much you love her."

She will try and come aground again, Behemoth said, showing me an icy bay and a rocky shore. I couldn't imagine a more inhospitable place to emerge, but I assumed she approached only uninhabited beaches. I hadn't seen any news reports about giant serpents rising from the surf.

I have to get there first, and stop her, Behemoth said. The prospect excited him. He believed that she could heal, if she stopped trying to reach him, and he wanted to tell her to wait. He would rather have her live away from him than die futilely, though he understood her desperation and frustration as well as his own. This way, at least, he would have the chance to see her.

I stopped stroking his head briefly, then resumed. He wanted to go to Leviathan, to whatever forsaken piece of northern shore he'd shown me. Since I couldn't recall an ice-locked bay in these woods, that meant a journey. Probably a long one.

Dean would want to go. A pilgrimage . . . that was right up his alley. "Where's Dean?"

Behemoth replied with the image of the jester again, but this time with a camouflage cap-and-bells and a grim, dirt-streaked face. In the woods, I think, Behemoth said. I could tell he didn't care. I need you, Adonis, Behemoth said. I do not want to make this journey alone.

I turned to the waiting acolytes. "Behemoth is going on a little trip. Who's with us?"

A dozen hands rose immediately.

I nodded. "Good. Can somebody point me in Dean's general direction, do you think?"

No hands shot up this time. Behemoth stood, silent. Finally, the willowy girl lifted a hesitant finger and pointed into the brush, in the direction of the setting sun.

I'm too old for trailblazing, I thought. One of the kids, with a scraggly beard and wide eyes, handed me a walking-stick. It had a snake carved on one side, all the way down its length. Every scale had been rendered perfectly, painstakingly.

"You made this?" I asked. He nodded, mute. "It's good," I said, and he grinned.

I set off into the trees.

"I'm staying out here, Harry," Dean said, two weeks after we graduated from high school. We sat on a dead tree not far from Behemoth's resting place.

I scratched my nose and tried to understand what he meant, exactly. "You were offered a scholarship. You graduated fourth in our class. Why would you stay in Pomegranate Grove?"

"I don't mean the Grove. I mean I'm staying here, in the woods, with Behemoth." He looked at me with dark, narrow eyes. Dean had grown up to be a lean, oily-faced young man. He made good grades in school because he applied himself there with the same dangerous intensity he directed at everything in his life. He'd been a clumsy kid, and I still thought of him that way, but he'd grown up frighteningly bright and dedicated. "You should stay, too," Dean continued. "He loves you."

The unspoken final phrase: "more than he loves me." I tore at the rotting bark on the log where we sat. "I love him, too. I've come out here every week all these years, haven't I? But I can't give him everything. Come on, Dean, living in the woods? Don't you want more out of life?"

I wasn't sure he did. Dean came to the woods several times a week, whenever possible. His devotion never flagged.

For me, seeing Behemoth had become like visiting a beloved but elderly relative. When he stirred and spoke to me, I enjoyed his company, but he usually slept his immovable sleep. As I grew older, I visited less and less often.

Dean didn't get bored. He would crouch beside Behemoth, sitting on his heels, for hours. I never really wondered what he thought about. Maybe I should have; maybe a better friend would have.

"This is the right decision for me," Dean said. "What about you? Are you going with Belinda?"

I could hear his sneer. Dean and I had grown apart until only our shared knowledge of Behemoth held us together. We didn't move in the same circles anymore. Dean didn't move in any circles at all. "Yeah. She's going to school in North Carolina, at Chapel Hill. I'm going with her." I grinned. "I didn't think I'd get accepted, but I guess all my extracurricular stuff made up for my grades."

Dean didn't answer. He did that a lot, trying to emulate Behemoth's silence, I guess. Dean didn't know how often Behemoth really talked, because more often than not the visions only came to me. I wish I knew why Behemoth loved me more than Dean. Maybe, in the end, it was because I acted from love instead of duty. Dean loved Behemoth like a cause, while I loved him like a friend.

"Go tell him you're leaving," Dean said at last. "He'll wake up for you."

"Sure. I'll be back, okay?"

Dean didn't even nod, just stared at a fixed spot in the trees.

I went into Behemoth's clearing and touched his snout. His eyes, green with black pupils, opened. "I came to tell you I'm leaving soon."

Behemoth didn't answer for a time, and then he gave me a picture of a leaping campfire with no one sitting around it.

"Dean's staying. You won't be alone." His skin felt unpleasantly rough under my fingers, especially compared to the smoothness of Belinda's body.

Why are you leaving? Behemoth asked.

I started to say something about growing up, moving on with my life, and starting a career, but I never told lies to Behemoth. "There's a girl, Belinda. We've been dating for a couple of years now, and I'm going away with her."

I am so happy for you, Behemoth said, and the force of that statement almost knocked me down. I saw a montage of images, mostly flashes of Leviathan and Behemoth together, her body twined around his, their heads close together.

Is she a wonderful girl? Behemoth asked.

"The best there is," I said. "I wish . . . " I didn't finish. I didn't know how to.

Behemoth understood. I will join Leviathan soon, he said. It cannot be much longer now.

I hoped, very selfishly, that it would be. I imagined a long life with Belinda, and I didn't want it interrupted by the end of the world. "I'll miss you, old monster."

Come back and visit me, Behemoth said. Bring your children, someday, and let them climb across my back.

"Of course I will," I said.

I didn't. I never had children. I married Belinda after our first year in college, as a desperate attempt to save our dissolving relationship. She finally left me after the second time I cheated on her. I can claim impetuous youth, but that excuse only goes so far.

I don't think I was ready for commitment, and whatever else I can say about Dean, he certainly never had that problem. After another year Belinda and I divorced and I transferred to another college. I got a business degree and started working for a big pharmaceutical firm, dated lots of women but never married, traveled a lot, and didn't return to Pomegranate Grove because my parents moved to Florida and I didn't see any reason to go back.

Sometimes Dean sent me cryptic letters, full of news about the acolytes and obsessively detailed descriptions of Behemoth's occasional movements. For a time Dean tried to divine knowledge of the future from Behemoth's occasional stirrings, but I never understood the system he used, and he never told me his predictions, only that he made some. I couldn't reply; Behemoth's woods don't have a mailing address.

Eventually he stopped sending letters, or maybe they couldn't make it through all my forwarding addresses. I didn't mind. I wanted to put that part of my life behind me and move on. Whenever I thought of home I thought of Belinda, the sun shining on her red hair in my back yard, the walks we took by the lake, the wild grapes we gathered together.

I kept moving on for years, and never got anywhere.

Until I came back to Behemoth's clearing, to the one love that stayed, and went with him across two countries to save the girl he loved.

Even with the stick, I moved slowly, but I didn't have to go far. I found Dean sitting on a fallen tree, not the same one we'd sat on all those years ago, but another. I imagined the first tree had long since turned to rot. Dean wore a ragged camouflage jacket and a grimy black beret, and had his back to me.

"Dean," I said, leaning hard on the walking stick. I could hardly breathe. My lungs resisted every inhalation, and ached when I exhaled.

"Harry." He didn't turn. His voice sounded the same, but tired. "They found you."

"Yeah." I walked slowly around the tree, favoring my right leg. My ankle hurt for no good reason. The joys of aging. I sat next to him, my heart pounding. "You surprised?"

"Not so much surprised they found you," he said. He still didn't look at me, but kept his eyes fixed on some invisible point before him. "Mostly surprised you came. Why did you?"

"Because he asked for me." Deep lines covered Dean's face. I barely recognized him otherwise, but the eyes were the same. Dark yet bright. Passionate.

"So that's all it took," he said bitterly. "He only had to ask. Didn't I ask you to stay?"

"Dean—"

"I stayed," he said. "And he never spoke to me. In fifty years . . . not once. Fifty years. Do you know how many days that is? Every day, hoping?"

I couldn't answer that. I'd filled my years with business and distractions, and they'd gone quickly. His years, I knew, passed more slowly. "Do you regret staying?"

"No. I guess I don't. Because I love him, even if he doesn't love me. I thought staying would make a difference . . . that he'd forget about you."

That stung, but I understood, and didn't get mad. "I love him, too," I said. "I came back, didn't I?"

"I didn't have to come back," Dean said. He finally looked at me, and as I watched, the brightness left his eyes. His whole face sagged, but his gaze held mine. "I never left." He looked away.

"Dean . . . "

"You'd better go, Harry. Behemoth is waiting."

There didn't seem to be anything else to say. I got up and slowly worked my way around the tree, through the broken branches and kicked-up underbrush, back the way I came. I turned once, and saw Dean still sitting, slumped. I don't think he looked back at all.

We left. I rode on Behemoth's shoulders, and the acolytes followed in two battered cars as Behemoth traveled down another dirt road that I'd never seen.

How is your wife? Behemoth asked.

I almost lied. Years of working in the business world made that natural. I didn't want to give Behemoth fifty-year-old bad news, but I don't lie to him. "The marriage ended pretty quickly. Mostly my fault, to be honest. The last I heard she got married again, moved to California and had a couple of kids. That was thirty years ago, though."

Behemoth didn't answer for a long time. He could never fall out of love with Leviathan, or vice versa—their love was like natural law. I wonder if any human can feel so strongly . . . and I'm afraid that some of them can. Not me, but some.

I am sorry, Behemoth said at last, and then didn't speak of Belinda again, as if the whole situation disturbed him too deeply to contemplate.

The acolytes occasionally drew alongside us and threw loaves of bread and bags of fruit for me onto Behemoth's vast back. Old men don't eat much. The acolytes brought me a blanket when it became clear we were going north. I marveled at the stretches of uninhabited land in this country. Behemoth walked a route that never touched a major city, and he only passed a few small towns. No one noticed us. In America, that's a pure miracle. I wonder sometimes if he bent the world somehow, to arrange that, if his own vast size could alter the very shape of the planet with its personal gravity.

As Behemoth walked, he got bigger, until I couldn't look over the side without a rush of vertigo.

The acolytes couldn't follow when we reached the Appalachian mountains, and we left them behind. They honked their horns and waved furiously. Behemoth didn't seem to notice.

By that time, Behemoth towered fifty feet high at the shoulder, and by all logic should have collapsed under his own tremendous weight. He trudged on (though with strides as long as his, it hardly felt like trudging) in defiance of the square-cube law. He stepped over rivers and gorges and left footprints deep as mineshafts in soft fields. We crossed into Canada in North Dakota, and didn't pass any significant human habitation thereafter.

Behemoth didn't want to stop walking, and before long the food gave out. At my age I don't eat much, and I drank when it rained. The water fell into my mouth, but it never touched Behemoth—just slid away a few inches from his skin, as if running down a sheet of glass. I wondered if that inviolability would protect him if he stepped into the sea, but I remembered the visions and knew it wouldn't. The powers that be accounted for rain, it seemed, but they wouldn't tolerate willful immersion. Pretty soon I noticed that rain fell, just for a little while, whenever I got thirsty. I didn't ask Behemoth about that. I developed a wheeze in my chest and a persistent cough. When my vision started turning red at the edges, I complained of hunger. Almost immediately, small brown mushrooms sprang up in the ancient dirt caked between Behemoth's shoulder blades. I ate them by the handful. They tasted a little woody, and a little like boiled eggs.

After countless days of travel, we reached the beach. I think we were somewhere in Alaska. Mountains crumbled into the sea, forming a protected cove. Gunmetal clouds filled the sky. The sound of waves crashing on rocks overwhelmed everything. I had never seen any place so simultaneously loud and desolate.

I'd never seen anything to compare to Leviathan, either.

Behemoth's vision had done nothing to prepare me for her size. Leviathan stretched long as a freight train, a hundred feet of her length exposed, the rest disappearing into the cold ocean. She thrashed in the shallows, her wet scales shining, every one a yellow jewel. White shore birds screamed and wheeled around her huge head. Whenever she moved, gouts of white water sprayed into the air, soaking jagged black rocks. The air stank of blood and salt.

Behemoth shrank as he approached. Eventually I had to cling to his shoulders to keep from falling off.

Leviathan lifted her golden, whiskered head. Her eyes were as vast as Behemoth's, but darker. She thrashed her way closer to shore. I saw the wounds on her underside as she heaved herself forward, ragged tears with white edges. Everything inside her spilled out as the earth scored her, and she crept forward along a path of blood.

Behemoth stopped a dozen yards away. The water lapped at his feet, and smoke rose where it touched him. I smelled burnt meat. He stepped forward again.

"No, Behemoth, don't," I said, gripping the loose skin behind his head. "It won't do any good." Wet, salty wind blew into my face, stinging my eyes and making them water.

Behemoth showed me a pair of images, parallel: The familiar love-embrace of Leviathan twining around his body, and an image of them melting into blood and meat together. He wanted to join her.

"Please, Behemoth," I whispered.

Leviathan lifted her head again and heaved. She came within ten feet of us. She blinked and exhaled, her head dropping. Her enormous jaw crashed into the rocky shore. The bones in her face splintered on impact, with a sound like dead trees falling. I squeezed Behemoth's skin harder. Leviathan's teeth, gleaming white pillars, broke against the ground. Her eyes, dark as tidepools in black sand, looked at Behemoth longingly.

He didn't move.

Her left eye closed, then the right. Her golden eyelids dropped as irrevocably as coffin lids closing. She didn't move again.

Behemoth wailed. I can't describe the sound, but I still hear it, almost, echoing off the rocks and the water. Echoing off the sky.

Leviathan's broken head brought it home for me. They would never twine together in the last days. Her blood had failed to make a path. If Behemoth wanted to die, all he had to do was step into the water. I imagined his blood mixing with Leviathan's, and that mixture somehow saving them both, repairing Leviathan's torn scales and his burned legs. I imagined resurrection and, prompted by their willing sacrifice, the long-awaited apocalypse.

But there were to be no more deaths that day, and no resurrections. I don't know why Behemoth didn't go in after her. His mind provided no visions.

He sank to his knees, shrinking, and rested his alligator's jaw on the ground. He stared at Leviathan. I touched his head, feeling the rough skin under my fingers. I shivered and coughed wetly. Shore birds landed on Leviathan's body and began to strut.

I looked away. "Come on, Behemoth," I said.

He stood, looked one last time at Leviathan's broken body, and trudged back the way we came.

Behemoth remained small on the return trip, never reaching the towering proportions he had on the way to Alaska. I rode his back the whole way, and he didn't communicate with me at all.

We eventually reached the woods. Behemoth settled down into his familiar depression in the dirt. He didn't send me an image for days.

The acolytes told me Dean had died shortly after we left. They wouldn't say how. They snapped at each other and walked on eggshells around me, and seemed relieved when I sent them away this morning. I told them to come back in a month with fresh supplies for me. They revere me as their founder (that was a kind legacy for Dean to provide, at least), so they obeyed. The willowy girl, crying, kissed Behemoth on the snout before she left.

This morning I went to Dean's grave. The acolytes marked it with a big water-rounded rock. I wonder if he enjoyed the life he chose, waiting to serve in ways Behemoth never required, providing for a creature that had no needs except love. Dean told me he'd made the right choice, and I hope he still felt that way at the end.

I sat by the rock for a while, trying to call up childhood memories, but nothing came. I never understood Dean's devotion. I chose other loves, and while I'll never know if I made the wiser decisions, I own those choices and accept them.

I returned to the clearing.

"Behemoth," I said. "I'm going to die soon, I imagine. I'm going to stay with you until I do." I spread my blanket and leaned against his side.

It's the middle of the night now. I woke myself up coughing. My back and kidneys ache, and my lungs burn with every breath. Death will come quickly if I stay in the woods, but I'm old, and I can imagine worse things than dying.

Like dying alone.

I wonder about the powers-that-be, whoever placed Behemoth and Leviathan on earth to await an apocalypse deferred, and why they let Leviathan die so pointlessly. If the powers intended it as a lesson, I don't understand the moral. Maybe in death I'll find some answers. If not, I hope the questions won't trouble me any more.

After I told him I planned to stay, Behemoth stirred a little. A moment later he showed me this: Me, leaning against him, sleeping while he slept.

"Good night, Behemoth," I said, and closed my eyes.

BONE SIGH

1

I sit at the table and work on my bonsai scar. I press the silver head of the meat tenderizer into my left thigh, stippling the skin. I do not feel pain; I scarcely feel the pressure. My nerves are dead, there on my left thigh, where I grow my scar. Matches, hot needles, knives, and time. I tend my scar, I do not control it. Skin and muscle are unpredictable—this is not like painting a picture, carving a piece of wood. The flesh knows its own logic, the bruises come strangely, the healing proceeds unevenly. I collaborate with my flesh.

The space between intention and accident, that is the place where God lives.

I put the tenderizer down on the white formica table and look at my bonsai scar. It is like a flower, a jellyfish, a pinwheel of raised flesh, yellow bruises, subcutaneous hemorrhaging.

Is it process, nothing but process, or someday will I be finished? Will I see the face of God, the expression of revelation? Or will I see the back parts of God, as Moses saw?

Only time and painful tenderness will tell.

2

I sit on a bench with a bored officer of the court while my daughter Crystal goes down the slide in the park, over and over.

My ex-wife was the only person who knew about my bonsai scar, my single devotion. When she decided to leave me, she told the court about my scar. She had taken pictures of my scar, while I slept, and she showed them to the judge.

The court decided that someone like me, who hurts himself so methodically, might try to hurt his own child. As if I do not understand the division between self and other, the difference between personal sacrifice and inexcusable attack.

My ex-wife left me and took Crystal, and now I only see my daughter in the park, with a chaperone, every few weeks.

My ex-wife has a new husband, a thin man who sells insurance, a thin man with a thin mustache and black hair slicked back with something oily that shines. He is secretly a monster, and I fear for my daughter, living in his house. I hope my scar will take a final shape soon, and guide me, for I feel close upon despair.

I have stepped up my devotions, and my whole left leg aches.

Crystal slides. Her pigtails fly behind her. She cries "Banzai!" as she slides.

3

My ex-wife has died. The brakes failed on her car and she plunged over a bridge, into a swamp. They found water in her lungs. She did not die on impact. She had to inhale swamp water, trapped upside-down in her car, before she could die.

I go to the funeral, in a small country church we never attended. The monster, my dead ex-wife's husband, sits in the first pew, holding my daughter's hand. I can see the truth about him crawling under his skin; his scalp bulges and ripples as the monster inside him shifts. No one else notices; perhaps God has given me the power to see monsters.

Perhaps God wants me to help myself.

The monster and my daughter walk past the coffin. Crystal weeps; the monster holds her hand and will not release her.

I realize that the monster cut my ex-wife's brakes, so that he could have Crystal all to himself. For some terrible purpose.

I wish my scar would advise me.

4

We named her Crystal because crystals start small, and then grow. Because they begin simple and beautiful and, over time, become complex and beautiful.

Like my scar. But we couldn't call our daughter Scar, and even if we could have, my dead ex-wife would have refused.

5

The scar does not guide me. I lash myself with coathangers and burn myself with lye, but more than ever before the window into revelation seems hopelessly opaque. I feel I have reached an impasse, that I have done all I can—now all my work is the equivalent of useless cross-hatching, obsessive shading, adding irrelevant details.

If my scar will not guide me, I must guide myself.

I will go to the monster's lair.

6

The front door is unlocked, and I go inside. There is some light from the windows, but it is dimmed by curtains. This is a squalid little house. My dead ex-wife was an excellent housekeeper, but in her absence the monster's house has reverted to type. I almost expect to see a heap of gnawed bones in the corner, a pallet made of rotting animal skins. But there are only old newspapers, empty aluminum cans. He is a subtle monster.

I have never been here before, so I creep in the dimness toward a hallway. The house smells of meat, of fat boiled with beans. I listen, and hear a voice. Crystal's. I want to scoop her up and take her away to freedom, away from the monster. But what if he is with her, right now? Who else would she be talking to?

I step softly to a half-closed door in the hallway and look inside. Crystal is sitting on the floor, talking seriously to a red-haired doll. Crystal's dress is soiled and torn. The monster is trying to dress her as if she were his own offspring, a monster herself.

"What the hell?" the monster says, behind me.

I turn. The monster stands in the hallway, dressed in boxer shorts and a dirty white t-shirt. He is unshaven, and his eyes are red. I can see the fires smoking inside his head, the tentacles coiled in his belly, the monster under his thin flesh disguise.

He has a large knife in his hand.

"Stay away from her!" he shouts, and runs at me. I throw up my hands to ward him off. He stumbles, tripping on an empty whiskey bottle on the floor.

I know what will happen before it does; it is like God grants me the vision, as a warning, or a courtesy.

When the monster falls, he stumbles into me, and drives his knife into my thigh. Into the heart of my bonsai scar.

Imagine a gardener, devoted to his bonsai, controlling its water, its nourishment, its temperature, its access to light—

—and then the bonsai is infested with woodlice, shredded by cat's claws, smashed with a fire poker, chopped with a hatchet. Imagine how I feel.

The knife sticks in my thigh, and all the dead nerves come to life, wake up and scream pain at me. There are arteries in the thigh, blood highways—did the monster cut one? Will I die? Will I see God's face (or even his back parts) when I die?

Crystal is screaming. The monster is on the floor, but he is getting up.

I pull the knife out of my thigh. That hurts worse than it did going in.

The monster turns his face to me.

His eyes are full of smoke, blood, fangs, shards of glass.

I put the knife into one of his eyes.

7

"Did he ever hurt you?" I ask.

Crystal sits on the edge of the bathtub, her eyes wide and vacant as I bandage my thigh, cover the bloody remnants of my ruined bonsai scar.

"Did he ever touch you, in a bad way?" I ask.

"No," she says.

But I know he would have.

8

Weeks after I saved Crystal from the monster, we sit in a motel room. She is better; talking more, glad to be with me. She feels we are on a grand adventure.

I have been careful not to let her see my bonsai scar, only changing the bandages in the bathroom, when she sleeps. But today I am taking the bandages off for good, and Crystal is curious to see my healed wound.

I remove the wrapping and look at the scar. There is a large, pale knot of scar tissue in the center, where the monster's knife went in. I look at my thigh sadly. The waste of all my work. The face of God, marred forever.

"Daddy," Crystal says, touching my scar gently. "It's an *eye.*"

I look at her, then at my scar, and I begin to smile.

She's right. The monster's stabbing wound has not ruined my bonsai scar, but has instead *completed* it, provided the final touch, formed the pupil of an *eye.*

"One eye. Like a Cyclops," Crystal says.

I think of the monster, the way I stabbed his eye out. Monsters have only a single eye, but my scar is not meant to reveal a monster's face.

I am blessed. The face of God is forming on my body, responding to my devotions.

But I have vastly underestimated the *size* of God's face. I will need more than one thigh to reveal it.

I will need my entire body; chest, arms, head, legs.

Looking at my daughter, at the fascination in her face, I realize something else—that the revelation is not meant for me. I am only the *medium* for revelation. I am the book, not the reader.

My body will become the face of God, and my daughter will look upon me and know the secrets of life, the ways and means of earth and heaven.

My disappointment is brief and selfish, and then I am glad. For what more could a father want? What better reason is there to sacrifice, but for the good of your child?

"Bring me my bag, darling," I say, and when she does, I take out a knife.

DAUGHTER AND MOON

The moon disappeared last week and the world is shuddering
like a wet cat. Cows sleep badly and the milk
is sour. The tides have gone insane, arriving and departing
without reason, like a secret alcoholic with a part-time job. Blood
flows (or doesn't flow) in unusual ways, streams
rush uphill and lovers bicker on park benches everywhere.

The moon is in my house. It is no bigger than a dinner plate
or a basketball, and is much grittier than it appears in the sky.
My daughter says she lured it with a trail of jelly beans (no
black ones) and that it will go home when it gets bored.
Meanwhile it eats the fresh butter, nestles in the bathtub,
rolls across the shag rug and chases our dog, who howls.

The farmers don't know when to plant. Our president
suspects the Arabs. Dubious astronomers check and re-check
foolproof instruments. People on the street shout that the end
is near, but the economy has never been better. All the spells
chanted under the dark of the moon are coming undone. My
daughter dresses our satellite in bonnets and her dead mother's
scarves.

Today I asked her (she is nine, with pig-tails and crooked
teeth) what it all means, why the moon came to us, and she

laughed. She ran down the hillside this morning
and the moon floated behind her. They play tag like old friends.
My daughter will never be this young again. I wonder
if the moon is telling her secrets. I suspect that it is.

CAPTAIN FANTASY AND
THE SECRET MASTERS

Shortly before I met Captain Fantasy, I sliced the end of my forefinger off while dicing cucumber for a salad. I shouted and shook my hand, splashing blood on the counter and tearing the thin strip of skin that held my fingertip on. The tiny lump of flesh tore loose and flew into the sink, down the garbage disposal, gone.

I cursed, then concentrated on my nerve endings, switching off the pain. My whole finger went numb. I had trouble controlling the nerves on such a small scale. Holding my finger in the air like a "we're-number-one" fan at a basketball game, I urged new flesh to grow over the wound. I'd make a few big hamburgers to go with my salad, supply some mass and calories for the healing . . . my new fingertip should be grown by morning, though the nail would take longer, and I'd have to either keep the nerves dead or be careful not to scrape the sensitive under-nail skin.

The phone rang. I answered it left-handed, clumsily. I expected my director, Jack Harrah, to call and remind me of that night's dress rehearsal, as if I'd forget. I was playing Orestes, the lead, at Harrah's Greek Revival theater. "Hello?"

"Hi, Li," Brady Doolittle said.

I almost hung up. But why bother? They'd found me. "Boss," I said, neutrally. "I tendered my resignation."

"Not accepted," Brady said cheerfully. "We need the best Metamorph available, and that's you. We let you run loose for nearly a year, never bothered you. Be grateful for that."

So they'd kept tabs on me all along. Well, of course. The Facility didn't lose track of people. "Tomorrow's opening night. Can't it wait until—"

"Your understudy, Bill Monroe, he can handle it. By tomorrow night, you'll be playing a much more important part."

Brady knew everything. Always. That's why he ran the Facility. I looked at the spots of blood on the counter and gave in. "When can I expect you?"

"A car's waiting outside. Pack a bag." He paused. "I think you'll like this one, Li."

"Sure." I hung up. I didn't have to pack a bag; I already had one ready, a change of clothes, travel-sized toiletries. Old habits die hard.

Walking to the car, an anonymous government sedan, I thought, "I'm like Orestes, trapped by cruel fate." I had to smile at that. Such melodrama. Even if I had to play the part of secret agent again, I didn't have to ham it up.

Several hours and a plane trip later, I found myself back in the Facility. *You never get away*, I thought.

"What did you do to your finger?" Brady asked, bushy eyebrows raised over his boyish face. He motioned me into the elevator. "Nice face, by the way. Very Greek."

I grunted and stared at the elevator doors, listening to the Facility hum around me as we descended. Brady didn't speak again, didn't try to draw me out, and I finally asked the question that had been plaguing me. "Is this about Kelli? Has she done something else?"

"Yep. Makes the rainy day affair look like tea time, too."

I had a hard time believing that. Kelli, with the help of the mad Dr. Nefarious, had wreaked havoc with the world's weather the year before, until I stopped them. We'd captured Dr. Nefarious, but Kelli, the mastermind, had escaped. What could be worse than endless rain drowning the world?

The doors opened and Brady led me down a long white corridor. "Is that why you said I'd like this?" I asked. "Because Kelli is involved? You think I want another chance at her?"

Brady shook his head. "No. I know you aren't the vengeful type. There's another reason you'll like it." Brady stopped at a reinforced door. He touched a palm reader, pressed his eyes to a retinal scanner, spoke his name loudly, and punched a long string of numbers into the keypad. I watched with interest and apprehension. Extreme security measures, even for the Facility, which meant—

The door slid open, revealing another corridor. Floor, walls, and ceiling were all the color of used motor oil, and cameras bristled every couple of feet. "Welcome to the Black Wing, Li."

I didn't step inside. "I heard you've got Bludgeon Man locked up in here. And Junior Atwater's brain, in a jar."

"Yeah, I've heard those, too," Brady said. "People believe any damn thing, don't they? Now come on. If this door stays open too long, alarms go crazy, and we'll be neck-deep in very tense guards."

I stepped over the threshold. The Black Wing was like the inside of a tumor. No wonder mental institutions favor soothing colors to pacify the patients. These walls had the opposite effect; they could drive a sane person mad. The Black Wing surely held a few mental patients, the ones with extraordinary powers. The ones who could enforce their delusions on the world, if they got free.

"Is Kelli here?" I asked as the door slid shut.

"No, but we've got a room all picked out for her. She's been here recently, though. She broke someone out." Brady smiled at my shocked expression. "That's top secret, you understand." He pressed a finger to his lips.

"That's impossible!"

"Yeah, we thought so, too, until she did it. She had inside help, of course, and it couldn't happen again, but once was enough." He led me around a corner, to a black golf cart. Brady got behind the wheel and I sat beside him. The cameras turned and followed our progress like the heads of watchful jackals. We drove past blank metal doors set at regular intervals.

"How many inmates are there?" I asked. I'd served with the Facility as a field agent for years, but I'd never seen the Black Wing. Metamorphs are masters of disguise, born impostors, and our usual assignments don't require access to the holding-cells for super-powered criminals.

"Way too many and not nearly enough," Brady said. We turned a corner, and I finally saw something that broke the monotonous black. One of the cell doors, bent and twisted, leaned against the wall across from a gaping doorway.

I whistled. "How did that happen? I don't see any marks from explosives."

Brady stopped the cart. "Carl Spandau, one of our guards, a Strongman with a titanium-alloy skeleton. We spent a lot of money giving him a set of bones that could support the strain his power put on his body. Then he betrayed us. We found him with his arms broken from tearing off the door, crying, but not from the pain. He'd disabled the teleport-dampeners, the quantum-entanglement disrupters, all the failsafes. Stuff he shouldn't have known about, codes he'd spent months ferreting out. Kelli bounced in, snatched up our prisoner, and teleported away—without Spandau. That's why he was crying. He said he loved her, and refused to believe she'd just been using him."

I nodded solemnly. Kelli could make you believe anything. I didn't ask what happened to Spandau. I know how the Facility deals with traitors.

"Who'd she break out?" I asked, not irritated at Brady's vagueness, simply needing to know so I could do my job. Seeing the Black Wing breached, hearing about poor stupid traitorous Carl Spandau's arms, had changed my resentful resignation to acceptance. I'd do what I had to.

"Josef Mengele got away," Brady said.

I stared at him, as uncomprehending as if he'd said Rasputin had escaped, or Vlad Tepes. "Mengele? The Angel of Death, the mad doctor of Auschwitz? But he's dead, they found his skeleton in '85, it was all over the papers!"

"People believe any damn thing," Brady said quietly. "We've had him for years. He's almost 90 now, frail but physically healthy, considering."

"Why?" I demanded. "He should have been tried at Nuremburg! He was the worst of the war criminals, so *cold*, and the experiments—" I broke off, staring at Brady.

Brady looked away. "Yes. The experiments. Mengele studied the limits of special powers, did things no ethical scientist could, but the knowledge . . . " He shrugged. "We needed it."

I nodded, disgusted. The Facility depended on people like me and Spandau, Metamorphs and Strongmen, as well as mind-readers, Pyrokinetics, Teleporters, Invisibles, all the extraordinary ones, and Mengele had studied our kind, dissected us, tested us to destruction. The Nazis, fascinated with the concept of supermen, had a special interest in such individuals. Just like the Facility did. "You want me to bring Mengele back."

"In a nutshell."

"But why me? What, I disguise myself as the Fuhrer, say 'I didn't die in that bunker, Josef, come with me?' Why do you need a Metamorph?"

"We need you to impersonate someone, of course." Then, sounding doubtful for the first time: "That's the part you'll like." Brady drove past the torn door. "I want you to meet somebody."

"Who else do you have in here? Stalin? Genghis Khan? Colonel Kurtz?"

"You don't want to know," Brady said.

Even without the familiar costume, I recognized him immediately. Hearing about Mengele had stunned me. Seeing this man, here, left me literally incapable of speech.

The Captain looked just as he had in the old pictures and newsreel footage from World War II. He should have been at least 75, but he looked no older than 30. *He doesn't age*, I thought, chilled and awed at the same time. No one had ever known the full extent of Captain Fantasy's reality-altering powers. In the war, he and his sidekick Spaceboy had routed the Germans time and again, though Baron Von Blitz managed to kill Spaceboy near the end of the war, and they said the Captain was never the same after that.

Captain Fantasy sat behind a white table. He was a massive red-haired man dressed in green clothes that resembled intern's scrubs. A red and blue plastic top spun before him on the table. He stared at the toy intently, his teeth clenched in concentration.

"Oh Captain, my Captain," Doolittle said.

The Captain looked up, and I glimpsed his bewildered expression, quickly replaced by a broad smile. "Why, you must be a doctor." The top fell over.

I looked at Brady, unease crawling like a worm in my stomach. In his jeans and black t-shirt, Brady looked nothing like a doctor.

The Captain lowered his voice. "Was it a mortar, doc? From Baron Von Blitz's artillery?" He tapped the side of his head. "I heard Spaceboy yell, and then, poof! Everything black. I must have taken one right to the head, huh?"

Brady didn't say anything, just stood with his arms crossed. I looked at Captain Fantasy, my childhood hero, and my throat closed up. Spaceboy had been dead for forty years. I remembered watching Captain Fantasy deliver the eulogy on television. That was before my time, of course, but even in the '60s, when I grew up, Captain Fantasy was a celebrity, with films and books, cartoons and lunchboxes, all chronicling his wartime glories.

When Brady didn't answer, the Captain's grin faltered, and that disturbing look of naked confusion returned.

Doolittle turned on his heel and left the room. With a last look at the Captain, I hurried after him.

"Is it amnesia?" I asked when Brady closed the door. But that didn't seem right. The Captain remembered Spaceboy and Baron Von Blitz, and I didn't doubt that he remembered Goebbels and the Hitlerbot and Mengele's homonculi ... just nothing after the battle when Spaceboy died. I narrowed my eyes. "Or did the Facility do this to him?"

"No, it wasn't us," Brady said. "Demonstrations work better than explanations. Come on." He went back into the Captain's room.

Feeling like an extra in a Chaplin film, or a Keystone Kop running in circles, I followed him.

The Captain still sat, his top spinning. He looked up, smiling. "Hey there! You must be a doctor!"

I gasped. The scene was too strange, too eerily similar to the first time we'd come in. Like someone had hit a great "Reset" button and started the whole encounter over.

The Captain looked at me. "Is Spaceboy all right? The Baron really got the drop on us, huh?" He ran a huge hand through his hair.

"Have you ever seen us before?" Doolittle asked.

The Captain laughed, a scattered sound. "Oh, I meet lots of people, you know, I've never been good with faces."

"Have you seen anyone else in the last few minutes?"

The Captain shook his head. "No, sir. I've been sitting right here since I woke up."

"Just take it easy, Captain. We'll bring you some food and fill you in on things."

"But Spaceboy, is he all right?"

"Oh, yes. He's fine."

I stared at Doolittle. Was he being cruel, or kind? And what had happened to Captain Fantasy?

Doolittle motioned me back into the black hallway. "Karsakov's syndrome," he said. "A rare neurological disorder. It's a nasty form of amnesia. Basically destroys the brain's ability to hold short-term memories. Long-term memory is unaffected, so he knows who he is and remembers his life, but he can't hold onto new memories for more than a few minutes. He lives in a perpetual present. He's met me dozens of times, but he can't remember. He doesn't even know anything's wrong, or if he does suspect that something's amiss, he doesn't know *what*."

I nodded, trying to process the information. It was like being a child and learning my parents were mortal, that they could make mistakes—a blow to my whole worldview. I'd always thought of Captain Fantasy as, well, *invincible*. "Why doesn't he remember anything after that last battle?"

Doolittle shrugged. "Sometimes Karsakov's is retrograde, and destroys a portion of the long-term memory, too. The Captain's memories stop in 1945."

"What causes it?"

"I'm no doctor . . . bad brains, I guess. I understand that if you're predisposed anyway, heavy drinking can lead to the onset of Karsakov's. You probably didn't know, they kept it out of the media, but the Captain went downhill after the war, and drinking was only part of it. He wanted to come out of retirement and help with the China problem back in '55, but then all that mess with Bludgeon Man and the Atwater Coup happened . . . then, in '75, we got word that Captain Fantasy had shown up at a pub in New York, dressed in full costume, demanding to know where Spaceboy was. The Facility picked him up, and he's been here ever since."

I sat on the golf cart. "This is a lot to absorb. He even looks the same."

"He doesn't think he's any older, so he isn't. We think that's why he's invincible, too. Most kids think they're invulnerable, they take stupid risks and get hurt. But the Captain *never* got hurt, because while he believed himself invincible, he was. He grew up that way, and never had a reason to believe differently. I guess he just never worried about his mental health . . . or, hell, maybe his power has a negative effect on his brain chemistry. Who knows?"

"This is sad," I said at last. "But what does it have to do with Kelli, and the rest of it? The Captain could help us with Mengele, I guess, if he were healthy . . . "

"This is the part you'll really like," Brady said. "You're going to impersonate Spaceboy, and, with the Captain's help, apprehend Kelli and Mengele."

I put my head in my hands. "You'd better explain how that's going to work."

"All in good time. First, let's get you to wardrobe."

Silver tights. Silver boots, even the laces. A silver shirt with long sleeves, accordioned at the elbows. Silver gloves, fortunately, to cover my damaged forefinger. A silver domino mask. Spaceboy's famous skintight costume, tailored perfectly to fit me.

I looked in the mirror and watched my facial muscles bunch, move, and tighten. Occidental eyes. A rounder chin. Snub nose. That rosebud, almost girlish mouth. I leached the pigment from my face, changing the Greek cast I'd affected for my part as Orestes. I compared my face in the mirror to a small photograph and nodded, satisfied. "I've got the face right, and the hair's okay, but I'm three or four inches too tall. There's nothing I can do about that."

"Close enough for jazz," Doolittle said. "The Captain is desperate to see something familiar, to find his bearings. We could wrap you in aluminum foil and he'd believe you were Spaceboy."

I plucked at the seat of the silver costume. "Foil wouldn't be so tight."

"If the Captain had a girl sidekick, she couldn't have gotten away with wearing something like that," Doolittle agreed. "Your costume's better than Spaceboy's original. Bulletproof, shock absorbent, and made of smartcloth, with its own musculature." Brady grinned. He looked like a wolf at a lamb-shearing. "To help you do the somersaults and shit."

I groaned. I'd kept in shape, but Spaceboy's famed speed and acrobatics were beyond me. Spaceboy had trained as a teenage gymnast, and during his three years with Captain Fantasy, he'd pushed his flexibility to the limit. "So we tell the captain that Mengele's hiding out, and we have to bring him to justice. Then we ride out in the Fantasy-copter and apprehend the villainous et cetera."

"You should write briefings," Brady said. "You're so good at abstracting the essentials from a plan." He led me out of wardrobe to the elevator.

"But he forgets everything after five minutes," I protested. "How is he supposed to remember the mission?"

Brady turned a key in the elevator and punched the buttons that would take us to the Black Wing. "In some cases of Karsakov's, surrounding the victim with familiar things provides a sense of continuity. In one case, a patient was driven to his old neighborhood. He perked right up, wanted to know how they'd put up a supermarket overnight, but otherwise he thought things were fine. They took him to his old house, and he sat in his favorite chair, tapped his barometer, read a book. He wondered why his wife had changed the drapes, but he didn't notice that his wife had aged five years." Brady looked at me pointedly.

"Close enough for jazz," I murmured. "So seeing me, and riding in a replica of the Fantasy-copter, you think that'll keep him in the present?"

"He'll still believe it's 1945, but that's okay. He's willing to fool himself a lot."

The elevator stopped. As we stepped into the hallway, I asked "What happened to that guy you were telling me about when he had to leave his house?"

"They took him back to the hospital. He cried and screamed, asked his wife why she'd brought him to such a place, why she was leaving him."

"God," I said, chilled by the image.

"Pretty awful. But ten minutes later he'd forgotten all about it." We entered the Black Wing and returned to the golf cart.

"Where do we begin?" I asked, sitting down.

Doolittle handled me an envelope. I wasn't surprised to find it addressed to me. The Facility had intercepted my mail. I opened it and removed the little card inside, decorated with balloons and party hats. "Come to My Party!" it read, in festive blue and red letters. Inside, it read "Join the Secret Masters in celebration of Kelli's birthday!" Under "Time" it read "As Convenient." Under "Place" it gave a set of coordinates.

"In the Atlantic Ocean," Brady said.

"Is she on a boat?"

"Not that our satellites can see. But we figure it's not a wild goose chase."

"Kelli likes to play games, but not that kind," I said. "What's this 'Secret Masters' stuff?"

"Well . . . It's just speculation, but a lot of high-powered fugitives and crazies have been inactive, dropping out of sight lately. Thunderhead, Brainchild, The Teacher, Broadside, Svengali Briggs . . . no activity for months. We think Kelli's gathering the bad guys together. The old Legion of Supervillians gag, you know?"

I nodded. "Seems like her style. Into the viper pit, huh?"

"At least you'll have the greatest hero in history at your side."

"I'd rather have a crack Facility squad."

"They'll be nearby. If things get out of hand, they'll try to contain the situation."

"Why take the Captain at all? I mean, if he had full possession of his faculties—"

Brady handed me another envelope. "Because she invited him, too. And Kelli's promised to do some nasty things if he doesn't show up. As a demonstration, she bombed Easter Island. Wiped it out, and we didn't even see how she deployed the weapon, though fortunately it seems to be a clean bomb. Some toy Dr. Nefarious made for her, probably, during the rainy day affair. She said Christmas island would go next, then a little town called Thanksgiving, Pennsylvania." He tapped the Captain's invitation. "In keeping with her holiday theme."

"That's crazy," I said. "What does she want with Captain Fantasy?"

"What does she want with Mengele? He's almost totally senile. Why does she do anything? Crazy's right."

When the Captain saw me in costume, disguised as Spaceboy, he rushed across the room and embraced me, lifting me off my feet. I expected to be crushed into bone jelly, but the Captain squeezed gently. "I thought you were done for," he whispered, reddish stubble rubbing my cheek.

I am, I thought, feeling lower than dogshit. *Blown to meat and splinters and scraps of cloth, 45 years ago.*

The Captain let go. "Not me, Captain," I said, pitching my voice higher than normal. My facility with vocal impressions has always been an asset on my assignments. I surprised myself by saying "Leaping lizards, Captain, they couldn't get *me*."

Leaping lizards. A classic Spaceboy exclamation, and it had simply popped out. Had I assumed the role so completely? Or did Captain Fantasy's ability to warp reality extend beyond his personal space, was he in some fashion transforming me into Spaceboy?

The idea bothered me, and I began to sweat. I shut off my glands so the Captain wouldn't notice. "Captain," I said gravely, wanting to get it over with. "We have a problem."

"Mengele!" Captain Fantasy said, walking quickly up the stairs, red cape flapping, black boots thudding on the risers. "I've been waiting for a chance at him. Is the helicopter prepared, Spaceboy?"

"Right on the roof, Captain," I said, hurrying after him. "And I've got the coordinates."

"God bless American military intelligence," the Captain said reverently, and then burst through the door, onto the roof.

A pale blue sky stretched above us, touching the low, scrub-covered mountains. The air smelled of desert sage. The Fantasy-copter, a low-slung two-seater in red and cobalt blue, crouched like a lethal dragonfly a dozen yards away. Captain Fantasy strode across the roof and opened the cockpit. I hurried around the other side to join him, ducking as the long rotors began to turn, lazily at first, then with invisible speed.

I belted in, light-headed. Captain Fantasy gave me a thumbs-up and took the controls. I grinned, feeling strangely exuberant. *I shouldn't be so excited*, I thought—*this is serious*. But I was in a helicopter with Captain Fantasy, about to fight the forces of villainy at his side . . . it was a childhood dream come true.

The helicopter lifted off, and we zoomed toward the ocean.

"It's nearby," I said, shouting to be heard over the helicopter's machinery. We skimmed close to the water, not moving very quickly. I looked at the placid expanse of blue-green water, seeking something out of the ordinary, some indication of Kelli's presence. "I don't—"

Something boiled up from the ocean, but before I could make it out, we'd flown past. Then the helicopter jerked, throwing me hard against my straps. I squawked and choked, unable to take a breath, and water rushed up at the cockpit's windshield.

We smashed into the ocean. I dangled in my seat, facing the water-occluded windshield, amazed that the impact hadn't hurt me more. The smartcloth in my costume had spread the impact evenly across my body.

Behind us, metal sheared as the rear of the helicopter parted from the front. I smelled smoke.

The Captain unhooked his harness and dropped to the windshield, which had taken the place of the floor. I followed suit. With the back half of the 'copter ripped off, the sky showed clear and blue above us, and the cockpit was transformed into a shallow cup floating on the ocean. The Captain reached under his seat and slung scuba gear toward me. I scrambled into the tank and mouthpiece. I'd just pulled on my flippers when something ripped the cockpit apart.

I saw tentacles the size of firehoses, and then the sea rushed in, bowling me over and dunking me. I forced myself to remain calm despite my heart's thundering and the shock of cold water. My silver suit began heating immediately. Captain Fantasy was treading water several feet away and I swam toward him, kicking hard against the undertow created by the sinking 'copter. I didn't see tentacles, but that didn't reassure me. If some monster inhabited the water with us, I wanted to be close to the Captain.

I looked up, expecting Facility agents to sweep in for the rescue. The sky remained clear. Were they so confident that we could handle this, or had Brady lied about our backup?

The Captain wrapped one gauntleted arm around my waist and held me up easily, my rear pressed against his pelvis. I blushed when I realized what I felt pressing against me through the Captain's wet tights. Evidently, danger excited him.

I forgot about the Captain's arousal when tentacles broke the surface again, a dozen waving in the air as if attempting some strange semaphore. Several of the tentacles were torn, gushing blood, probably ripped off when they grabbed the Fantasy-copter and brought us down.

The tentacles were bad, but then I saw the rest.

A blunt shark's head broke the surface, four feet across, with ten-inch-long teeth marching back row-by-row in its gaping mouth. Crude black stitching crossed its head. One saucer-sized eye stared at us, black, and a cobwebby cataract gummed the other. A small metal lens glinted between its natural eyes.

I wet myself, and if the Captain hadn't held me, I would have swum away as fast as possible. I hadn't signed up to face monsters—at least, not inhuman ones—and my thrill at fighting by the Captain's side didn't include facing something like this.

The Captain tossed me aside with a bellow. I hit the water, sank, and emerged in time to see the Captain leap from the water and drive his arm up to the elbow in the shark's good eye. He crouched on its snout, heedless of its snapping jaws, and pulled out a handful of red and gray matter. The tentacles lashed spastically, and I occupied myself with avoiding them. After a few seconds they stopped moving, and I looked back at the Captain.

His arms were bloody to the shoulders. He waved jauntily at the dead shark-thing's camera-eye, then ripped out the metal and tossed it into the water. He jumped off and sidestroked casually toward me. The shark rolled over and floated, belly to the sky, tentacles trailing beside it like catfish whiskers.

"Looks like one of Dr. Morlock's creatures," the Captain said.

I blinked at him, looked at the shark, and said "Jumping jackals, Captain, you're right." Dr. Morlock had worked with Mengele, but his experiments involved "enhancing" natural predators. One of his creations had killed him in '46 or '47, if I recalled, so he couldn't be responsible for this monster. But if he hadn't made this shark, why the crude stitching, Dr. Morlock's signature?

I looked at the Captain. My bowels clenched. The Captain believed it was 1945. Had the force of his belief acted to alter local *time*? Could he be so powerful? Had he plunged us into a long-past sea battle with Dr. Morlock?

It's impossible, I thought, but knew with Captain Fantasy anything could happen.

The Captain tenderly pulled my face mask down over my eyes. He touched my cheek and smiled. "Come on. I think Mengele and Morlock are below us." Then, without so much as taking a deep breath, he dove beneath the waves.

I've always wanted to see a U-boat, I thought miserably, and followed.

If I hadn't already emptied my bladder, I would have wet myself again.

Not a submarine, as I'd expected. A submerged *city*.

Specifically, the squat metal starfish of the Nazi Unterseeburg, the Reich's main submarine base, the bunker to which Goebbels fled during the German collapse. The Captain swam toward the dimly phosphorescent building and I frogkicked after him, letting the smartsuit do most of the work. Faced with this impossible artifact from the past, my mind reeled. I stared at the dark metal sprawl, thinking "No, no, no."

The Unterseeburg clung to an artificial reef, only a few hundred yards below the surface. The Allies had torpedoed that stronghold, and Goebbels with it, at the end of the war. There should have been ruins, twisted metal beams grown thick with barnacles, but not a complete city. Its presence confirmed my fears. Captain Fantasy's delusion had become reality, and we'd gone back in time.

Would I become Spaceboy, next?

Before I could give in to despair, or simply freeze in light of the situation's enormity, frogmen streamed from an airlock, and I had to fight. I dodged speargun bolts, astonished and terrified by my own agility, seeing it as another indication that I was becoming Spaceboy. The smartcloth alone couldn't account for my new lightning reflexes and dexterity, astonishing even underwater.

The Captain moved more ponderously, but dealt with the divers efficiently, tearing aside their antiquated (to my eyes) gear, slamming their heads together, kicking them in the stomachs. When the last frogman fled toward the surface, I joined the Captain at the divers' airlock. The Captain punched through the reinforced steel and peeled it back, gesturing for me to go through the hole. I slithered in, and the Captain widened the hole and followed.

Once inside, he tugged the ragged edges back into place and rubbed his hand rapidly in circles across the torn metal. After a few seconds a red glow appeared beneath his hand, and the water around the door began to boil. The steel under Captain Fantasy's hand turned molten in the cracks, and the Captain stopped rubbing. He'd created enough friction to melt steel and make the airlock watertight again. He hit the decompression button and the water level in the lock sank.

I felt triumphant, just being with the Captain, forgetting for a moment the temporal situation. It occurred to me an instant later that the exultation I felt might be Spaceboy's, and wondered how the change might happen, a transformation of my personality into that of the Captain's dead sidekick. Would I feel it happen, the last of my self dissolving, finally becoming my role as I'd never managed in the past?

The Captain kicked right through the interior door, tearing a wide opening. I followed him into a well-lit, narrow corridor that curved away after a few yards. Clunky surveillance cameras observed us. The Captain whooped and smashed the cameras, hopping to reach them.

I grinned around my mouthpiece. The Captain had so much *fun* fighting the forces of evil—that joyfulness accounted for most of his popularity.

When he'd killed all the cameras in that deserted length of corridor, the Captain took me in his arms and kissed me full on the lips.

Stunned, I didn't react at all, even to resist. The Captain's stubble dug into my chin, and his huge arms held me tight. He put me down, gently, and said "Let's go get Mengele." Then he ran, boots pounding.

I followed, things coming clear in my mind. That first embrace, the Captain's extremity of grief when the real Spaceboy died, the way he'd raged and destroyed Baron Von Blitz and his artillery on that sad day, the Captain's bachelorhood, maybe even Spaceboy's skintight silver costume, all those things made sense, now. In the '40's, homosexual heroes wouldn't have been tolerated, and even now no one would accept a seventeen-year-old boy lover. I doubted Brady knew about this, or that anyone else did.

I probed myself for signs of arousal. If I felt attracted to the Captain, would that indicate a step in my transformation? I couldn't discern any reaction other than shock.

Somewhat reassured, but much more conscious of my skintight suit, I followed him.

Several corridors later the Captain battered his way through another door, and shouted in triumph from the other side. I hurried after him, and at the far end of a low oblong room, I saw Dr. Morlock and the Storm Troupe waiting for us.

That proved it. We'd gone back in time.

We faced the German Ubermenschen, the high-profile PR warriors, the Reich's answer to the Allies' Captain Fantasy and Fat Man and Corporal Justice. Baron Von Blitz stepped toward us, sneering in his blue uniform, silver lightning bolts on his sleeves, huge black goggles covering half his face. His lieutenants flanked him, Krieger and Alder, massive twins, one a Strongman, the other a Flier. They wore contrasting red and white costumes. The rear guard, Brickhouse, didn't move. He'd once been an American citizen, but had become a Nazi sympathizer and defector. His invulnerable skin gleamed like red metal under the harsh lights. Off to one side, the diminutive Dr. Morlock in his white lab coat rubbed his hands together and giggled.

I stopped a few paces behind the Captain, and for a long moment we faced the Troupe. *This is it*, I thought, a tight ball of fear in my belly. The sort of thing I'd dreamed of as a stupid kid—fighting genuine villains beside a true hero.

The Captain, that unparalleled man of action, broke the pause. He charged them.

I noticed the long slots in the floor then, laid at right-angles, a crazy gridwork that made no sense but alarmed me anyway. I shouted a warning, and in mid-cry metal walls rose from the slots with the sound of smooth hydraulics. I jumped aside to avoid being cut apart, seeing the light gleam from the razor-sharp edge on top of the wall in front of me. I stared at my reflection in the mirrored wall and understood. The slots in the floor, the bizarre gridlines; this was a maze, separating me from the Captain. I tried to remember the layout of the slots, but I'd only seen them for a moment, and couldn't recall anything useful. Would the Captain maintain continuity without my presence, faced only with his reflection, or would he wander lost in the maze? Did he even need me for continuity anymore, since his delusion had become reality?

A great crash and the shriek of stressed metal interrupted Dr. Morlock's continuing titter. I grinned, unable to help myself. The maze hadn't daunted the Captain at all. He simply smashed his way through, not altering his course a bit. I wanted to join him. With my smartsuit (and a hint of Spaceboy's agility) I could clamber over the walls . . . and be sliced in two by the razor-sharp edges. But wasn't there a trick to mazes, taking only right turns, or something? If I could reach the place where the Captain started busting through walls, I could follow his route. The crashing sound of his progress went on.

I hurried down the corridor and turned right into a cul-de-sac. But not an empty one.

Baron Von Blitz leered at me. My heart hammered. He'd killed the original Spaceboy, and now he'd kill me. I had to run, to escape—

—and then he reached out, holding a stunstick, and struck me over the heart. My muscles contracted, and I fell to the floor, blacking out. My last thoughts weren't panicked, or angry, or regretful. Instead, my mind made a cool observation.

They didn't have stunsticks during World War II. They hadn't been invented yet.

I woke up slowly, like a man swimming out of a black pool into the light. I jerked against the cords holding me to a straight-backed chair, startled by the closeness of Dr. Morlock's pale face, his watery eyes staring at me.

Up close I could see through his disguise. Not Dr. Morlock at all. I couldn't remember his real name, but he called himself Brainchild, and he occupied a respectably high position on the Facility's Most Wanted List. In my time. He'd shaved his head and put on horn-rimmed glasses, heightening a natural resemblance to the infamous doctor, but the disguise didn't hold up under scrutiny. Still, close enough.

Close enough for jazz.

I began to understand the whats, though the whys still escaped me.

"He's awake, Kelli," Brainchild said, his breath puffing the smell of butter and cheese into my face. He pinched my cheek, hard. "You look just like Spaceboy. Good job, scout."

I barely heard him, straining against my ropes to look for Kelli. Author of my despair, the pretty stiletto, the birthday-girl playing some bizarre party game of her own devising. Playing with the world, but playing more immediately with me.

Brainchild scuttled away and Kelli stepped into my field of vision. Beautiful, made up like a '40's movie star in a sea-green silk party gown. She looked like Veronica Lake, full blonde hair falling to her shoulders, a just-so beauty mark over the corner of her mouth. She laced her hands together and smiled at me maternally. "David," she said, then wrinkled her nose. "I finally found out your first name. It's too boring! Let's stick with Li. So macho, so . . . monosyllabic. You probably wonder why I brought you here—and in such a complicated fashion."

"You wanted the Captain," I said, trying to sound bored. "You knew about his condition, you knew how to create continuity by surrounding him with familiar people and things. You built this replica of the Unterseeburg, you got your cronies to dress up like famous period Nazis . . . " I inclined my head, as much as possible against the ropes, toward Brainchild. "I figure Thunderhead is the one posing as Von Blitz . . . I'm not sure about the others. And it worked. Where's the Captain now?"

"In a white room, of course. Living in the now." She seemed amused. "Anything you don't understand, oh wise Mr. Li?"

Lots of things, but I asked the question most pertinent to my mission. "Why did you free Mengele?"

"To execute him. We ejected his body—what remained of it—into the water this morning." She lifted one elegant eyebrow at my surprise. "Shocked? He was hopelessly senile, worthless to us anyway. Mengele's execution came as a condition of Brainchild's cooperation. Without him, we couldn't have built this base, or engineered that monstrous shark we used as a prop . . . Brainchild wanted Mengele dead, and I could deliver, so we made an arrangement."

I remembered Brainchild's real name, then. Itzak Goldberg. I didn't know anything about his relatives, or where they'd been during WWII, but I could make certain guesses, and even sympathize, a little.

"I got an hour alone with him," Brainchild said, looking down at his pudgy hands, making fists and then relaxing them. I shivered. Monster or not, war criminal or not, I didn't want to think of senile Mengele in Brainchild's vengeful hands.

"I thought it made a nice bit of misdirection, too," Kelli said. "Let them think I had some plans for Mengele. His relationship to Captain Fantasy, however tangential, served to make the distraction plausible, don't you think?"

I grunted.

Kelli leaned forward, put her hands on my shoulders, and looked into my face. I could read nothing in her green eyes. "There are things Brady didn't tell you, Li. Imagine! Your own superior, lying to you! Did he tell you about the Tourette's? About the neurological disorders?"

I didn't answer. Name, rank, serial number, I thought. That's the way the Captain would play it. I'd said too much already.

"I know he didn't. Captain Fantasy has Karsakov's syndrome, you know that. And he warps reality, you know that, too. You had no reason to think of those facts in combination. It's a well-kept government secret. Prolonged exposure to Captain Fantasy results in neurological damage, Li. It's like a radiation he gives off." She smiled. "Spaceboy, the original, had Tourettes. You know about that condition? A brain disorder. Symptoms include vocal and physical tics. 'Leaping lizards, Captain!'" She mimicked Spaceboy with vicious accuracy. "Touretters often have amazing reflexes, too. They're attracted to shiny things, and things that move quickly. Some of them make a game of darting in and out of revolving doors, they're that fast. Ah, the light dawns. Been feeling frisky and fidgety, have you, Li? Yes, you've got Tourettes, too, though not as severely as Spaceboy did."

I blew air hard through my teeth. It all made sense, and it made me furious. Brady had known, he'd exposed me to brain damage, and he hadn't told me. For the greater good, right. That's the Facility's excuse for everything, and the worst thing is, it so often holds up.

"It could be worse. You could have developed aphasia, or lost your kinesthetic sense, or even gotten Karsakov's yourself. Do you see, Li, how your masters would have wasted you?" She took her hands off my shoulders, touched my face. "Join me. Let's wreck the governments, teach them all a hard lesson. They deserve it, and I wouldn't waste you."

I smiled a little. "Fuck the world, right, Kelli?"

She smiled back, indulgent, pleased. "Yes, Li. Fuck the world."

"I can't do it."

Her smile disappeared. "You remain loyal to the Facility, after all this? Then you're a fool."

I shook my head as much as the bindings would allow. "I don't care about the Facility, you're right, they're bastards. But you want to use Captain Fantasy, somehow, and I can't go along with that. Because he's a real hero, even if he is sick, even if he makes other people sick. He'd die to save the world, Kelli . . . I won't help you use him to hurt it."

"Then we'll have to use you," she said, sounding regretful. "Because you're right. He would die to save the world . . . but he'd kill to save Spaceboy. I'd hoped you would cooperate, but we can do what's necessary anyway. Dear Li. My worthy opponent." She kissed her fingers and touched my cheek, then walked away, swaying beautifully in her gown, sinuous as a cobra.

Brainchild drugged me, and after a while I woke in the central hub of the Unterseeburg, suspended twenty feet above the floor. The transparent dome overhead revealed the vast dark water, and creatures moving in it, Brainchild's creations. I looked upward groggily for a long time before noting my surroundings. I moved my arms and legs experimentally, found myself unbound. They'd put me inside a transparent glass box, coffin-sized but upright, hanging from the ceiling. I lowered my head, taking in the narrow platform under my feet and the people below.

I saw Captain Fantasy first. He looked up at me, veins standing out in his neck, huge fists clenched. The impostors stood a respectful distance away, Morlock and Blitz, with Kelli clinging to the Baron's arm like an airhead showpiece.

My head began to clear. I heard a click, and then the crackle of a hissing speaker. How nice of them to let me listen to the conversation. The Baron spoke, loud, haughty, with a terrible German accent. "Do you agree to our terms, Captain? Will you do as we say, strike where we tell you? If you do not . . . " I could imagine his sneer, the only bit of mimicry Thunderhead did well. "Your little sidekick dies." He gestured imperiously, and Brainchild pulled a lever, giggling like Dr. Morlock.

I heard the sound and understood before I looked down.

Plates in the floor slid aside, revealing a dark pit full of spinning silver blades. I couldn't see the area directly below my feet, but I imagined more of the same, enough circular saws to make me into luncheon meat. *Such drama*, I thought, knees weak, suddenly very aware of the flimsy metal platform under my feet. I twisted enough to look down and see the hinges, built to let the platform swing open and drop me. Probably another lever to control that. One pull by Dr. Morlock and down I'd go.

Great job. Full-time hostage.

"Don't hurt him," Captain Fantasy said. He raised his voice. "Spaceboy! I'll get you out of this! Don't worry!"

But he wouldn't get me out of this, and I knew it, and he knew it too—I saw the anguish in his broad face, so open, so easy to read. He couldn't fly up here to save me; he'd never believed he could fly. They had him cold, and he'd do anything they said to save me. To save Spaceboy, the one he loved, the one he hadn't been able to save before, even if he didn't remember that failure.

"Do you accept, Captain Fantasy?" Blitz insisted.

"Yes," he said, his voice small. "Don't hurt him."

"No, Captain!" I shouted. "Don't do it! Tear them apart, forget about me!"

No one below reacted. They let me listen, but not transmit, for obvious reasons. And they could play this game again and again, I realized—just stick the Captain in a white room for a while until he forgot everything, then stage the scene again. He wouldn't get fed up, he wouldn't realize they'd never free Spaceboy. They probably wouldn't bother with me after a while, just dress someone else like Spaceboy. Wrap somebody in tin foil and the Captain would believe it was Spaceboy from this distance. This had been Kelli's plan all along, to get the Captain, the most powerful being in the world, to work for her.

I couldn't allow that. Spaceboy had died once, at Baron Von Blitz's hands, and when he died Captain Fantasy went berserk, destroyed the artillery, killed the Baron, broke the entire German tank line . . . and changed the course of the war. That death, the death of his boy lover, drove the Captain to perform feats of heroism unparalleled.

I didn't think about it for too long. I knew I'd talk myself out of it. I refused to dwell on the small possibility of my own survival, either—I'd live, or I wouldn't. The result would be worthwhile either way.

All that talk at the Facility about the greater good must have gotten to me.

The glass box was strong, the platform below me well braced, but Kelli hadn't known about my smartsuit, about the built-in musculature. To help me do somersaults and shit, Brady had said, but it could do more. I braced my hands on the glass walls, lifted my legs, and kicked straight down. The Captain and the bad guys looked up at the thud, but I didn't stop. I kicked again, felt the metal shiver. One more would do it. I looked the Captain in the eye, and I blew him a kiss.

I kicked the platform as hard as I could, the smartsuit driving my legs like pistons. I screamed when my left femur snapped, and thought of poor stupid Carl Spandau, arms broken for love.

The hinges snapped, and the trapdoor fell open. I held myself up with the pressure of my arms against the walls for a moment and looked down at the whirring blades. They didn't fill the whole pit—there were gaps—but they filled enough of it.

I let go and fell, twisting mightily in the air, pushing my Touretter's speed and the smartsuit's agility to the limit.

The last thing I heard was the Captain, calling his dead lover's name.

When I woke, Brady Doolittle sat beside my hospital bed holding my hand. "Li," he said, hoarse. He looked like he hadn't slept, red-eyed with mussed hair. "You bastard."

I looked at him, then at my hand. Pink, unscarred, soft. New tissue. "I lived," I said, a little surprised.

"It's a miracle," he said. "You lost your arms and legs, right up to the shoulders and the thighs. The blades nicked your head and torso, but you lived."

A miracle. I didn't argue. I'd done what I intended, twisted so the blades wouldn't damage anything vital, just my extremities. The shock rendered me unconscious, but bodies are smart, especially Metamorph bodies. My wounds sealed as soon as my limbs came off. "How long?"

"Four months," Brady said. "We've been pumping you full of food, Li, right into your veins. It was damn creepy, watching your arms and legs grow again. Like watching parts of a baby grow up in time-lapse."

"Ever the apt metaphor," I said, voice raspy from long disuse. "What happened . . . ?" I didn't know what I meant, Kelli or the Storm Troupe or the Captain. Probably all of it.

"The Captain went batshit, Li, he destroyed *everything*." He shook his head. "The Most Wanted List has been considerably revised. Lots of names got crossed off that day. Our boys were nearby, they rushed in when the base went boom and got you and the Captain out."

"Kelli?"

Brady shook his head. "We don't know. The Captain has never killed a woman. He didn't think she mattered, he said. Thought she was a girl-friend, and didn't chase when she ran off. We didn't find Mengele, either."

"Mengele's dead."

"You're sure?"

I nodded, tired of talking, then thought of something else I wanted to say. "The Captain's back in his white room, I guess."

Brady grinned. "No, hoss, he's not. He's still our guest, but he's recovered."

I didn't breathe for a moment. "What?"

"We don't know how, but he's all better, since shortly after we got him back here. He remembers everything, pretty much, and what he didn't know we told him. He wants to meet you." He looked at his watch. "It's time for your pills right now, though."

"What kind of pills?"

He shrugged. "I'm not a doctor, Li."

I nodded, swallowed what he gave me. Some of them were drugs to regulate the Tourette's, I figured. I wondered how long it would take Brady to tell me about that. Whether he'd admit that Captain Fantasy gave me the syndrome, or just say it mysteriously developed. Time would tell. I tried not to expect too much from Brady.

The Captain being okay . . . that was good news. Very good.

A few days later I got to see the Captain. The room where we met differed from the white room in particulars; it had a nice dark carpet, wallpaper, armchairs . . . but essentially it served the same function. A place for a powerful, dangerous, wonderful man to wait.

He wore jeans and a dark blue sweatshirt now, his hair a red crewcut, and he looked at me for a long time. "You don't look a damn thing like Spaceboy," he said at last.

I smiled. "I had a different face, then." I sat gingerly in the chair. My new appendages were tender.

"I tore all the bugs out of this room," the Captain said matter-of-factly. "They haven't had time to put in new surveillance equipment. We need to talk in the meantime."

I nodded slowly. "Okay."

"I apologize for kissing you. Understand, I mistook your identity. Looking at you now, I have to say, you aren't even my type." He smiled, a ghost of his go-to-hell grin.

"Understood, sir." My face wanted to blush, but I wouldn't let it.

"I loved Spaceboy in a special way. Most people don't know that. Nobody but you and me, now. I'd like to keep it that way."

"Your secret's safe, Captain."

"There's something else most people don't know." He sighed, looked contemplatively at the wallpaper. Seeing him like this, so weary and passive, struck me as wrong. He should have been out busting heads for God and country, not sitting tired in a small room. "I have a lot of control over my own mind, my own *brain*. I don't get hurt, I don't get old, I can see farther than most, hear better . . . mostly I don't think about how I do it, I just do. But I *can* think about it, and control things." He looked me in the eye. "When you met me, I didn't know what year it was, and I didn't know Spaceboy had died. I liked it that way, Mr. Li. I had a hard time after the war, as you may know. One day, in the '70's, I decided I didn't like my life anymore. Suicide always seemed like a coward's way to me, and I didn't know if I could die anyway. The prospect of living forever, without *him* . . . It didn't appeal. So I thought about my brain for a while, read about some things, amnesia, Karsakov's syndrome . . . " He crossed his legs, clasped his hands over his knee. "See where I'm going with this?"

"You gave yourself Karsakov's syndrome," I said, both surprised and not surprised. It made sense.

"The best days of my life ended when Spaceboy died, Li. I wanted them back." He shrugged. "After seeing *you* get cut up, that trauma repeated, something shook loose in my head, and I remembered it all. I thought I'd try to make a go of my life again . . . " He shook his head. "It's no good. I just feel too heavy. But I wanted to talk to you. To tell you, to ask you to keep my secrets. I want to go back, Mr. Li. They'll say I had a relapse. Nobody but you will know different." He held out his hand.

I took it. He shook my hand gently. "Sir," I said. "Sir, I never told you, I grew up reading about you, and—"

His face brightened. "Are you a doctor?" he said. "Say, that must have been some knock on the head I took!"

I disengaged my hand from his, carefully, and stood. I turned my back to leave, then stopped. I faced him. He'd only remember for a few moments, but that would be enough.

"Sir," I said. "You're my hero."

He smiled slowly, his whole face lighting, like the sun filling the sky. "Thank you, son. Thank you."

I shut the door behind me.

ENTROPY'S PAINTBRUSH

Lucifer walked slowly across the moon's dusty surface, looking at the sharp stars pinpricking the sky. He seldom approached anyone as petitioner, and felt nervous doing so now. Pausing before the thin dome, he considered turning back. But he'd come this far, hadn't he? He shouldn't let pride stop him from going on.

He passed through the dome's transparent walls without setting off the perimeter defenses. The single building looked gray and squat as a sleeping toad. Laying a hand on the steel door, Lucifer focused a fraction of his energies.

The metal pinged with heat as the security system burned up, and the door swung open. Lucifer adjusted his heavy black robes and stepped inside.

The building housed a single dim room. Large objects draped in gray cloth stood here and there in the shadows. A man sat at a long table, his workspace illuminated by a bright lamp. He seemed oblivious to Lucifer's entry.

"Are you the artist, Bogatryev?" Lucifer asked, knowing perfectly well he was.

Bogatryev swiveled his chair and looked at the angel, one bushy eyebrow raised. He grunted, then turned back to his table, where he patiently braided lengths of colored wire. "Yes. Who are you?"

"I've come to have my portrait done," Lucifer said.

Bogatryev looked at him again. "Oh. Why did you come to me?"

"You are the greatest artist in history."

"Michelangelo Buonarotti is the greatest artist in history. He lived on Earth, a long time ago. Paroxys Mien, the Morelian, is a close second."

Lucifer waved an impatient hand. "Certainly you're the greatest living artist."

Bogatryev shrugged. "Doesn't matter. I don't take commissions anymore."

"Name your price." He's so old and stringy, Lucifer thought. Temporal human decay always made him feel ill.

Bogatryev laughed. "I don't need anything. I bought this moon for a studio because I wanted to be left alone."

"Surely you still seek models," Lucifer said. "Especially those that might challenge you."

"You think you'll constitute a challenge? All right. Take off your robe and let's see."

Lucifer let the robe fall away. His wings opened, and his luminescence filled the room with harsh brightness. Bogatryev squinted, then picked up a piece of cobalt glass from his worktable. He put it over his left eye, then grunted again, more appreciatively this time. "Come back in a week, I'll have something to show you." He returned to his task.

Lucifer's wings drooped. He considered burning Bogatryev to a cinder for daring such a dismissal, but his fury passed. The artist had agreed to do the portrait, and nothing else mattered. Long ago God had forbidden Lucifer the sight of his own reflection, as punishment for his original vanity. If Bogatryev created an accurate portrait, Lucifer could look upon himself again. He left his robe on the floor and stepped out of the studio, then sideways through space to Dis, his palace.

"It's just a glare," Lucifer said. "Just a pillar of fire!"

Bogatryev nodded, arms crossed over his thin chest. "Put these on." He handed Lucifer a pair of glasses, smoked almost to opacity. Lucifer put them on, scowling.

He looked, and after a moment sighed, the sound of a dying man's last breath, bringing release from pain. A perfect angelic shape rotated inside the cylinder of light, visible now that the dark glasses had cut the glare. Fairer than all the angels in heaven . . . "Is it an accurate representation?" Lucifer asked.

"It's not a bad likeness," Bogatryev said. "You can take it with you."

"How can I repay you?" Lucifer said, unwilling to take his eyes from the slowly turning angel.

Bogatryev didn't answer for a moment. Then, thoughtfully, he said "Tell your friends. I appreciated this challenge. I'm willing to take commissions from special clientele."

When the demon-king Puzuzzu came, Bogatryev fashioned a machine of bear-traps, pincers, and saws. "It captures your essence," the artist explained, and Puzuzzu gibbered happily from his thousand mouths.

Not to be outdone by his fellow archfiend, Beelzebub came in his most fearsome shape. Bogatryev spent the best part of a year cloning genetic specimens, hybridizing, and rebuilding skeletal structures with nanomachines. In the end he presented Beelzebub with a creature part rhino, part kraken, part mantis, and part allosaur. It shambled on nine legs and slobbered over Bogatryev with affection.

Beelzebub, repulsed by the mindless creature that so perfectly matched his favorite form, declined to take possession. Bogatryev killed the animal with a painless injection, then stuffed and mounted it. He put it outside the dome to scare away trespassers.

Word of Bogatryev's infernal portraits spread across the pantheons. Alien gods came to him haughtily and left proclaiming his genius. Stroud, the carrion god worshipped by the scavenger peoples of Eblis, left with a twice-life-size sculpture of himself made of rotting, worm-riddled meat. Bogatryev released holographic projections of his work to the public, and critics hailed them as his most brilliant work yet. He did not tell anyone the pieces had been commissioned, and ignored all offers from wealthy collectors to buy his originals.

Then, abruptly, Bogatryev withdrew, turning away all divine and infernal commissions. Lucifer, who had become something of a friend, visited him. Seeing Bogatryev slumped at his work table, Lucifer once again marveled at human frailty. Bogatryev wheezed, a pallid caricature of himself. "I'm dying," he said, stick-thin elbows planted on the table.

"Would you rather stay alive?" Lucifer had to ask. Humans had odd notions about dying, sometimes.

Bogatryev laughed, but it turned into a coughing spasm. "Very much, but I didn't think that was your area. I thought you worked in the receiving department."

Lucifer put a glowing finger to his lips. "I can't do anything for you personally, but I know the right people."

Leaning on his bench, Bogatryev nodded. "I'd appreciate anything you can do."

"Man," the voice said. Bogatryev shivered from more than his fever. The voice summoned images of dust and airless spaces, of the pause between breaths. It had nothing to do with birth or regeneration, only cessation. The voice of final entropy, Bogatryev thought.

The artist lifted his head from the bench, but saw nothing except a shimmer in the air beside him, like hot air rising from a vent. "I hear," he said, his voice a creaking whisper, his lungs clenched in his chest.

"You will make my portrait," the voice said, "and you will live."

"I have to see you. Unless you want to be a skull in a black robe, or a dancing skeleton."

"No. This time metaphors will not do. It must be an accurate portrait. Look on me, man, and create."

Bogatryev's eyes, trained to find form, color, and simple shape in everything, rebelled when the air opened and Azrael (the Finality, the Undoing, the Last Cause) stepped through.

Darkness blotted over him, and Bogatryev saw nothing.

"Man," Azrael said. "I am pleased."

Bogatryev felt exhausted in every joint and muscle, but his lungs worked painlessly, and his fever was gone. He looked around blankly. The voice came from the shimmer in the air.

Momentarily forgetting the gift of health, he frowned. "I don't remember seeing you, much less doing a portrait. How can I learn from my work if I can't remember it?"

The air rippled. "Whether you remember or not, it is a good likeness. You saw the truth of my nature, and your art described it. You may live for a while yet."

"But what medium did I use? Paint? Light? Metal? Flesh? Something else?"

Azrael was gone (though not far, the artist thought; he is never far). Bogatryev inventoried his studio's supplies and found nothing missing. He checked his chronometer. He'd only been unconscious a few hours, hardly time to do a work of any complexity. His portrait of Azrael remained a mystery, even to its creator.

Lucifer visited him a few days later. "You seem better, my friend."

"Yes," Bogatryev said, carefully slotting fossilized shark's teeth into a carved wooden head. "Please tell everyone I'm willing to take commissions again."

She came to him three years and a hundred works later. She came mocking and teasing and sure Bogatryev could not do her portrait. When she told the artist her name, he only nodded. He'd known it already. "I thought you must have died, when people stopped worshipping."

"Everyone worships beauty, by whatever name. I am Beauty. You cannot make my portrait, artist. Your fame has spread far and wide, but I have come to demonstrate your limitations."

"Give me time and your presence, and I will do you justice," Bogatryev said.

Aphrodite frowned and worlds trembled. "My husband Hephaestus would be jealous if I brought you to Olympus." She smiled (though she had no face, properly; she existed beyond shape, approaching essence). "I'll take you with me right away. He has grown too complacent lately. But your portrait will fail, artist, and you'll go mad trying to capture me."

"I accept your challenge," Bogatryev said.

Before beginning his work on Beauty, Bogatryev created a portrait of surly, club-footed Hephaestus. Bogatryev didn't want the jealous god's hammer to crush his head and ruin this opportunity.

Bogatryev made an animate statue from precious metals, designed to sweat mercury, piss molten lead, and sing bawdy songs at the forge. Hephaestus loved it. He grew quite fond of Bogatryev, and welcomed the artist to his house, often showing him bits of ornamental ironwork, which Bogatryev praised.

Aphrodite never formally sat for him. It wouldn't have helped. She had no single shape, no form Bogatryev could sketch and elaborate on. He simply watched her when she drifted near, and thought, and after a hundred years began working.

Finally, many centuries later, he completed Aphrodite's portrait. He considered it the final fruit of his talent. The portrait contained every great work of art (personally and perfectly reproduced by Bogatryev), images of every natural splendor (from the high peaks of Sevon to the last remaining grotto on Morel), every shape of woman, man, and alien that pleased any eye, and many other beauties besides. The images, carefully phased out of normal time and space, flickered at the rate of a thousand per second, and still it took a dozen years to complete the cycle a single time.

Bogatryev presented his portrait to Aphrodite.

"It's my masterpiece," he said, standing against the wall in his Olympian studio. Aphrodite watched the portrait for a long time (long enough for Bogatryev to sleep and wake and sleep again many times).

"It is perfect," she said at last, her voice strange and flat. "You are the greatest artist of all time, and you have captured my image. But now you must destroy it, and leave Olympus, for I cannot bear to have my perfection reproduced, and I grow angry."

Bogatryev gladly complied. He had made the portrait of perfect Beauty, and it didn't matter if the work remained. He never needed to create anything else. His time as an artist had passed.

He returned to his moon, which Lucifer had maintained over the past several centuries, and slept for three days.

When Wotan, god-father of Valhalla, petitioned him for a portrait, Bogatryev graciously declined, explaining that he had retired.

When the Valkyries appeared, armored and bearing spears, Bogatryev was irritated but not surprised. He went with them quietly to Wotan's hall in Valhalla.

"Well?" Wotan demanded, his single eye blazing, leaning forward in his ivory throne. "Will you make my portrait, or not?" The two ravens on his shoulder flapped their wings in sympathetic agitation.

Bogatryev could do it easily enough. The sculpture should idealize Wotan's broad shoulders and chest, and Bogatryev could weave tiny war hammers and battle axes into the statue's white beard. A pair of live ravens would be a nice touch.

He contemplated the work, and found it tedious.

"I am retired, all-father," Bogatryev said respectfully. "I appreciate your interest, but I no longer make portraits." Lucifer lounged conspicuously at one of the feasting tables, and he nodded to show his support.

Wotan quivered, furious. The Valkyries and Wotan's huge-muscled sons bristled on the edge of violence. Let them kill me, Bogatryev thought placidly. I have done my greatest work, and I'm not afraid to die.

"You will do as I say, or you will be bound under the rock with Loki. You will bathe in venom and writhe on coals." Wotan's face gleamed red with sweaty impatience.

"That is not so," a voice said from the back of the hall. Everyone recognized the voice, even those who'd never heard it before.

"Azrael," Lucifer said, and shivered.

"How dare you come into my hall uninvited?" Wotan demanded.

"I go where I will, and I am seldom invited. This man is not yours to dispose of."

"I only wanted a portrait," Wotan muttered, settling down on his throne, gripping one of the skulls on his armrest. "Everyone else had one. Why not me?"

"Your vanity is unimportant now. All your vanities. Things have passed beyond that."

"Do you mean—" Lucifer began, but didn't go on.

Wotan licked his lips. "Is it the end, then? Ragnarok?"

"Basically," Azrael said, and Wotan jolted in his chair. Bogatryev stood close enough to see his single pupil dilate, and the white of his eye cloud with blood. Wotan slumped. The ravens flapped their wings and pecked at his eye.

The warrior-gods shouted in alarm, but only Thor had the bravery (or foolishness) to rush Azrael, his hammer raised. The shimmer in the air darkened with a streak of blackness as Thor fell face-forward onto the floor.

"Make your peace," Azrael said, and the gods fell. Lucifer slouched with a strangled gasp, radiant to the last.

Bogatryev closed his eyes and swallowed, waiting for death, hoping it would come without pain. He hadn't feared dying in the abstract, but now his legs shook and his bladder felt full of needles.

"You will live, man," Azrael said. "There is a final work for you to do."

"I'm retired," Bogatryev said, opening one eye. Cracks appeared in the high gray walls. "Is this happening everywhere?"

"Everywhere," Azrael agreed. "Things have come to a close."

Bogatryev touched his chest, his arms, his own face. "But why me? Why am I still here?"

"Come with me," Azrael said, and Bogatryev found himself in darkness. He could no longer feel his body, only the nothing pressing in from all sides. He had come to terminal time, entropy's last result. He felt Azrael's cold presence, a frigid eddy in the neutrality, but sensed nothing else.

"This is your work, man. Your portrait of me. You made it well."

The nullity made Bogatryev want to scream, but he had no breath, and there was no air to hold sound. Even Azrael's voice somehow conveyed sense without breaking the silence. "You understood that I am just a blankness, and you created a picture of this place that is not a place, this place beyond everything. This was your true masterpiece, not your portrait of brief beauty. Yet there is another work for you to do, and it may be a masterpiece as well."

"I can't do a portrait," Bogatryev said without voice. "There are no models here."

"No. This work must come from inside you, man. I am the end of it all, and I have brought this inevitable nothing, but nothing is only half the universe. It is only one end of the continuum. A painting begins as a blank canvas, does it not, Bogatryev? A space to be filled."

"Then, this last work—"

"Is really only the first. I trust you will do it justice." Then he was gone.

Bogatryev stretched his nothing limbs in the emptiness. He considered. Then, with a pallet of stars and blackness, he began to paint the nothing into light.

MY NIGHT WITH APHRODITE

I met Aphrodite in a bar and picked
her up (I asked her sign and she showed
me her constellation—you know what
starry nights do to women). We went
back to my place and had a few drinks
and went to bed. She was perfect, tongue
like honey, body like love, and she said
all the right things. I was done in no time
(she is a goddess) but I helped finish her off.

In the morning she was still perfect. My breath
tasted sour and she flinched away when I went
to peck her cheek. I pissed and shaved and she
watched like somebody seeing a snake eat
a rat for the first time. I sucked in my
stomach, brushed my hair, took a shower.

She followed me to the kitchen and didn't
want breakfast. She gagged at the smell
of frying sausage. She was still naked.
Her breasts defied gravity. I was hungover
and felt like dogshit on a bootheel. I noticed
that her feet didn't touch the floor. She

suggested that I could be a better housekeeper,
wrinkling her pretty nose at the dishes in my sink.

I walked her to the door. She didn't want
a ride. My car, she said, smelled like cigarettes
and fast food. She would fly. "You can
call me if you want," she said doubtfully.
"Just light a white candle, scented with
rose and jasmine, and invoke my name five—"

"Sure," I said, and closed the door.

UNFAIRY TALE

Molter Keen gamboled in the field: small, purple-ragged and clouded with flies. His nose wiggled, scenting the dry flowers and the bodies rotting in air. He hopped onto a sandy boulder beside the corpse wall and crossed his legs. The wall rose twenty times his own height, a terraced cliff-face. Molter craned his head and counted broad stone shelves. Ten, fifteen, twenty-five. Every shelf held a naked body and a contingent of fat crows.

And on the top shelf: The beauty, sleeping.

Wasps built a nest at the base of Molter's skull. The back of his neck burned red from repeated stings. He opened his mouth and flies buzzed out, zipping in close formation to feast on the bodies. They flew to the wall's top and circled the beauty's perfect unrotting head. Round and round they went, unable to strip her bones, and returned to the plague victims, the broken-backed old, and the infant with the too-big head.

Molter picked a wing from between his teeth and spat. Clouds streaked the sky black and dark blue, the wall was stacked with the dead (and the beauty), and the fleas in his hair slept. A blessed day in the no-longer-desert. Who cared if the air was too wet? Who cared if flowers grew where only stones had flourished? Not Molter, not today.

Mosquitoes boiled forth from his navel and flew across the sandy field. They returned quickly, full of blood, and bit him in the crook of the elbow.

Other blood mixed with his, and he grinned. Corrigan's blood. Molter did not love the new wet not-desert, but he accepted it in exchange for the gifts of the green folk from beyond the misty veil. He'd once been a

169

wandering djinn, companion to scorpions, capable only of making a temporary body from blowing sand. After a meeting with the king of the green folk he came away with buzzing insects and a beautiful body of imitation man-skin. In exchange, he only had to defend the beauty, and accept the greening of the desert.

Corrigan approached, his white scarves fluttering, his yellow hair streaming. His eyes were the pure blue of the desert sky before the clouds came. "Hail, djinn," he called. "Do you have any word of the mortal?"

Molter spat. Spit! Water from mouth to earth! "He doesn't come. He will not reach the desert, I think."

Corrigan shook his head. "He wants the beauty. He pursued us over an earthly continent, and then across the misty veil to the island of my people. A journey to the desert will not stop him, though we hope *you* will."

"He will not pass me," Molter said. A long millipede slipped out of his mouth and started to crawl down his chin. He slurped it back in.

Corrigan covered his face with a scented handkerchief and glanced at the corpse wall. "Perhaps you should bury those bodies," he said. "Haven't you noticed them swelling and starting to stink?"

Molter had noticed. The local tribes always put their dead on walls for the vultures and elements to reclaim. The corpses normally dried to stringy husks and dust, but since the green folk had brought flowers and grasses and rain, the bodies puffed and rotted. "There can be no burying. The sands shift, and uncover the graves."

Corrigan sighed and sniffed his handkerchief. "In a few more months, we'll have good digging soil here, and the humans can dispose of their dead properly."

Molter wanted to protest, to say "The sands sing at night, and whisper with shifting." But he owed Corrigan's king service, and so kept silent. "The mortal has not come. No sign of sword or lips or pure heart. May I return tonight to the caravan trails, to whisper madness and make bargains with humans?"

"We gave you a body," Corrigan said, turning his back to the wall. He looked over the spreading blot of flowers and grass. "You may not leave until your service is completed. I thought your kind were used to strict conditions, being sealed in clay pots and bound in caves for a thousand years, things like that."

Molter didn't answer. He wished to say "I am Il-a-mo-ta-qu'in, and no man has ever bound me," but he no longer owned that name. The green folk called him Molter Keen, and they owned his service. He laced his fingers together and smiled as mites crawled from beneath his fingernails. A good trade, he thought. This flesh will outlast my service.

"I've been thinking," Corrigan said. "Before the mortal comes to wake the beauty, you should prepare obstacles. Perhaps construct a castle, and put her in a tower? You could surround the tower with thorns, or thick trees that grow more quickly than he can cut them down. Or a stream full of snapping, biting fish."

"A stream?" Molter said. He knelt and took a handful of sand. Despite the flowers and the rain, the earth still sifted brown through his fingers. "There is a pool to the south, but the sand will not hold much water or . . . trees?"

Corrigan kicked at the sand, uprooting several small flowers. "Damned desert. In other countries, we could arrange proper obstacles."

"Why didn't you? Why bring beauty here, then?"

Corrigan looked at him, then at the cloudy sky. "We tried the obstacles. The mortal overcame them, and nearly reached the beauty. So we brought her here, crossing distance quickly through the land beyond the veil, in hopes he would not follow. But he has. He is implacable."

"I'll tear him arm from chest, head from neck, when he comes," Molter said.

"What?" Corrigan said. "Is that how you do things here? Such an attack is out of the question. Have you no grace, no honor? If he can reach the beauty and kiss her, he will break the sleeping curse and have her love. We may impede his path, but we cannot harm him directly."

Molter pondered. A beetle crawled from under his tongue and he bit down on it, chewing. The carapace cracked between his molars. Corrigan looked pointedly away and muttered something under his breath.

"I will stop him," Molter said at last. "If not head from neck, another way." He hopped from the boulder and scampered away from the small patch flowers, into the desert proper. The huge crows had driven away the local vultures with their numbers, but many still flourished over the sands. Molter had spies among the bald, reeking birds, and he wished to consult them.

I hope the mortal approaches, he thought. So that I can return to the desert, and the wet green folk will take their flowers away.

Days later, Molter sat again before the wall with Corrigan. The sweet stink of bursting bodies wafted from the shelves. Molter's bright rags hung dirty and disheveled, and grubs fell from holes in his imitation skin. "Obstacles *all* failed," Molter said. A big scorpion trundled slowly from a rip in his stomach, waved its claws, then scurried back inside. "The dunes moved and filled the spike-pit. Boulders poised to fall, instead sank into sand. He jumped over the poison stream, one hop." Molter had damaged his new body often while setting the obstacles.

"I was against this from the start," Corrigan said. "If we couldn't stop the mortal from his quest, of course you desert kind couldn't."

"I could have gutted the mortal," Molter said. He crushed a rock in his hand savagely, tearing his fingers. Stupid flesh, he thought. He looked up. Stupid clouds. "Could have filled his throat with sand. Torn out his eyes. Not stupid *obstacles*."

"He's coming," Corrigan said. "He's almost here. He's passed the trials, and nothing remains but the kiss, the revival, and the triumphant return." He smirked. "Enjoy your body while you can, djinn. My king will surely take it away once beauty wakes. Your petty obstacles failed."

Obstacles, Molter thought contemptuously. Corrigan didn't understand that djinns worked differently than his own kind. Molter scurried up the rock shelf, shedding insects as he went, until he crouched on the highest point, beside the beauty.

Corrigan compared her skin to snow, her lips to roses, but Molter did not know these things. He saw her skin was white as bleached bone, her lips red as the sunset seen through dust. Her hair was yellow as snake's bile, and soft as camel's hair. Corrigan rose slowly, levitating smoothly, until he hovered with his head above the level of the shelf.

Molter thought of the approaching mortal and smiled. A cockroach fell out of his mouth, onto the beauty's unmoving face, and scurried away. "She cannot be hurt, yes?" Molter said.

"She is beyond the touch of time and death," Corrigan agreed. "Until the pure-hearted mortal kisses her."

Molter bent his head and pressed his mouth to the beauty's. He thrust his tongue between her red lips, parting them.

"That's disgusting!" Corrigan said. "Stop it. *You* can't wake her, djinn. You've no heart, pure or otherwise."

After a long moment, Molter raised his head. He smiled, then jumped off the shelf, straight at Corrigan.

Corrigan floated backward. Molter landed in a crouch on the sand, jarring lose a small rain of insects.

"Fool," Corrigan said. "This is no time for games." He settled onto the boulder.

Molter didn't answer him. He sat on the rock and watched the fat fluffy clouds float by.

"There," Corrigan said. The mortal crested a dune and approached them. He wore a white cloth over his head, like the tribesmen in the area. A waterskin hung across his chest. He stepped on the flowers.

"Are they all so big and pale in his country?" Molter asked.

Corrigan shrugged. "Some."

The mortal reached them. He hesitated, hand on the hilt of his sword. "Do you challenge me, fair folk?" he asked.

"You pursued us to this desolate place," Corrigan said. "You overcame our obstacles. We will not prevent you from touching beauty. We are bested."

Molter watched as ants ran across the backs of his ravaged hands.

The mortal came to the wall, keeping his eyes fixed on Molter and Corrigan. He climbed the shelves, stepping on bodies as he went.

He tread on a bloated woman's body and nearly slipped. The mortal recovered his grip, but the body rolled from the shelf and fell a dozen feet to the ground. Molter started toward the body, angered by the casual sacrilege. He didn't especially care if humans died, but their bodies belonged to the creatures of the air, not the earth. He stopped himself before he reached the body and gave Corrigan an open-mouthed grin. Biting flies emerged from his mouth and flew into his nostrils.

"Let's watch the kiss," Molter said. He climbed a mound of boulders for a clear vantage.

"I don't see why," Corrigan said, but he floated to the top of the boulders anyway.

The mortal wasted no time touching the beauty's face or making pretty words for deaf ears. He knelt and bent to kiss her.

Several scorpions emerged from the beauty's mouth before the mortal's lips touched her. Corrigan gasped. The scorpions ran across the mortal's face and plunged their stingers into his lips, cheeks, and eyes. The mortal shrieked and lurched back. He clawed at his face, and rolled from the shelf, falling heavily to the ground.

Molter put a finger in his mouth. A scorpion crawled out and sat in his palm. Molter kissed its stinger, then set it on the rock.

"You did that," Corrigan said, awestruck. "Not an obstacle at all, but a trap."

"I favor traps," Molter said.

Corrigan made as if to touch him, then drew his hand back and wiped it on his chest. "Well done, djinn. The king will be most pleased. He may allow you to caper at his feet when he comes to take his holidays here—"

"No," Molter said. "Take the beauty, flowers, wet, clouds, take it all away. The desert is done with you." He watched the mortal thrash at the base of the wall.

"You don't understand," Corrigan said. "I'm offering you a place in the king's court."

Molter stripped a layer of skin away from his arm and let it flutter to the ground. A puff of sand rose from the hole in his flesh. "I am Il-a-mo-ta-qu'in. I refuse your flesh and obstacles. Go. Tell your king."

Corrigan tightened his lips. He floated to the corpse wall and took the beauty in his arms, then returned to the ground. He walked across the flowers and over the dunes.

Molter tore away great flaps of his skin. The wind rose at his wish, and scorpions scurried from his body, devouring the smaller insects. Sand covered the flowers, and the clouds moved swiftly toward the horizon. The crows took flight, following Corrigan to his green land beyond the veil.

Molter left his imitation skin lying on the ground. Returned to his pure form, he built a brief body from dust and stone. He kicked sand over the convulsing, dying mortal. He knelt by the bloated woman-corpse that the mortal had displaced. Reverently, with hands of golden sand, Molter returned her to her place on the wall.

DOWN WITH THE LIZARDS
AND THE BEES

I dreamed monitor lizards were eating my face; it was one of *those* dreams, so I got up off my futon, dressed by the gray dawn light from the high windows, and went out. I wore fingerless gloves, so no one could cross my palm with silver when I wasn't paying attention—I'd been bound once too often *that* way. The trains were crowded, but people moved away from me, though I don't look particularly derelict or mad; they could sense my difference from them, that's all. I changed trains at three different stations, though I could've gotten to my destination in one. I wanted good omens, even manufactured ones, some charms spinning a little in my direction.

I walked ten blocks from the station into a weedy, broken-down part of Oakland. Even the houses looked dispirited. I'd been here dozens and dozens of times. I never saw anything new anymore.

I climbed over the ruined rubble of foundation blocks coughed up by the ground in some long-forgotten earthquake, and walked the ragged path I'd worn through the broken glass and wildflowers over the years. I crouched down by the sewer grate where H. lived. I ran my finger along the iron bars, furred with rust; my fingertip came away powdered red. A square sewer grate, 18 inches to a side, darkness and sometimes a stink beneath. A gate to the only underworld I'd ever really believed in.

"Hey, H." I said.

His voice came up from beneath the grate, cool and low. "B. You motherfucker. It's been seasons."

"Five months," I said, looking at the ruined wall across the lot, jagged bricks like the silhouette of a stegosaurus made of Legos. "Good months. No dreams."

"Until last night." H.'s voice was like candy wrappers blowing along the ground in a parking lot. "Now you need me. Now you come see me."

"We agreed," I said, trying to hold myself aloof, trying to remember I was basically talking to a hole in the ground, a loquacious absence, nothing more. "It's better if I stay away."

"Shit. I changed my mind about that."

"The dream," I began.

"Right down to business, huh?" H. said. "Gimme gimme." His voice was greedy, deeply desperate. I'd known that side of his personality when he was alive, but it was stronger now that he was mostly gone, nothing left but an intelligent echo, a talking aftertaste, a splash of memory and blood.

"I brought you some weed," I said, reaching for the bag in my pocket.

"Fuck that. I want rock."

I sighed. "Weed was good enough last time."

"That was a long time ago. It's a new season now. Gimme rock."

He was punishing me. Well, why not? And maybe he really did want rock. It couldn't hurt him now, but I still hated doing it. I'd given him enough drugs when he was alive. "I'll be back."

You'd think crack houses would change locations, float around to avoid trouble, but I knew one that had been in the same place for years. I knocked on the door, and the man I wanted was home, and awake, having not gone to bed at all the night before. He stood in the doorway of the bedroom, smiling at me. "White boy. Superstar. Been a long time."

We exchanged the ritual pleasantries, and I handed over some money, and returned to H.'s lot with a vial of crack. I dropped the lumps of crystal cocaine through the grate. They splashed.

"Okay," H. said. "Tell me your dream."

I settled back comfortably on my heels. "I was on the back of a truck, a flat-bed semi, sitting on some splintery timbers, facing backwards, looking at the road behind. The truck went into a tunnel, total blackness, for a while, then it came out, and we were on a dirt road. The truck slowed down. I saw things running along both sides of the road, pacing us."

"Us?"

"Yeah. Somebody was driving the truck. I banged on the window to get the driver's attention, to tell him about the things following us, but he didn't look back. We slowed down some more, because the road was muddy. Then the things jumped on the truck. They were monitor lizards."

"No shit?"

"Yeah. I wouldn't even know what a monitor lizard was if it wasn't for you." I expected him to say "I wouldn't even be dead if it wasn't for you," but he didn't. "The lizards jumped on me," I said. "And . . . well . . . they ate my face."

H. whistled. "Maybe you were just missing me. Lizards and guilt . . . "

"No. It was one of *those* dreams. For sure."

"Yeah. Okay. You're going on a journey, with a companion who will choose the path. The destination will matter to him more than *you* do. There will be terrors and trials. The lizards . . . hell, monitor lizards were my favorite . . . they might just symbolize monsters, but maybe they mean you'll have to deal with guilt, or something from your past . . . maybe even me?"

He sounded so hopeful. I didn't have the heart to remind him that he was dead, and unlikely to have any bearing on my life anymore, beyond these hollow conversations.

"I can't back out? I can't avoid it?" I asked.

"No, bro. You're on the truck." His voice changed, became playful. "Oh, there's one other thing the dream means."

"Yeah?"

"Yeah. Classic symbolism. Straight outta Freud. It means you're gay." He laughed. It was a terrible laugh, because it sounded almost exactly like he had when he was alive. "Hate to break it to you."

"Mom and Dad will freak," I said. "Thanks, H." I got up to leave.

"B.," he said, softly, serious.

"Yeah?"

"I love you, B."

My throat closed up. I shook my head. "Damn it, H. We agreed we weren't going to say that anymore."

He didn't answer.

I left, trying to shake off the emotional aftereffects of the conversation, wondering when this thing would happen, when someone else's destiny would hit me like a truck.

I went to a coffee shop, got tea and a bagel. I can't stomach coffee anymore, not even really milky espresso. It gives me the jitters.

I sat, leafing through a newspaper. Somebody said "Hey." I looked up. A skinny guy stood nearby, with a big nose and kinky hair, dressed all in black. He was ugly in an arresting way, with big, light blue eyes. He had nice hands, I noticed that right away; long fingers. I've always liked nice hands.

"You're him, the guy." He snapped his fingers. "Bradley Bowman."

"Yeah." I looked down at my paper again, but it was too late. This was the guy. The one driving the truck in my dream.

"I loved you in *The Glass Harp*," he said. Most people said that. Then he surprised me. "And that spoken word thing you did, *Underwater Monologues*, that was great."

"Thanks," I said, and meant it. I'd been nominated for a Grammy for *Monologues*, but not many people had heard it. It was the one decent thing I'd ever written myself.

"I didn't know you lived around here."

"Pretty close." I hesitated, but H. had said it—I was already on the truck. "Want to sit down?"

"Yeah!" He put down his bag, pulled out a chair, and sat down. "I'm Jay."

"Good to meet you. Call me Brad."

"So, uh." He fidgeted with a coffee spoon. "You, uh, doing anything—"

"No," I said. "Pretty much out of the business, since that thing with that director."

He actually blushed. "I heard about that, yeah."

My last acting job. Jesus, six years ago. Fourth day on the set, I attacked the director, tried to strangle him, people said. He didn't press charges—everyone figured I was just fucked up about H. dying, and that I was on drugs—but no one wanted to work with me after that, and I didn't audition, didn't return my agent's phone calls. I'd been living off residuals from *The Glass Harp* and my other movies ever since.

In truth, I'd saved the director's life. He was hag-ridden, a thing like a fat lamprey clinging to the back of his neck, feeding on him, backwashing poison into his brain. No one else could see the creature, but I could see all kinds of shit, after H. died. In exchange for a bottle of quaaludes poured down the sewer grate, H. told me how to make a nasty broth to soak my hands in, and then I could touch the lamprey thing as well as see it. It worked. H. is always right, now that he's dead.

The dead know things, but the living have to do the work.

I killed the lamprey, ripped it away from the director's neck and tore it apart, and people thought I was trying to kill the director, so I killed my career, too. It was a corpse I didn't mourn much.

"If it's not too personal," Jay said. "I mean . . . your partner died, right?"

I nodded. "A long time ago."

"I only mention it because my girlfriend died a couple of months ago." He looked at the table. I couldn't read anything into his expression at all. "She got stung by a bee, when we were having a picnic, and it turned out she was allergic." He shook his head. "She died in the ambulance."

"Oh, Jay, I'm so sorry." What a shitty, out-of-nowhere thing. No one was surprised when H. died the way he did. He'd been doing more and more drugs, and I was buying them for him, I had all the connections, and he shot up too much and he died. Simple, straightforward. But to die from a bee sting . . . that was bad shit.

"But I think . . . " Jay said, and then trailed off. He looked up. He looked into my eyes. "I think I can bring her back."

Any other day, I'd have figured he was crazy, and excused myself, and taken off. And for *me* to think someone's crazy, with the things I've seen, that's serious. But I'd had one of *those* dreams, and Jay had driven me into the darkness, so I just said "How?"

And he told me.

We managed to hide in the BART station in Berkeley, which is no mean feat, crouching a little way down the tunnel (well away from the third rail) after the last train of the night passed by. We listened as the BART cops shooed out the stragglers, and heard the metal gates rattle down, blocking us from the world above. We waited for a while, in the dark and the silence, then helped one another back up to the platform. We sat against the wall, our eyes gradually adjusting to the dimness.

Jay ate potato chips, every crunch as loud as the trump of doom. He didn't seem nervous at all, like he did this kind of thing all the time.

"How'd you hear about this train?" I asked.

"Somebody at a party was talking about urban myths, new ghost stories, shit like that."

"Huh," I said. Thinking I'd never heard about a ghost BART train. Thinking the guy Jay heard at the party had probably made it all up on the spot. Thinking maybe that didn't matter, that the confluence of Jay's need, and my presence, and my dream, would be enough to call something

179

imagined into being.

"It's good of you to come with me," Jay said. "It would be harder to do, if I was alone. I might not have come down here at all. Maybe . . . maybe your old boyfriend is down there, too."

I didn't answer. I'd thought of that, sure. But H. had been dead a lot longer than Jay's girlfriend. Did that matter? Could we bring Jay's girlfriend back, but not H., because she was fresher, or because she hadn't earned her death like H. had? I could visit H. any time I wanted, sure, right in the empty lot where he'd died, by the sewer grate he'd puked blood into. But that ghost was residual heat, a fading photograph, not H. himself. If H. had a soul, something essential and eternal, it was . . . somewhere else. Maybe where we were going tonight. I didn't want to think about that.

"What's your girlfriend's name?" I asked.

"Eunice. She hated that name. Her middle name was Ethel. She hated that worse. I called her E."

E. And my H. And him Jay, and H. always called me B., though no one else did. I tried some anagrams, didn't come up with anything. Decided it was a coincidence. Some things were nothing more than that, after all.

We talked about trivial things—my movies, the band he played keyboards for, his job debugging code. After a while I said "When do you think it'll come?"

Then we heard the hum and rattle, felt the air come pushing down the tunnel. We both stood up. A headlight appeared in the dark, a strange pale white light that illuminated Jay's face. He looked absolutely terrified.

The train pulled up before us. Just one car. The front compartment was all dark glass, the driver (if there was one) hidden. The train was white, not silver like a normal BART train, and it was streamlined, organic, all of a piece. It looked like it had been carved from a single enormous thighbone.

The doors slid open with a hiss of compressed air. I stepped forward. Jay didn't move. I looked at him. He was on the edge of running away, though he wouldn't get far, since we were locked down here. Jay had never really believed the train would come. I guess he thought this was going to be a ritual, a vigil, a night spent in E.'s honor, with no consequences.

Maybe it would have been, if I hadn't joined him. It was more than that, now.

"Coming?" I asked. Not impatient. Just asking. This was his journey, though I never really thought he'd walk away.

He nodded, squared his shoulders, and walked into the dimness inside the train. I followed.

There were no seats, and instead of metal handrails on the ceiling, there were large bone hooks. I grabbed one. Jay did the same.

A voice, cold as dry ice, whispered "Doors are closing," over a speaker.

Aren't they always? I thought, and the doors hissed shut.

The train accelerated smoothly through the dark. Jay hung from the hook, his eyes closed, swaying. "I wonder how far we have to go?"

"I think it's always a short trip to the underworld," I said, looking at the window and seeing only my reflection against the blackness outside.

"You'd think there'd be a cost," Jay said, opening his eyes. "You know? Two pennies each, like in the old stories."

"That buys you a one-way ticket. I guess there's a different price for a round-trip."

"What kind of price?" Jay asked.

I shrugged. I figured we'd have to pay afterward.

We didn't travel for very long. The train stopped, and diffuse light shone in through the windows, faint like the glow of bioluminescent mushrooms. There were bare trees and swirling fog, and more than anything the place looked like the set of a B-grade horror movie. The doors hissed open.

We got off the train, Jay first. "Where to?" I said. The trees were petrified, black, or else they were stone carvings of trees.

"I guess we follow the buzzing," he said, his hands shoved deep in his pockets as he stared into the trees and the fog.

I heard them, then. Bees, off in the distance, sounding angry and busy, just like the clichés say.

"Is it dangerous here?" Jay asked.

It was, in many ways, a silly question, but I answered it seriously. "I think this place is normally beyond danger—this is where you go when the danger *gets* you. It's the land of the lowest energy level. But we're here to change things, to take someone out . . . so, yeah, I think it's dangerous." Though I wasn't sure how. I knew things like this—magic, the supernatural, everything outside of, over, and under the reality most people inhabit their whole lives—could be unpredictable.

"I read Dante in college," Jay began.

"Don't think that way. Dante wrote a political treatise, a love poem, a spiritual meditation. He wasn't drawing a map. You can't map this place." I pointed. "Let's follow the buzzing bees. If there's a path, stay on it."

We passed through the dark wood. Was the sky empty of stars, or were we in an enormous cavern underground? It didn't matter, really, but my mind worried at the question, to keep from wondering where H. was, I guess. This wasn't my journey. I was the catalyst, the facilitator, nothing more, and I wanted to keep it that way.

Pretty soon we came to a clearing, a circle surrounded by trees, and there was E.

Jay gasped. I just stared.

E. was a beehive. I couldn't tell if she'd ever been pretty, or if she was short or tall or fat or thin; her body was changed beyond such things. She leaned against a tree (it looked like she was *fused* to the tree), and her chest was filled with hexagonal chambers dripping honey. Bees flew around her like a black-and-yellow poison aura.

"Jay," she said, or else the bees buzzed and made a sound like words.

"E. Are you . . . " He shook his head. "I came to get you. To bring you back."

The buzzing increased in volume, and the bees moved faster and more erratically. I wondered if someone would get stung, and what a sting from an underworld bee would do. I hung back. This wasn't my journey, and I wanted to stay out of the way. It seemed to me, though, that E. was at peace. Like she'd left her troubles behind.

"I'm full of honey now," she said.

"Baby," Jay said softly. "I've come such a long way . . . "

But he hadn't, not really. Where were the trials? The tests, the bargains, the obstacles? Or were they still ahead? If this was it, if he just had to lead E. out of here now, it was too *easy*. If this was all it took, the world would be full of the rescued dead, and no one would ever have to mourn again.

Something slinked into my peripheral vision, and when I turned my head, I saw monitor lizards. Big as wolves, with dark green scales, wedge-shaped heads, watchful unblinking eyes. They flickered their tongues. They beckoned me.

I knew the lizards could take me to H. The real H., or what was left of him, whatever essential part had passed on.

"I can come back with you," E. said, a dreamy buzz. "But only if you don't look back. You can never look back."

"Like Orpheus," Jay said.

I knew that story. Learned it in school. Orpheus went into the underworld to bring back his dead lover, and he was told she would follow him back to the land of the living—as long as he didn't look back on the way out. And, of course, Orpheus didn't hear her behind him, and he doubted, and he looked over his shoulder, and that was that. She sank back into death forever. I always thought Orpheus was an idiot, having one rule and breaking it, but now, *here*, I suddenly understood.

Don't look back. It wasn't meant literally. It didn't mean "Don't turn your head," it meant "Don't *remember*." Because how could your lover live, if you knew she had died? How could you go on loving her, with the weight of that knowledge, with all that interrupted grief clogging up your head? You had to *forget it all*, drink the waters of Lethe, the river of forgetfulness, and afterward you'd never understand why your lover was afraid of subway stations and cemeteries, why she refused to go to your aunt's funeral with you, why she wept on gray days and stared off into the middle distance as if she were looking at things you'd never be able to see. Because *she* wouldn't forget about her death. Just you.

I thought about all the gray, hollow people I'd met in my life, shuffling through their days, as if they were swathed in shrouds no one else could see, and I wondered how many of them had been dead, once upon a time, and come back, and remembered.

I looked at the sinuous lizards, at their indifferent grace. They would lead me to H., if I let them. I would find my dead lover holding a needle full of Lethe-water, more potent than any drug we'd taken in the old days, and then what? Would we go back in time? Would I be a star again, with H. by my side? A strangely quiet H., still doing drugs but for a different reason, trying to forget something he knew I would never remember again?

Because the dead know things, even if they come back to life, and because it is still up to the living to act, to *choose*.

Was I willing to forget all the pain, everything I'd learned since H.'s death, in order to bring him back, to have him suffer, and remember, and be lost to me again someday?

"The bees can sting you," E. said to Jay. "They can sting the loss away, and then I can follow you back. If you want." She sounded totally indifferent.

"Don't you want to come with me?" Jay asked.

"It's up to you."

"Of course I want you back," he said, and walked into the black and yellow mist of bees.

I turned and walked away, taking big ground-eating steps. The lizards followed me, paced me, and I started running to get away from them, from their cool green temptation. I wept as I ran. I wondered if H. would understand why I was running away, if he would want it this way, too.

I found the train, and its doors hissed open at my approach. The lizards hung back among the stone trees, watching me.

I looked back at them, for a long moment, then wiped the tears from my eyes. I got on the train. Jay would find his own way back, into the sun, and E. with him. But he would never understand why she didn't want to go outside, why she was so afraid of bees and dark places, and he would leave her eventually, I think, because the strange sad girl who came back would not be the woman he'd loved. *That* was Jay's trial, his price to pay.

"Doors are closing," the driver whispered over the speaker, in tones of warning. These doors wouldn't open again, not for me. This was my one and only trip on this train, at least while I was alive.

"Let them close," I said, and rode back through the emptiness in the belly of the night, toward another morning, having nothing but my memories, but holding tightly to those, holding them as though they were worth all the rest of my life.

ORPHEUS AMONG THE CABBAGES

She picked up a pomegranate, squeezed
it hard, sighed. She'd always preferred golden
delicious apples, but they were all
mushy today. Someone called out
from the direction of the cabbages,
not her name, just pleading. She pushed
her clattering cart toward the greenest
part of the produce department.

A man's head rested among the cabbages.
He had black hair, and the kind of olive skin that
some women find exotic when they don't know
better. "I am Orpheus," he said, "cursed to live
forever, bereft of love, and now left
among these living green things
that by their fecundity mock my living
death. My woe is legend . . . "

She resisted the urge to thump
his forehead like a melon. She called
to a beefy old man wearing a
supermarket smock. "What's this head
doing in among the cabbages?" she asked.
He walked toward her, looked at Orpheus,

grunted. "I just unload the crates," he
said. "The quality of the vegetables
is none of my business."

"Did these cabbages come from Greece?"
she asked.

"Olives are what come from Greece," he
said. "Cabbages come from places like
Ohio." He wandered away.

"Long I sought my love," Orpheus said.
"Long I wandered singing in
the lands below the earth."

She looked at the sign. "Cabbages, 89 cents
a head." She picked up Orpheus by his
hair. He didn't seem to mind. If his neck
had been bloody she might have left
him there, but his wound was smooth
as cut cucumber. She dropped him
in her basket, paid for him at the register,
thinking "Of all the places to find
true love."

In the car, on the way home, Orpheus went
on and on about his dead wife from inside
the grocery bag.

She wished he would stop; a girl could
start to feel like an afterthought. She decided
he would never love her after all.

A mile from her house he started singing.
She wept. So did a dog in the street, a mailman
passing by, and a stop sign. She decided to keep
him after all.

When she got home she put the rest
of the groceries away, but took Orpheus
into her dusty bedroom, swinging him
gently by his hair. "Long I sought my love,
and an end to loneliness," Orpheus said.
"Long I searched to find the gates
of my paradise denied."

She undressed, surprised to find
herself trembling. She stretched out
on the bed and bent her knees, then
tucked the murmuring head of Orpheus
between her thighs.

"Sing out," she said, and he did.

A bit later, so did she.

PALE DOG

Marla carried a drawstring bag containing a dozen kidney stones recently passed by an elderly clairvoyant named Bainbridge. She swung the bag and hummed, almost dancing down the alley. She'd taken Rondeau along with her to see Bainbridge, and Rondeau had been the one to actually fish the kidney stones out of the toilet. Marla wasn't averse to doing her own dirty work, but given the choice, she'd let Rondeau do it for her every time.

Now Rondeau had his hands shoved deep in the pockets of his jacket. He wore a vintage purple zoot suit with a gold shirt—a suit which he claimed was haunted by its former owner. Marla had yet to see any evidence of a ghostly presence, though Rondeau had been wearing the suit for a week straight, ever since he bought it.

Rondeau looked up at the looming brick walls on either side of them and sighed. "It seems like we're always skulking down alleyways. Why can't we take a nice stroll down a broad avenue, all with . . . " He waved his hands in a vague gesture. "With trees and shit. Happy little lampposts."

"Alleys are shortcuts," Marla said. "Shortcuts are our business."

"So me having my hands in a filthy toilet, that was in the service of the Great God Shortcut?"

"It beats cutting Bainbridge open and taking the stones out that way, doesn't it?"

"At least you would have done the cutting yourself," he muttered.

A white dog trotted into the alley. Marla didn't know much about dogs, but if pressed she would have said it was partly shepherd but mostly mutt. The dog was neither big nor small, but medium-sized—just exactly the right size for a dog, Marla thought.

"Lovely pup, Rondeau said, squatting to pet the animal on the head. The dog panted and wagged its tail. Marla crouched and ruffled the fur behind the dog's ear. "Good boy!" It looked at her with peculiar, honey-colored eyes, and licked her hand. "It looks well fed, but it might be a stray. Do you need a home to go to, little pup? Do you? Do you need a Mama? I can—" Marla stopped the rush of baby talk she felt welling up within her. Slowly, she lifted her hand from the dog's neck. The dog didn't seem to mind the end of attention, just kept looking at her, panting and wagging.

Marla eased away from the dog. "Rondeau," she hissed.

Rondeau looked up. "What?"

"Why are you petting that dog?"

"What do you mean? It's a nice dog. Aren't you a nice doggie? Aren't you just?"

"*Rondeau*," Marla said, in her most sandpaper-on-nerve-endings voice. When she had Rondeau's attention, she said "Can you think of any two people *less* likely than us to stop what we're doing so we can pet a stray *dog*?"

Rondeau stopped patting, his hand hovering a few inches over the dog's head. He looked at the dog, at Marla, and back at the dog. "Ah," he said. "Right." He eased away to stand beside Marla. The dog didn't move, or seem troubled by their behavior. It just kept wagging its tail, looking at them expectantly.

"I still want to pet it," Rondeau said. "And I *hate* dogs. A dog stole my dinner once when I was a kid, living under the Brandon Street underpass."

"I don't hate dogs," Marla said, keeping her eyes fixed on the animal. "I don't even *think* about dogs. They're pointless. I have no opinion about them. But I want to take this one home, and give it a nest of blankets at the foot of my bed, and . . . and feed it *steak*."

"Do you think it's some kind of a . . . dog god?"

"I hope we haven't sunk that low, Rondeau, to get pushed around by a *dog* god."

"Well, what, then? Somebody's familiar?"

"Maybe, but it would have to belong to someone pretty damned power-ful. Who runs a dog show? Some out-of-towner? It's nobody local; I would have heard." Marla was the head sorcerer in the city, chief of chiefs, first among equals. Not much slipped through her information network.

"And *I* would've heard if anyone of consequence came to town." Rondeau ran Juliana's Bar, and all gossip of relevance to the city's sorcerous population passed through there eventually.

"So."

"So."

"Shapeshifter?"

Marla snorted. She could tell a shapeshifter from a real animal. Only ordinaries and amateurs were fooled by shapeshifters.

"Maybe it's just a sport, a fluke." Rondeau looked down at the dog, whose tail had not slowed in its wagging. "An otherwise normal dog that was born with some psychic twist. It happens to people sometimes, so why not dogs? It makes us want to love it and take care of it . . . that seems like a reasonable, beneficial adaptation."

"Maybe," Marla said. "But then why is it out on the street with no collar, no tags? If this were my psychic dog, I'd take better care of it."

Rondeau shrugged. "Maybe the collar broke. Maybe—"

The dog moved, and Marla and Rondeau both stepped back warily.

The dog turned and trotted out of the alley.

"See?" Rondeau said. "Off to seek other suckers."

"I don't know . . . "

Rondeau shook his head. "You just don't like my theory because, if I'm right, the dog is harmless, and you don't know how to deal with anything harmless."

"Maybe that's it," Marla said. And maybe it was. But as they walked back to Marla's apartment, she kept her eye out for the white dog. She didn't see it, but she wondered if it could see her.

Marla set the last jar on the counter, the one holding Bainbridge's kidney stones. Another jar held the toenail clippings of a man with amazing regenerative properties. A third (and this jar was made of cobalt glass, to mute the brightness) held a dram of the shining lymph of Mother Abbot. The remaining jar contained a goiter cut from the throat of a sacred cow.

"That stuff's nasty," Rondeau said, wrinkling his nose at the jars. He twiddled with the radio on the counter until he found some big band music. Marla didn't like that kind of music, but it was an improvement over the hard-driving dance-music Rondeau usually preferred. He hummed along with the radio for a moment, then took a sip of his gin and tonic and grimaced. "This drink is nasty, too. How can you stand this stuff?

Tastes like pine needles."

"I like the taste of pine needles." Marla checked the seals on the jars. "That's it, we're set. Now we go to see Langford."

"Why can't you do a divination on your own? Why go to all this trouble?"

"The only divination I'm any good at is reading entrails, and I don't have the stomach for that anymore."

Rondeau swirled the ice in his glass. "You don't have the stomach. For reading entrails. Marla, have you just made your first joke?"

"It's my second joke at least. Don't you remember that knock-knock joke?"

"Ah, yes. I must have repressed the memory. But really, why are we going to see Langford? There are other methods."

She waved at the jars. "This is specialized stuff, to answer a specialized question, and for that, we need a specialist. Hence, Langford. Most of the Seers in this city are cryptic and obscure. They can't help it—that's just the way the information comes to them, the way it gets filtered through their minds. I don't have time to puzzle out secret meanings, though, and Langford can give me clear, unambiguous answers."

"He's creepy," Rondeau complained.

"This from the man with the haunted zoot suit?"

Rondeau looked at his sleeves worriedly. "Shh. You'll wake him up."

"I thought the dead didn't sleep?" She put the jars into a satchel. "Or else they don't do anything *but* sleep."

"Yeah, well, he's quiet sometimes, at least." Rondeau smoothed his lapels.

"Let's go. We have to catch the 7:35 train."

"Why do we ride the subway, when we could take the Bentley? We never take the car." His eyes became dreamy, faraway. "I like cars. I want a big one, like you see in old movies, all chrome and curves, like a torpedo, a rolling bomb . . . "

Marla frowned at him. He'd never rhapsodized about cars before. "Cars are for ordinaries, Rondeau. We're underground people."

"Goddamn shortcuts."

Langford owned big property, and kept his headquarters beneath one of the city's largest medical testing facilities. The place was like a hospital, without the inconvenience of actual patients. Marla and Rondeau walked

191

down white hallways, past gray doors. People in lab coats passed by and gave them quizzical looks—Marla in her milk-white cloak with the silver clasp in the shape of a stag beetle, Rondeau in his gold-and-purple zoot suit. The two of them looked disreputable, fundamentally out-of-place, but people who worked for Langford doubtless became accustomed to the occasional odd coming-and-going.

Marla led Rondeau down a dim stairway to a steel door with no discernible seams or apertures. A red button set into the wall glowed faintly. Marla pushed it.

"Yes?" Langford's voice came crisp and digitally clear from a concealed speaker

"It's Marla and Rondeau."

The door buzzed and swung inward. Marla and Rondeau stepped inside. Marla had been to Langford's lab before, so she knew to breathe through her mouth. Rondeau, however, was a newcomer, and he gagged. "It smells like a barnyard in here!"

"I always thought it smelled like a yeast infection," Marla said, her voice nasal. "But I've never smelled a barnyard." They stood in a small, featureless room, with another door at the other end. "This is the anteroom, too. It *really* stinks in the main area. Langford says you get used to it. I never have."

The inner door opened, and Langford smiled and beckoned them in. He wore a lab coat, too, but his was spattered with strange stains, yellow and green and red. His round rimless glasses seemed on the point of sliding off his nose, and his brown hair was cut short. He might have been a cute young medical student, but Marla knew he was fifty years old at least, his youthful looks just one of the consequences of his dabbling in biological esoterica. Langford was commonly known as a Biomancer, and his early studies had, indeed, been almost exclusively concerned with the effect of magic on living organisms (his menagerie of "transformed" creatures was supposed to be astonishing, though Marla had never spoken to anyone who claimed to have seen it firsthand). In recent years he'd expanded his field of inquiry, however, dabbling in quantum mechanics, superconducting technology, and other endeavors, applying the torque wrench of magic whenever traditional scientific approaches proved too slow or ineffective.

"Are you ready for the divination?" he asked.

Marla nodded, holding out the satchel.

"Oh, good," Langford said, grinning. His glee for the work he did never seemed to fade; he was the most consistently happy person Marla had ever met. She wondered if he'd done something to step up endorphin production in his brain.

Langford took the satchel and preceded them into his workshop. In contrast to the gleaming, humming sterility of the labs upstairs, Langford's personal workshop was a riotous mess, part junk-shop, part science lab, part *brujo's* hut. One wall was covered with a particularly virulent green mold, and the last time Marla had visited, Langford had introduced her to the mold, and told her he was experimenting with "aggregate sentience." Innumerable shelves held pickled oddities, as well as terrariums filled with all manner of live creatures, from hissing roaches to fire newts to water dragons.

Rondeau was clearly spooked by the towering proximity of so many nasty, chitinous, slithering things, but Marla chose to ignore his discomfort, and Langford was wholly oblivious. The scientist led them to a lab table (its surface remarkably clear of clutter) and put the jars down beside a large metal mixing bowl filled with a viscous black substance.

"I've been thinking about scrying bowls," Langford said. "And quantum computers. The difference, really, is only one of perspective and application—"

"I don't need to know the details," Marla interrupted. "You know this stuff is beyond me."

"Oh, only the math," Langford said. "You could understand the outlines, if you wanted."

"I'm not interested in how you get the answers, just in the answers themselves."

"Of course," he said, and started taking the jars out of the bag. "The goiter isn't bad. I'd have preferred a goiter from a white buffalo, but this will do."

Marla laughed. "If I had a white buffalo, I could work up a magic big enough to get rid Sweeney of forever, and I wouldn't need this divination."

"I can make a white buffalo, of course," Langford said, gnawing his lip. "But the naturally occurring ones are so much more effective."

"Sweeney?" Rondeau said. "You're here to ask a question about Todd Sweeney? But he's *dead*."

Marla shrugged. "He's supposed to be dead. Everyone said he was dead. But one of Hamil's spies saw him in the lobby of the Whitcroft-Ivory building, alive and well. I'm here to figure out how that happened."

"Shit," Rondeau said, with no little awe. "Todd Sweeney's alive. That's impressive. If as many people wanted me dead as want *him* dead . . . Well. I'd be dead."

Todd Sweeney (and the name was a pretentious affectation, one of many the man entertained) had come to town the year before. It was obvious to everyone that he was a player, and he claimed connections to heavy operators in Thailand and French Guyana. He wanted what everyone wanted—money and power—and he was charming enough to get both.

But Sweeney had no qualms, no scruples, and no manners. He'd connived, cheated, and screwed-over everyone in the city to get what he wanted. *Everyone*, even hardcases like Gregor and Hamil. Marla was the only one who hadn't done any business with him. When the council of sorcerers decided something had to be done about Sweeney, that a message had to be sent, Marla was the obvious choice to carry out the sentence. She was the only one who didn't have a personal stake in Sweeney's downfall.

But now, somehow, Sweeney had survived Marla's efforts.

That was a mistake on Sweeney's part. His survival made things between him and Marla a personal matter. "Yeah," Marla said. "I take his continued life as a personal affront. He tricked us somehow, or else tricked death itself. Langford's going to tell me what's what."

"Wow." Rondeau said, shaking his head. He walked over to one of the shelves, scowling at insects in a terrarium, then wandered toward a shelf of books.

"You have the question all worked out?" Langford said, opening the jars. "My, this is exceptional lymph!"

"Yes," Marla said. "Nailed-down and unambiguous. I went over the wording about a hundred times. It's airtight."

"Good. Because you only get one chance to ask, and—"

"I know, Langford," she said, not without affection. She liked the Biomancer. His ambitions were incomprehensible to her, but they were also completely tangential to her own. That meant he was no threat. That meant they could be friends.

Langford added the contents of the jars, one by one, to the bowl of blackness on the table, stirring with a wooden spoon. The toenail clippings swirled away, as did the kidney stones, and the goiter appeared to actually *dissolve.* "It's like programming a computer," Langford said. "Inputting the parameters. If you assume that everything physical has a spiritual analogue—" He glanced at Marla, who had her arms crossed with impatience. "Ah. Sorry." He held the blue jar of lymph in his hand, light shining from the jar's open mouth. "After I add this, ask the question. Don't take any unnaturally long pauses, or the scrying bowl will think—well, not *think*, I don't mean *think* exactly—that you've finished. It's fascinating, really—as near as I can tell, the vibrations your voice cause in the air are transmitted to the scrying fluid, which then performs some operation which is at bottom mysterious to me, and the answer *emerges* . . . I don't think the bowl is at all concerned with the *content*, it's like the thought experiment about the Chinese-language-translating machine . . . " He glanced at Marla. "Well. Anyway. Onward."

He tipped the jar of shining lymph into the bowl, where it disappeared, not even changing the substance's color.

Marla drew breath to ask her question.

"What the hell is this dog doing here?" Rondeau shouted.

Marla's mouth fell open in shock and dismay. She looked at Langford, who was staring fixedly at the bowl. "That's it," Langford said. "That's the question it's going to answer. I'm sorry, Marla." He slumped his shoulders for a moment, then stiffened. "*What* dog?"

Rondeau hurried back to the table . . . followed by the white dog they'd seen in the alleyway. "Marla, it's that dog again, I don't know what—"

"Rondeau," she said, her voice full of ice and spines. "You ruined the divination. Why can't you keep your mouth shut?"

"It's impossible," Langford said. "How did this dog—nice doggie—get in here? There's no possible entrance, no conceivable way, unless it came in with you two, but it couldn't have—oh, good dog!—it couldn't have, because I let you out of the anteroom myself . . . " He frowned. "Why do I want to name this animal 'Snowflake' and take it home with me?"

The scrying bowl spoke, then, in Rondeau's voice:

"The dog is here to guide the undying spirit to its final rest," it said.

Marla, Rondeau, and Langford all looked at the bowl.

Then they looked at the dog. Which was wagging its tail.

"So," Marla said, feeding the dog a huge hunk of rare steak. "Do you think it's come to get Sweeney? That he managed to fool death somehow, and now the dog is on his trail?" The dog sat on a chair beside her, eating happily off his own china plate.

"It's possible," Hamil said, looking at the animal thoughtfully. Hamil was Marla's consiglieri. An older sorcerer, and a man of considerable *gravitas* (as well as considerable physical bulk), he had the experience to temper Marla's sheer-power approach to problem-solving.

"Then why's it keep following us?" Rondeau asked from the other side of Hamil's table. He'd been sitting beside the dog at first, but it kept sniffing at his armpits, which made Rondeau nervous, mostly because he found the dog's behavior adorable, which was a wholly unnatural response for him.

"Perhaps it recognizes you as allies. It is surely a creature of great wisdom and perception . . . " Hamil trailed off as the dog began licking its own testicles, with evident pleasure.

"That's so cute," Marla said, and then scowled.

"That dog is too creepy," Rondeau said. "Mostly because I don't find it creepy at *all*, when I know I should. What do we do now?"

"We go see Todd Sweeney, and let the dog get a whiff of him, and drag his ass to hell." Marla patted the dog. "I always thought hellhounds were black and breathed fire and such."

"Death rides a pale horse," Rondeau said. "Maybe this is Death's pale best friend."

Hamil chuckled. "Psychopomps—beings that guide the dead from earth to the afterlife—come in a number of guises. They appear as birds, quite often. Why not a dog?" Hamil took a bite of a chicken leg, then offered the drumstick to the dog.

Rondeau reached across the table and slapped Hamil's hand away, though under normal circumstances he never would have struck a sorcerer of such power. Rondeau's only strength lay in his ownership of Juliana's Bar and his friendship with Marla, and those could only offer so much protection.

Hamil looked at Rondeau with the implacable patience of a glacier.

"I'm sorry," Rondeau said, looking down at the table. "Really. But you can't give chicken bones to the dog. It might choke."

"We've got to find Sweeney," Marla said.

Marla and Rondeau went to Sweeney's old place, a Victorian townhouse in a nice neighborhood. The house had been ritually defiled, the walls covered with lethally mis-drawn spray-painted runes, the corners filled with sea salt, the mirrors all shattered. Bird-shit covered the floor from the flock of pigeons that had been released inside, that now lived raucously in the living room chandelier. The house had been turned into one huge bad-luck death-omen. That had been Sweeney's first warning, which he had disregarded. As if he had nothing to fear from threats of death.

"I don't think he's been back," Rondeau said, noting the undisturbed dust. The dog sat down by his feet and scratched behind its ear. The pigeons twittered, and the dog barked. It was an adorable bark, a bark that would never annoy neighbors or frighten children.

"Let's check the bedroom," Marla said, and went upstairs. She opened the closet, which was empty but for a few wire hangers. "He came back for his suits. He was always vain about his suits." She glanced at Rondeau. "You're vain, too, but he had good taste. Has, I guess."

Rondeau tugged at his purple cuffs. "My taste is unimpeachable. How do you know it was Sweeney, and not some looter, who took the suits?"

She pointed to the carved designs over the closet door. "If anybody else passed so much as a finger through this doorway, zap! They'd be burned."

"That's pretty extreme wardrobe protection."

"I told you he was vain."

The dog trotted toward the closet door.

"No!" Marla and Rondeau shouted simultaneously. But the dog passed through the doorway without visible harm; the runes over the door didn't even glow. It was as if the dog wasn't even there. It trotted back out, whining, seeming unhappy for the first time since they'd met it.

"So where do we go next?"

"Sweeney doesn't seem to be covering his tracks particularly well," Marla said. "He doesn't seem worried that we'll find him. Where would you stay, if you wanted to thumb your nose at the whole council?"

"Heaven forbid I should do such a thing . . . " Rondeau considered, then snapped his fingers. "Sauvage's place."

Marla blinked. "Oh, he wouldn't." Sauvage had been the chief sorcerer in the city, before Marla. He had been murdered, and he was a heroic, almost totemic figure in the city's history, its most accomplished and well-loved secret ruler. His former residence, a lavish apartment above the nightclub he'd owned, was practically a museum piece, preserved and untouched, the nightclub closed, the property owned by the council of sorcerers.

"Sure he would," Rondeau said. "Sweeney's an asshole."

The dog barked again, as if in agreement, though it might have been barking at a stray pigeon that had made its way upstairs.

"I haven't been in here since the day Sauvage died," Marla said, pausing with her hand on the door handle. "It's been a long time."

"He was a hell of a guy," Rondeau said, tugging at his shirt collar. "My goddamn ghost is waking up."

"So long as it wakes up quietly."

"Like that's up to me. I'd rather it never woke up at all."

The dog scratched curiously at the door. Marla pressed her hand against the metal, closed her eyes for a moment, and nodded. "No traps. Not magical ones, anyway. I guess Sweeney could have a shotgun in there, with a string tied from the trigger to the doorknob."

"Cheerful thought."

Marla took a big, old-fashioned keyring from her pocket and unlocked the door. She eased it open and stepped into the dimness, her eyes quickly adjusting to the lack of light. Rondeau and the dog followed, the one muttering and tugging at his lapels, the other wagging its tail. They went past the shrouded jukebox, dusty chairs, and covered pool tables. "The stairway to the apartment is through the curtain, in the back." Marla led them through the curtain and up the stairs, ghosting silently. Rondeau followed, still fidgeting as if his suit itched, but doing so quietly. Only the dog made a sound, a low growl that Marla took as an encouraging sign. Sweeney must be upstairs. With luck, Marla wouldn't have to do anything to him herself—the dog would do its otherworldly messenger thing and drag Sweeney's spirit away.

Marla paused outside the apartment door. Inside, someone walked around, singing to himself. Marla touched the knob, found it unlocked, and shoved it open.

Sweeney stood in the middle of Sauvage's living room, wearing one of the dead sorcerer's oversized flannel robes. He held a glass of something amber and probably alcoholic in his hand. Sweeney raised a bushy eyebrow at Marla and lifted his glass in salute. "Ah, you tracked me down." His voice rolled majestically; that was half his charm.

Rondeau stood beside Marla, taking no notice of Sweeney. "Fucking ghost," he muttered. "It's all . . . fluttery."

Marla ignored him, stepping toward Sweeney. "This is the end."

"You've come to kill me, then? Really kill me? Not like your bully-boys did? You think you'll have more luck than they did?" Sweeney didn't seem to be blustering. The whole situation appeared to amuse him mightily, which only incensed Marla further.

Marla touched the dagger at her belt, its hilt wound with bands of white and purple electrical tape. It was her dagger of office, symbol of her position as chief sorcerer, custodian of the city.

The dagger was very sharp.

"What I kill, stays dead," she said.

Sweeney sipped his drink, then belched softly.

The dog trotted around Marla's legs, cocked its head, and looked at Sweeney.

Marla grinned. "Have you met this nice pooch, Sweeney?"

The dog sprang.

But it didn't jump at Sweeney—it jumped at Rondeau, a shocking lateral move that caught Marla by surprise. The dog hit Rondeau in the chest, and despite its relatively small size, managed to drive him to the ground. The dog snapped its teeth near Rondeau's throat—and, abruptly, Marla's could see the ghost that haunted the zoot suit. Rondeau *wasn't* paranoid or full of shit—there was a paranormal infestation. The ghost flickered and shimmered in her vision, like a black-and-white film projected on a billowing curtain, but it was undeniably there, black hair slicked back, dimpled chin, desperate eyes.

The dog dug its claws into Rondeau's stomach and pulled, holding the ghost by the throat. Rondeau was quiet, perhaps knocked unconscious by the fall, perhaps simply shocked into silence.

"That's unusual," Sweeney said. "And it looks like such a nice dog."

Marla glanced at Sweeney, then back at the dog. They'd been wrong, she realized—the dog wasn't here for Sweeney. It was here for the ghost in Rondeau's suit. The ghost must have been sleeping before, or dormant, or *something*, somehow beneath the dog's awareness, but now it had woken up, and the dog was on it. No wonder the dog had sniffed at Rondeau so intently; it must have faintly sensed the ghost.

Well, this was unexpected, but it wasn't really her problem. Let the dog have the ghost. She'd take care of Sweeney. Since the dog wasn't after him, perhaps Sweeney hadn't worked some dark magic to cheat death. Maybe Marla's bully-boys had simply made an error, and believed Sweeney dead when he wasn't. Maybe they'd even killed the wrong man by mistake. She would make no such error now. She unsheathed her dagger.

Then Rondeau screamed. Marla whipped her head around and gasped in horror.

The ghost wasn't the only thing being pulled away by the dog's relentless tugging. A flickering image of Rondeau himself was coming out, too, tangled up with the ghost. At first Marla thought the ghost was holding on to—to what? Rondeau's spirit? The ghost seemed to have its arms wrapped around Rondeau's spirit, like a shipwreck victim clinging to a piece of flotsam. But then Marla saw that the ghost's arms *disappeared* into Rondeau's spirit, that she couldn't tell where one left off and the other began. They were joined like Siamese twins, the ghost and Rondeau's spirit somehow *grown together.*

The dog was pulling out the ghost, and in the process ripping Rondeau's spirit from his body.

Marla didn't think. She took a few short running steps and kicked the pale dog in the head as hard as she could. The moment her foot connected, she was wracked by remorse—how could she have done such a thing, kicked a poor, sweet dog? The intensity of her guilt made her double over, gasping.

The dog spun off Rondeau with the force of Marla's kick, releasing the entwined spirits, which snapped back into Rondeau's body. The dog hit the carpet, rolled, then gained its feet. Marla expected it to growl and snarl, but it only lolled its tongue, wagged its tail, and raced off down the stairs.

But it would be back. Supernatural messengers weren't the quitting kind.

Sweeney could have escaped at any time during the confusion, but he was still there, half-smiling. "Damnedest thing I've seen all week," he said. "Wish you hadn't kicked the dog, though. I liked it."

Marla drew her dagger, bared her teeth, and rushed at Sweeney.

He died like anyone. Nothing special. But she had Rondeau (who was sweating, shaking, and clearly frightened by his ordeal) wrap the body in a blanket. They would hold onto Sweeney's corpse for a while, to make sure it didn't stand up and walk away.

Marla called Hamil, and told him to send a car. She sat on the couch smoking a clove cigarette, looking at the wrapped bundle on the living room floor. Trying not to look at Rondeau. He didn't speak, either, just sat shivering in a chair.

Marla's cell phone rang, once. The driver was here. She picked up the wrapped corpse and slung it over her shoulder. "Let's go."

"Marla," Rondeau said, voice trembling. "That thing . . . what happened with the dog . . . "

"We'll talk about it later," she said, more disturbed by the whole thing than she wanted to admit. Marla wasn't particularly good when it came to seeing around corners, and she didn't see a clear-cut way to solve this. That made her nervous.

And, somewhere out there, the dog was waiting. Wagging its tail.

"He's quite dead," Hamil said, tugging the blanket back over Sweeney's face. He frowned at Marla. "You executed him rather . . . enthusiastically, didn't you?"

Marla sighed. "I wasn't in a very businesslike frame of mind. But he's dead, really dead, and that's what matters."

"Yeah, all our problems are solved," Rondeau said morosely. "Except for the dog that's after me."

"The dog is only a symptom of your larger problem," Hamil said. "From what Marla described, this is more than a simple haunting—this ghost is parasitic. This is a possession-in-progress. The ghost is devouring your spirit, fusing with it . . . and once the process is finished, you will be gone. Only the ghost will remain, in your body. Every minute you wear the suit, the possession progresses a little farther. I'm sure it's very difficult work for the ghost, taking you over this way . . . that probably explains the periods of dormancy. It's psychic recuperation time."

It also explains Rondeau's recent fascination with flashy cars and big band music, Marla thought. The ghost was already partly assimilated, its personality bleeding into Rondeau's own.

"Already the ghost is so entwined with you that the dog cannot drag one away without taking the other," Hamil said.

"I should've never bought this suit," Rondeau said. "But it was only *four dollars*! And once I put it on . . . hell, I could tell it was haunted, but I looked so sharp! I figured, it's just a ghost, it's harmless, it's a psychic burp, an aftertaste, an echo. Nothing to worry about. I mean . . . " He looked at his shoes, frowning. "I haven't taken this suit off since I got it. I haven't showered in a week. I thought I just . . . liked the suit a lot. But now I think I was compelled to keep wearing it, just like I was compelled to be nice to that dog."

"So take the suit off now," Marla said. "Arrest the process."

"I doubt it will come off so easily," Hamil said.

Rondeau nodded. "It's like its part of my skin."

Marla touched her dagger's hilt. "So we cut the suit off."

Hamil shook his head. "Won't work. Unless you're prepared to take the skin with it."

Marla considered that. "Last resort," she said finally. "Other options?"

"I'm looking into it," Hamil said. The expression on his face told Marla that he had ideas—just nothing he wanted to mention in front of Rondeau.

"Go lie down in the spare bedroom, Rondeau," Marla said. "Get some rest. We'll keep an eye out for the dog."

"Go away and let the grown-ups discuss things," he said, with just a trace of bitterness. "Got it."

"So," Marla said once Rondeau was gone. "Give me the bad news."

"Your knife," Hamil said. "It's . . . special, as you know. I realize you largely limit its usage to assaults on the material, but under the right circumstances, the knife can also be used to cut the *immaterial* . . . even the flesh of the soul."

"So you're saying . . . "

"You can cut the ghost out of Rondeau."

Marla stood up. "Hell, let's do it!" Seeing his dour expression, she sat back down. "What's the catch?"

"Think of the ghost as a cancer, and of Rondeau's spirit as healthy tissue. It's an imperfect analogy, but it will do. Imagine trying to cut away the cancer. Part of the tumor is easy to excise, and comes away cleanly. Sometimes, though, you have to cut away some healthy tissue along with the cancer. And sometimes . . . " He shook his head. "Sometimes, there's no way to cut out the cancer, because it's spread too far, and can't be removed without destroying vital parts of the healthy tissue. Without killing the patient."

Marla nodded. "So I can cut away some of the ghost, but not all?"

"Yes. Fortunately, unlike a cancer, the remaining parts of the ghost—those you can't cut away—will not continue to grow or spread. But those parts left behind *will* have an effect. A few of the ghost's memories, perhaps, or the ghost's taste in food, or movies, or sex. Or larger personality traits may carry over. And in the course of cutting away the ghost, you may unavoidably remove pieces of Rondeau's spirit, slice away sections of his memory or personality . . . " Hamil shook his head again. "It's an ugly business."

"What do we need to get started?"

Hamil waved his hand. "Herbs, oils, tinctures. We must create a charged atmosphere, one in which you can see and interact with the spirits. I'll get you a list of what we need."

"Do it. I'll go get the ingredients. You keep an eye out for the dog." She looked toward the spare bedroom, her gaze softening. "And try to make Rondeau comfortable, as best you can."

The best *brujeria* in the city had no fixed address. Hypotheses and explanations for that fact abounded—some speculated that the owner suffered under a curse that made her endlessly restless. Others said the owner was pursued by one of the infamous Slow Assassins, and that the killer had drawn close enough that if she stayed in the same place for more than three or four days, he would find and kill her in her sleep. Marla suspected there was some magic involved—that the *brujeria's* impermanence added to its potency. In those stories about magic shops, weren't they always changing locations, appearing and disappearing without warning? There had to be something to that. Old stories almost always began in the mud of truth.

Today the *brujeria* was located in one of the huge old sewer pipes by the bay. The tunnel was big enough to ride a horse or motorcycle through, but as usual, Marla walked. It didn't take her very long to reach the shop, even though she was traveling by foot; she knew all the shortcuts.

Her boots squished in a trickle of water as she walked down the dark sewer pipe. When the river flooded, this pipe carried the overflow off into the bay, but it was relatively dry, now. Marla approached the light at the end of the tunnel, where the *brujeria* was.

Wind chimes tinkled in the breeze, dangling from the roof of the pipe over the *brujeria's* wooden shelves and tables. A man poked through the leaves and fronds piled on one of the tables, his back turned to Marla. The owner of the shop, a woman called Cecily, bowed slightly when Marla approached her. Cecily's face was painted kabuki white, the lips sharply outlined in red. She wore a sky-blue silk robe. Cecily did not speak. She never did.

Marla reached into her pocket and took out the list Hamil had made. She passed it to Cecily, who looked at it thoughtfully, then nodded and turned to a shelf filled with jars.

Marla looked at the other customer's back. She wondered if it was anyone she knew. There were plenty of apprentices, amateurs, and cantrip-throwers in the city that she didn't recognize; probably it was no one she knew, though even the lowest of the sorcerous kind would recognize her.

This guy had a nice suit, at least—

Marla narrowed her eyes. She tapped the man on the shoulder.

He turned, holding a bundle of herbs in one hand. When he saw Marla, he stumbled back against the table.

It was Sweeney. Here. Alive and well, even though Marla had left his body at Hamil's an hour ago.

Marla grabbed him by the throat, choking off his smile. "Cecily," she said. "Get me rope."

Sweeney's eyes widened.

"I'm not going to kill you this time," Marla said. "Not right away. I'm going to figure out what the hell your game is first. I might *hurt* you, to make you talk, but it'll be a while before I open your throat again. It never seems to work anyway."

Cecily brought her a coil of rope that, upon closer examination, proved to be a supple vine. "Tie his hands behind him," Marla said, and Cecily complied, then bound his feet as Marla instructed. Marla shoved Sweeney down, leaving him to lie on his side by the trickling water, wetness staining his suit. He whimpered. She kicked him, rather gently, all things considered, and his noise subsided.

"Get that stuff together," Marla said to Cecily, and she did so, her face completely serene, though that may have been an effect brought on by the white makeup. Marla poked through the jars on the shelves until Cecily tapped her on the shoulder. She handed Marla a brown bag with the top rolled down, and a piece of paper—a neatly itemized bill. She'd even charged Marla for the vine used to bind Sweeney, but it was a reasonable price, so Marla didn't complain.

Marla tucked the bag under her arm and bent to pick up Sweeney.

That's when she noticed that he was dead. Sweeney was face-down in the trickle. Somehow, he'd managed to drown in an inch of running water. He'd rolled over onto his stomach and stuck his face in the flow. That couldn't have happened by accident. That took *effort*. Marla said she wasn't going to kill him, so he'd killed himself.

He still clutched the bundle of herbs in his bound hands. Marla checked her bill, and saw that Cecily had charged her for those, too. Fair enough. Let Hamil have a look at the herbs. Maybe they were a clue.

The two dead bodies of Todd Sweeney lay together on Hamil's long library table, one wrapped in a sheet, the other still bound with vines.

"Most odd," Hamil said finally. He took the herbs from the second Sweeney's hands. "I'll find out what these are." He nodded to the bodies. "And I'll find out what those are, too. I'll get Langford to do an autopsy."

"And in the meantime . . . " Marla said.

"Yes. Rondeau. I've set up the ritual space, the circle is primed. Once Rondeau enters the perimeter, you'll be able to see his spirit, and the ghost's. Cut carefully."

"Will there be . . . I don't know . . . any mess?"

Hamil smiled grimly. "Not even ectoplasm. Though if the knife slips, and you cut his body, Rondeau will certainly bleed."

"What will happen to the ghost, once I slice it out?"

"It should stay with the suit. You're only cutting it away from Rondeau, not out of the place of its original haunting. Be sure to strip the suit off Rondeau right away. The ghost will begin re-attaching itself to his spirit very quickly."

"Okay. I'll get started.

"Watch out for the dog, Marla. Your cutting will almost certainly excite the ghost, and that could draw the dog's attention. Can you handle it?"

"As long as I can kick it before I start wanting to snuggle it."

Hamil stood. "I suggest drugging Rondeau, knocking him out. Having someone carve on your soul is probably quite unpleasant, if you're conscious to experience it."

Rondeau rested on the library table, his suit wrinkled and more than a little rank from constant wear.

Marla lit the candles and the bowls of herbs and whispered the incantations, words that seemed to twist in her mouth and wriggle off her tongue. Marla washed her hands in a bowl of wood alcohol and spring water, reminded of the scrying bowl at Langford's. She'd intended to ask for a way to effectively kill Todd Sweeney, but she hadn't gotten the opportunity. She still had to figure out how to get rid of Sweeney permanently, but saving Rondeau was more important.

When Marla said the last words, the light in the library changed, became crystalline; light with edges, with texture. As though Marla were looking at the world through a sheet of slightly prismatic glass.

And she could see spirits.

Her own, clinging to her skin like a pale aura. Rondeau's, which hovered a few inches above his body, drawn out because he rested at the focal point of the spell. And the ghost, all tangled up with Rondeau's spirit, melted into his chest.

The plants had spirits, too, and a few of the books on the shelves. Marla wondered if Hamil knew about those.

She washed her dagger in the bowl, then held up the blade and tilted it. The knife didn't have a spirit. It only glinted, wet and sharp.

The ghost muttered and shifted, then melted into Rondeau's spirit a bit more deeply.

Marla put the knife against the ghost's neck and felt resistance. She grinned. This would work. With a steady pressure, she bore down on the blade. It was like cutting through a stomach, the resistance of muscle, but nothing bone-hard, nothing too unyielding.

The ghost's eyes sprang open and rolled toward Marla. It scrabbled at the knife, and its fingers sheared away when they touched the blade. The severed fingers fell on the suit and melted into the fabric. The ghost swung its other hand at Marla, but she felt nothing—the hand just passed through her. For the ghost, only the knife was tangible. Still, it writhed, distracting her. She bit her lip and cut slowly, carefully slicing at the place where Rondeau's spirit and the ghost were joined. At least she couldn't *hear* the ghost, and Rondeau was unconscious, unaware of what she was doing to him.

Fifteen minutes later, perhaps halfway through the surgery, Marla heard the "tick-tick" of claws on the wooden floor.

She turned. The white dog stood on the floor, tail wagging, exuding benevolence and adorability.

But now, for the first time, Marla could see the dog's spirit.

Dark and looming, the dog's spirit was a vaguely defined manlike shape with eyes like distant stars and long, multi-jointed arms that terminated in grasping fingers, the digits sprouting a profusion of hooks and barbs. Its squat, powerful legs ended in blunt feet with toes like ice-axes, feet that would dig in and not be moved. That was the essence of this creature, then—a beast of function, something made to grasp things and drag them away.

The dog filled Marla's head with summertime and protective love—she couldn't hurt it. Even the memory of kicking the dog oppressed her, filled her with twisting snakes of guilt.

But the dog's spirit—that was monstrous and terrifying, and Marla could focus on it, the claws, the feet, the squat body. Never mind that it was *part* of the dog, the *essence* of the dog. She could keep them separate in her mind.

She could attack the dog's *spirit*.

Marla rushed the dark thing, lashing out with her dagger.

The dog howled as a great rip appeared in its spirit, spilling darkness like a cloud of ink expelled into water. The dog turned around quickly, snapping at its own flanks

—and disappeared, with no fanfare.

Marla had wounded it, and driven it away.

She had little doubt that it would return, and that it would be angry.

Marla finished cutting the ghost off Rondeau intently, quickly. She felt certain she was being watched.

Rondeau wore a bathrobe and sat sipping tea from a white porcelain cup. He'd been in the shower for nearly an hour, cleaning away the stink from his body. "I feel normal," he said. "But then, I felt normal when I had the suit on, too, so who knows? But I feel like *me*." The suit was on the floor in the corner, a wrinkled pile of purple and gold.

"Good," Marla said. They would have to wait to see how much of the ghost was left, and how much of Rondeau she might have accidentally cut away.

The door opened and Hamil rushed in. "Homunculi!" he said triumphantly. "Duplicate bodies, grown in great yeasty vats of meat!"

"No shit?" Marla said. "So those bodies weren't Sweeney at all? Just decoys, copies?"

Hamil shook his head. "Copies, yes, but not the usual sort, not just stupid doppelgangers. Sweeney's been moving his mind, his *soul*, from one body to another."

Marla whistled. "That's insane."

"There are dangers and repercussions, yes. The soul can be lost in transit. But even if the transfer goes perfectly, there's *wear*. Attrition of the soul. The edges get ground away, the substance of the spirit thins out. Every time Sweeney switches bodies, he loses a little of his humanity. He'll become more and more monstrous, until one day the thing looking out of Sweeney's eyes isn't really Sweeney at all—isn't even *human*. But it's one of the paths to immortality, if you're stupid enough to follow it."

"Doesn't he need a charm, something to loosen his mind from his body?

I didn't see anything like that on him . . . "

Hamil cleared his throat. "Well, yes. The herbs he bought at the *brujeria* are used to make that charm, actually. To be effective, the charm must touch skin. Normally such a thing would be worn as a medallion, against the chest, but that's risky, of course—the medallion can be snatched away, torn off. Sweeney found a more clever place to put his. He wore the charm on the *inside*."

Marla looked at Hamil blankly. "He ate it? Aren't those herbs poisonous?"

Rondeau laughed. "I think what Hamil means is, Sweeney shoved the charm up his ass, like a mule taking cocaine across the border."

Marla shook her head. "The things people do to live forever. So. He has a freely migrating spirit. But he can't just hop from body to body at will, can he?"

"His current body has to die, before he can relocate. But he doesn't seem to have much trouble dying at will. He probably has poison and razor blades secreted on his person, things he can use to kill himself, in a pinch."

"So we knock him out, get the herbs out of him, and cut his throat, right?"

Hamil nodded. "Hardly glamorous work, but that seems to be the only course of action."

"Okay," Marla said. "Let's find him. I bet he's at the best table in the best restaurant in town."

"Bastard's probably a terrible tipper, too," Rondeau said.

"Todd Sweeney, sleeping the sleep of the wicked," Rondeau said. He wore a powder-blue tuxedo jacket over a black t-shirt and faded corduroy jeans. Marla almost found his attire refreshing, after the horrible monotony of the zoot suit.

Sweeney lolled in a wingback chair, his hair disarrayed, his jaw agape, quite unconscious. "What did you give him?" Marla asked.

"Some cocktail of Hamil's. One whiff of a soaked handkerchief, and he passed out. Hamil says he'll be down for hours yet." Rondeau grinned. "You should have seen me. I crept up behind him in the men's room at the Chatterly Club, and I dragged him out the *window*. Slick as can be. Nobody saw a thing."

"I don't suppose you, ah, removed his talisman, did you?"

Rondeau wrinkled his nose. "Look, I fetched kidney stones out of a toilet, yes, but I have my limits. I'm not going butt-fishing in Todd Sweeney."

Marla sighed and pulled on a latex glove. "This is what being chief-of-chiefs leads to, Rondeau. The dirtiest of dirty work. But once we get that charm out of his bottom, he'll be as mortal as you and me. Assuming we can get every sprig of leaf out of there. I don't look forward to the process." She took a step toward Sweeney, then paused. Slowly, she smiled. "But then again, maybe there's another way . . . Strip him for me."

Rondeau began to protest.

"No, no," Marla said. "I just need you to make sure he doesn't have poison, or anything he can kill himself with."

Rondeau stripped the body, finding a vial of blue liquid and numerous razor blades.

"Now get some rope," Marla said. "We're taking him to Langford's clinic. There are observation rooms there, places where we can keep Sweeney, where he won't do any harm to himself."

"You're a fiendish bitch," Rondeau said with admiration. He leaned against the unbreakable glass, watching Sweeney begin to stir. Sweeney had been in the bare white cell for several hours already, his hands cuffed behind him, lying unconscious on his side. "But what if the dog doesn't come?"

"It'll come," Marla said. "It's been to Langford's clinic before. It knows the way."

Sweeney opened his eyes, blinking stupidly at the light. He squinted toward the wide window, then nodded. "Hello, Marla," he said, his voice transmitted to a speaker on Marla's side of the glass. "You've caught me again. You're certainly persistent." He looked down at himself, frowning, then lifted his gaze to Marla, somehow meeting her eyes through the one-way glass. "Imprisonment is one thing. But why have you dressed me in this hideous gold and purple suit?"

"Is it a good fit?" Marla asked.

Sweeney glanced up at the speaker in the ceiling, where Marla's voice emerged. "It fits all right, yes. But it smells terribly of body odor. And it's . . . itchy. Almost as if the suit is moving against me."

"That's how it starts," Rondeau said with authority.

"There's been enough time for the ghost to get its hooks into him, don't you think?" Marla said.

Rondeau shrugged. "Hamil said it doesn't take long to get started. So now . . . we wait for the dog."

Sweeney struggled to his feet, leaning against and sliding up the wall. "Well," he said. "It's been a pleasure. But I have other engagements." Sweeney lowered his head and ran toward the far wall, hitting his head with such force that the *crack* of collision was transmitted clearly through the speaker.

"Shit!" Marla shouted, and ran for the door. "Why didn't we tie his feet?"

"We were too busy being pleased with ourselves," Rondeau said.

Marla wrenched open the door while Sweeney sat, dazed, on the floor. "Bugger," he muttered, and tried to stand up so he could make another suicidal run. Marla reached for him—then stopped as the sound of claws on tile came from behind her.

She turned. The dog stood in the doorway, its tail wagging like a metronome. Curls of blackness wisped away from its pale back. Its eyes were as dark and unreflective as lumps of coal. Its adorable form was coming apart at the edges.

Marla backed away, holding her hands before her, palms out. "Nice doggie," she said softly.

Rondeau was backed all the way up against the window, flattened out, unmoving, his eyes fixed on the dog. "I should be terrified," he said, hardly moving his mouth. "But it's still *cute*, black eyes and all."

"I know," Marla said.

The dog sniffed the air, its head swinging toward Sweeney.

Sweeney blinked at it, still dazed from his collision with the wall. "Dog," he said. "White dog. Care to sic me, doggie? Put those pretty teeth of yours in my throat, so I can get on with my evening?" He laughed. "But you're a nice doggie, aren't you? You wouldn't kill me, no matter how I—"

The dog jumped, landing on Sweeney's chest, driving him to the ground. It snapped its jaws at his throat and began pulling.

The ghost in the suit came out, eyes wide and empty of intelligence. The traumas the ghost had recently experienced—the first assault by the dog, the sharpness of Marla's dagger—had ruined its vestige of a mind.

But even with its sense wholly removed, the ghost had tried to take over Sweeney's body. Its hands disappeared into Sweeney's chest, as if gripping his ethereal heart. As the dog dragged the ghost out, Sweeney's spirit came with it. The spirit-Sweeney looked around, bewildered, the face of a man who has been living high, unable to comprehend that the good life has come to an end. That *life* has come to an end.

The spirit-Sweeney mouthed a single word—"Bugger"—and then both of them, the ghost and Sweeney's spirit, were torn from the body and the suit.

Marla expected the dog to drag them away. Instead, it began to *gobble* the ghost, taking great bites and swallowing the spiritual substance. It swallowed Sweeney, too, unable to—or uninterested in—telling the difference between the two. Marla and Rondeau watched in sick fascination as the spirits were consumed.

The dog finished eating and licked its chops. It trotted toward the door, and Marla and Rondeau both relaxed.

Then the dog stopped. It turned its head to look at Marla, its black eyes terribly intent. It trotted toward her, and Marla swallowed. She wanted to whimper, but if this was the end, she wanted to go with some dignity. "I'm sorry I kicked you—" she began.

The dog growled, and Marla stopped talking.

With great deliberation, the dog lifted its leg, and pissed all over Marla's boots. It pissed for a very long time, looking at Marla all the while, as if daring her to move, daring her to kick. Marla simply stood, glad she'd waterproofed the boots.

When the dog finished, it walked out of the room without another glance.

Rondeau exhaled. "I thought you were dead for sure."

"I am dead for sure." She gestured toward the puddle around her feet. "Dogs piss to mark their territory. I've been marked."

Rondeau's eyes widened. "Oh, shit."

Marla shrugged. "I didn't expect to live forever." Then she smiled. "But I kicked the hell out of that dog once already, and I'm not afraid to do it again. No matter how cute it is."

Rondeau laughed. He went to Sweeney's body and crouched. "I wonder how much I can get for this zoot suit at the vintage clothing store?" he asked.

THE HEART,
A CHAMBERED NAUTILUS

(For Heather)

Because the night is old, and she's alone now, wearing a little black dress for no good reason anymore, Lynne surrenders to impulse and drops a dime in the strange unmarked machine, a squat thing like a dorm fridge, gray, no words or symbols adorning it at all, just a coin slot too small for a quarter. The dime rattles down inside, and Lynne waits, crouched in the space below the stairway in the empty train station, expecting nothing, but hopeful all the same.

With a pop of air escaping, the front of the machine swings open on secret hinges, revealing a man inside, folded in an impossible yoga pose. His eyes are the color of burnished copper, and he holds Lynne's dime between his smiling teeth. He eases himself out of the box in half a dozen slow moves, unfolding before her like a Japanese fan. He takes her dime from his mouth, wipes it carefully on his sleeve, and offers it to her.

Lynne stands from her crouch and says "No, keep it."

He nods and places the coin in his pocket. "How may I serve?" he asks, and Lynne comprehends instantly, completely; this is not so different from stories she has heard, and yet it is a disappointment, this impersonal genie, fey spirit available for ownership by anyone with a dime, not special, not just-for-her.

"What can you do?" she asks.

He counts on his fingers (long, neatly manicured, ringless): "I can make wine of memories. I can fold the space in small closets and make them open into cathedral vastness. I know the source of all potions, and the binding of uncertainties into chosen shapes. I sup with owls and learn their stories; I gather the mist and mend magical garments; I served as cobbler for twelve dancing princesses. I designed the nautilus shell and furnished the heavens with their constellations." He spread his hands.

"Can you interpret dreams?" she asks.

"Of a certainty."

"I have dreamed this dream a hundred times. I sit in a soft chair, with my feet up, in a small, airless room. The walls are aquariums, filled with prehistoric fish, all long snouts and protruding teeth, claws and spines and eyes that bulge, lashing through the murky water, watching me. I sip a drink, good Scotch, but it doesn't soothe me. I know the glass will break, the aquariums will shatter, and I'm just waiting to drown or be devoured. Then I notice that my footrest is actually a wooden box—this surprises me, every time—and I try to open the lid. It is heavy, but I manage to lift it, and inside I find a staircase descending through the floor, down into the earth. Then I hear a door open below, and light spills out—"

"And a man steps onto the stairs," he says, his voice nearly trembling. "And he calls to you, and asks you to join him, in a palace bigger inside than the whole of the world, a place full of gems and silks, but empty of love, of laughter, of you."

"Yes," she says. "That's it exactly. And then I wake up. Can you tell me what it means?"

He closes the door on the gray box, turns it over onto its back, and when he sets it down it changes from metal to wood, cherry-red and rich. He opens the lid, and soft yellow light pours out. "It is, you know," he says. "Bigger, inside, than out. It really is."

"Like a heart," she says, and takes his hand. "Like all the empty rooms inside a heart."

They go down, inside, together.

AFTERWORD

Perhaps I'm in the minority, but I've always loved reading introductions, forewords, afterwords, story notes, and all manner of back-and-front matter. I'm not sure if it's the insight into the writing process that I love, or the occasional chatty anecdotes, or simply the thrill of glimpsing the wizard behind the curtain. For whatever reason, such notes are often the first thing I read, even though I know I *shouldn't*, since they tend to give things away. I can't resist the opportunity to write some such notes of my own, but I'll try not to give anything too major away, in case, like me, you're in the habit of eating your dessert first.

Little Gods

This story has done a lot of good things for me. It was one of the first stories of mine to get any notable critical attention, it was well-reviewed, and it even appeared on the Nebula final ballot in 2003. I began writing the story at Wiscon, the annual feminist science fiction convention, in 2001, after attending a panel (actually just a bunch of people sitting around on couches and the floor, talking) hosted by Terri Windling and Midori Snyder. We were discussing ways to make the mythic resonate with the personal without trivializing the one or pointlessly aggrandizing the other, and their suggestions and insights opened a lot of doors in my head. I'd been trying to figure out how to write about a recent break-up, and the pain I was feeling from that separation—in other words, I wanted to write a story about grief, and especially the grieving process. "Little Gods" is what emerged. The self-proclaimed King of Grief, with his beautiful, hurtful lies, is one of my favorite characters, and one of the scariest I've ever created, I think.

The Fallen and the Muse of the Street

I wrote this after my first trip to New Orleans, having gotten the idea for it while sitting in Jackson Square, watching the unicyclist who appears in the story. My friend Donna Bond actually created the character of Samaelle, but not in writing—Donna paints and draws, and the winged, wicked, curvaceous angel of death appears in many of her works. She graciously gave me permission to translate her creation into writing. This was my first sale to *Strange Horizons*, when that magazine was only a few months old, and I think it's a fun romp, if not quite as profound as it might wish to be.

The Witch's Bicycle

Junior high was Hell. There's a lot of autobiography in this story: the terror of going to the bathroom; the dark alleyway at school called "The Tunnel" where kids got beaten up on a regular basis; the overloaded buses that had to make two trips to ferry all the students home; the empty hours hanging around school grounds waiting for the bus to return; the roving bullies. I never had anyone as cool as Heather come to my rescue, but then, I was never preyed on by anyone quite as sociopathic as Rocko, so I suppose it all balances out. When I was in junior high (and the first year of high school, for that matter), I remember the disgust and disbelief I felt whenever I heard adults talk about how easy kids had it, not having to worry about jobs and bills. I promised myself that I would never forget how hellish and terrifying those middle-school years were, never forget the gauntlet I had to run just to get to class, never forget the bullies and boredom and hatred and fear. I didn't forget. I wrote it all down here, so I wouldn't.

Being an adult is way easier than being a kid, incidentally. Having a day job is a breeze—I don't have to worry about getting the shit kicked out of me when I go to the bathroom, after all. I can eat anything I want, stay up as late as I wish, and go out whenever I like. What's not to love?

Annabelle's Alphabet

This is the little story that could. I wrote it in 1998, and it's far and away the oldest story in this collection. I sent it to lots of magazines, big and small, and after about 20 rejections I was ready to give up on trying to sell it. Then I read a few issues of *Lady Churchill's Rosebud Wristlet*, edited by Gavin Grant & Kelly Link, and thought "Maybe they'd like my strange little story." So I sent them "Annabelle's," and they did like it (though they had me rewrite "U"—it was originally "U is for Urges," and was a bit heavy-handed). The story was subsequently chosen for inclusion in *The Year's Best Fantasy and Horror* and *Best of the Rest 3*. Proof, if any were needed, that persistence is a virtue for a writer.

I wrote the story for a friend and lover named Adrienne, who made my college experience many times more interesting than it would have been otherwise.

The Scent of Copper Pennies

My friend Susan calls this my "Quantum physics voodoo love story," and that's obviously pretty apt. I wrote it during the year I lived in Santa Cruz—a wonderful time, in many ways, but also a lonely one, because I didn't know many people, having moved there from North Carolina essentially on a whim when I got out of college. The story begins as a typical wish-fulfillment romance, but I like to think it goes to unexpected places after that. The coffee shop where the story begins is Caffe Pergolesi, the best coffee-and-beer joint in Santa Cruz. In terms of inspiration, I've always been fascinated by many-worlds theory, and the Borgesian notion of the world as a garden of forking paths, and the figure of Papa Legba ("the opener of the way") in *voudon*. All those fascinations came together in this piece, along with a sense of profound dislocation at having moved 3,000 miles from the place, where I grew up. I wish I could've met a woman like Merrilee during that lonely year. Maybe, in some other somewhere, I did.

The God of the Crossroads

While the speaker of this poem is not the protagonist of "The Scent of Copper Pennies," the two pieces are related thematically and in terms of the presiding deity. I've spent a lot of hours in my life worrying about choices and weighing possibilities, and paralysis is always a danger in situations like that. Looking back on my life, I see a series of lulls and sudden surges of movement. Those sudden surges—moving to California for no particular reason, moving in with my now-fiancée after having known her for only a few months, and so on—have always turned out rather well. But who knows what would have happened if I'd chosen differently? The question endlessly fascinates me, and it's one that I deal with frequently—sometimes consciously, sometimes not—in my work.

Fable from a Cage

I went to Clarion in 1999, and while at the workshop I set myself the task of writing against my strengths. I tend naturally toward writing contemporary fantasy, so I tried to write humor, and satirical horror, and science fiction. The results were decidedly mixed (though a couple of stories I wrote at Clarion made it into this collection—"Behemoth" and "Unfairy Tale"), and the worst story I wrote, by far, was a sword-and-sorcery story called "Charm." It was justly torn to shreds by the other workshop participants, and afterward I shied away from writing that sort of faux-Medieval fantasy. A couple of years later I got the idea for this story—just the opening, of a man in a cage telling a story—and decided to give sword-and-sorcery another try. This is the result. And, in truth, it's more of a pointy-stick-and-sorcery story. I'm quite fond of the magical system here—the notion of "you are what you eat" taken to a grotesque extreme.

Bleeding West

I like Westerns. From spaghetti Westerns to *Tombstone* to the comic-book series *Preacher*, I've always been fascinated by these dusty tales of ambiguous heroes. I wrote this story after reading about the death of the battle-chief Tecumseh, and his unhappy fate at the hands of the Kentucky Volunteers. It features one of my favorite characters, Cosmocrator, who appears in the writings of Valentinian gnostics as the demonic ruler of the material world. I took considerable—rather, total—liberties with the mythological facts of the figure, and turned him into the cursed water demon you find here. In many ways this story was a prototype for a Western-tinged novel I recently completed, called *The Strange Adventures of Rangergirl*. The story and the book don't have much in common, but that central figure—a spirit of the ugly side of the mythic West—appears in both.

Behemoth

Blame it on William Blake. Or on the class on Blake I took in college. Blake's writings are uneven (the Proverbs of Hell still thrill me, but some of his more visionary works can get a bit ponderous), but his illustrations are almost all fabulous. He did an illustration for the Book of Job that features a downcast-looking Behemoth in the upper half and a lashing Leviathan beneath. My fascination with that painting led me to research those two primordial monsters. There's a wealth of largely-contradictory information about them, some of it deeply weird (like the notion that, in the afterlife, spirits will feed on the self-replenishing flesh of Behemoth and Leviathan—a sort of heavenly surf n' turf, if you will), and I took the parts I liked and ignored the rest. The notion of Leviathan as a symbol of the feminine principle and Behemoth as the opposite masculine principle led me inevitably to think of them as star-crossed lovers. Michaela Roessner (who provides the introduction to this collection) gave me some wonderful advice on how to fix the flawed, shredding-itself-apart first draft of this story, for which I am grateful. This was first published in a neat anthology called *Brainbox II*, in which each author supplied a story and an essay about how the story was written. I'd reprint the essay here, but it was almost as long as the story itself, so I'll spare you.

Bone Sigh

This is the only story in the collection that is, arguably, not fantasy. It's horror, certainly, but I think it achieves a sort of sweetness by the end. It's about love and madness. I wrote it in a week, one section per night, and I'm proud of the deadpan narrative voice, the speaker's total sincerity, his questionable madness, his obvious love for his daughter.

Daughter and Moon

This is one of my favorite poems to read aloud, and when I perform it, people often ask me afterward if I have a daughter (I don't), which means, I think, that I did something right. I wrote this after reading a fair bit about the function of the moon in making spells, and about the moon's connection to the feminine principle, thinking how that connection could be potentially bewildering for a well-meaning father, seeing his daughter begin to grow up and away from him.

Captain Fantasy and the Secret Masters

Every writer should have a gay superhero vs. Nazis story, right? This is mine.

I wrote this before I ever read Alan Moore's brilliant comic *Watchmen* and long before the movie *Memento* was made, though I realize it reads like a sort of mutant hybrid of the two. I first learned about Karsakov's syndrome from Oliver Sachs's first-rate essay collection *The Man Who Mistook His Wife for a Hat*. I've written a couple of other stories about the protagonist, Mr. Li, and may write a novel about him one of these days.

Entropy's Paintbrush

This is an odd little story, inspired largely by Neil Gaiman's *Sandman* series, particularly the way he had every god from every culture uncomfortably co-existing, which I think is a wonderful way to deal with the problem of multiple, conflicting mythologies. I wrote it in college, while taking a class on the Renaissance and after reading Vasari's *The Lives of the Artists*, which taught me about the difficulties of creating art under a system of patronage. Since Lucifer is a being of great vanity, it seemed natural that he would, at some point, commission someone to create his portrait. Since I wanted my artist to have access to technologies far beyond those available today (and because I liked the idea of letting a misanthrope live on his very own moon), I had to set it in the far future. And that's where the entropy came in . . .

My Night with Aphrodite

This is another favorite to read aloud, always a crowd-pleaser. Perfection in a lover is pretty amazingly daunting, isn't it? I've dated two women (neither, admittedly, perfect) with neo-Pagan tendencies, who considered Aphrodite their goddess of choice. This poem isn't exactly *for* them, but it's certainly *because* of them. The poem can be read as a comment on Aphrodite as she appears in "Entropy's Paintbrush," too, which is why they're placed next to each other here.

Unfairy Tale

I read a lot of mythology and folklore and fairy tales (gee, could you have guessed?), and this is a story of mythological culture-clash. I've never liked stories where a kiss brings a dead person back to life (even if they're only metaphorically dead), because that feels like such a terrible lie to me, so I decided to write a Sleeping Beauty story where the beauty never wakes up. And why should she? This isn't *her* story, after all. She's just sleeping in it.

Down with the Lizards and the Bees

I inevitably set stories in the places where I live. The flavor of my environment always seeps in. This story takes place in North Oakland and Berkeley, where I've lived for the past two years, and in the underworld, where I haven't spent much time. The coffee shop where Bradley Bowman meets Jay is the Temescal Café, on the unfashionable end of Telegraph Ave., where I occasionally drink Italian sodas and eat cheap bagels. I've spent more hours than I'd care to count waiting for trains in the downtown Berkeley BART station, and I've wondered more than once what I'd do if a decidedly non-standard train pulled up to the platform. It's another story about grief and loss, and contains my answer to the question that's always bugged me about the Orpheus story—why the hell *did* that idiot look back?

Orpheus Among the Cabbages

And here's a rather more playful take on the Orpheus myth. It was very difficult to restrain myself from including an explicit "giving head" pun in this poem, but I succeeded. Except to the extent that the entire poem is a dramatization of that pun, of course . . .

Pale Dog

This is the treat of the collection— a previously unpublished novelette full of ghosts, sorcery, vintage clothing, death, dogs, and divination. Marla is one of my favorite characters (and the protagonist of the novel I'm currently working on, *Blood Engines*), and I think this is one of my best stories. I jokingly call my Marla stories "sorcererpunk," because I like to think they have the sort of information-density that made cyberpunk such a pleasure, lots of bizarreness and eyeball-kicks.

The Heart, a Chambered Nautilus

I wrote this for my fiancée Heather Shaw, for our first anniversary. If I say much more, the afterword will be longer than the story itself. We published it in December 2002 in a limited edition chapbook called *Floodwater*, along with a short-short of Heather's, and a collaboration we did together. When she read it, she cried, so I succeeded. I don't expect it to make you cry, but I hope you like it.

Thanks for reading these stories and poems. I'll keep writing them, and I hope you'll keep reading them.

Finally, thanks to Heather Shaw, for being with me these past years, listening to every idea, proofreading everything I give her, being my greatest fan, and supporting me in every way; to the many editors who have published and helped me polish my work, especially Shawna McCarthy, Jed Hartman, Susan Marie Groppi, Kelly Link, and Gavin Grant; to Nick Mamatas, the godfather of *Little Gods*, who encouraged me to put this collection together in the first place; to my colleagues at *Locus*, who help provide me with the best day job a writer could hope for; to my editor Sean Wallace at Prime, for making this whole process so pleasant; to Michaela Roessner, for the lessons, the advice, the conversations, and the introduction; to all my many writing teachers, from Clarion and elsewhere; to my writer-pals, always there with feedback and encouragement, particularly Michael Jasper, Greg van Eekhout, Jay Lake, Jenn Reese, and Karen Meisner; and to my family and friends, especially Megan, and Adrienne, and of course Scott and Lynne, who always have a place for me to crash in Santa Cruz. Since I do most of the actual writing in a small room by myself, it's good to have these people to keep me company in the rest of my life.

COPYRIGHT INFORMATION

Printed in the United States
1495200001B/147